Endpapers: *The Sky-goddess Nut from the gold-covered innermost shrine of Tutankhamun's tomb.*

The mystery of the Pyramids

Pyramids at Giza.

The mystery of the Pyramids

Humphrey Evans

Marshall Cavendish London & New York

The god Ra

Designed by Graham Beehag

Published by Marshall Cavendish Books Limited
58, Old Compton Street
London W1V 5PA

First printing 1979

Printed in Great Britain by Redwood Burn Limited

ISBN 0 85685 709 2

Preface

The pyramids are among the most remarkable technical
achievements of civilization and yet they come close
to being as old as civilization itself. Ever since they
were built by the pharaohs, the god-kings of
Ancient Egypt, they have been a source of wonder and
amazement. Since the nineteenth century, archaeological
excavations have done much to explain the history
and the culture of the people who produced them.
The phenomenal wealth of material, in addition
to the pyramids themselves – monuments in stone,
artifacts in gold and alabaster, furniture in ivory
and wood, not to mention the grisly evidence
of the mummies themselves – points to a
civilization of extraordinary richness and complexity.

The Mystery of the Pyramids presents the fascinating
evidence which the archaeologists have amassed:
how the pharaohs ruled, the rites of the religion of which
the god-kings were the centre, the vast building
programmes of which the pyramids were part,
and the practices of mummification.

But of equal concern are the unanswered questions the
pyramids pose. By what means were the pyramids
built if it is true that the Ancient Egyptians did not
have the pulley? Do they still contain
treasure in chambers as yet undiscovered? Do their
hieroglyphs still hold unfathomed messages? Are their
orientation and proportion keys to mysteries as
yet only dimly perceived? And is there any
convincing evidence for the widely held belief that a
curse lies on those who disturb the sleep of the mummies?
It is these enigmas which have given the pyramids
their enduring hold on the imagination.

Contents

Introduction

MYSTERIES, PYRAMIDS AND EGYPT, the three cling together in the mind. Here is an ancient civilization, splendid in its powers; its kings and pharaohs appear fabulously rich amid their hoards of gold; its people record their presence with inscriptions in graves and tombs; its temples and religious cults offer esoteric knowledge; its art astounds and its style of hieroglyphic writing intrigues. And yet the symbol for this complex flux is the simple shape of a pyramid set against the empty desert.

Each pyramid is a massive brooding presence. Seen as a diagram, or as a model in a museum, it seems easy to comprehend: four faces, four edges, a point and passage-ways leading to a chamber within the structure. The reality is different. Stand close beside a pyramid, raise your eyes towards the summit and thoughts of faces, edges and points become irrelevant. Half the world is stone, the other half is sky. Climb inside and the cramped and humid passage-ways will confuse and disorient you. Pyramids are big. The British sculptor Henry Moore has emphasized the point: 'Imagine the pyramids if they were no higher than a house. It's their size that counts.'

And the pyramids are old, built during a period of a thousand years that ended seventeen centuries before the birth of Christ. When Napoleon rallied

On the plateau of Giza, near Cairo, the Great Pyramid of King Cheops, on the right, and the almost equally large pyramid of King Chephren stand as they have for forty-five centuries. Despite the discoveries of archaeologists, there are still unsolved mysteries about their purpose, how they were built and secrets they may yet hold.

his troops at the Battle of the Pyramids he told them 'Think of it, soldiers; forty centuries of history look down upon you.' The thirteenth-century Arab traveller and physician Abd al Latif turned all the influences round when he wrote: 'Time itself experiences the eternal duration of these extraordinary edifices.'

Largest and most glorious of all is the Great Pyramid of Giza built by King Cheops, whose Egyptian name was Khufu, in the twenty-sixth century BC. The ancient Egyptians called it *Akhet Khufu*, the 'Splendour of Khufu' or 'Khufu in the Horizon'; the powerful sun, the personal deity of these god-like kings, rose and set in the horizon. The Egyptian word for any true pyramid was *mr* or *mer* and when writing this in hieroglyphs they followed the letters with a determinative, a tiny picture of a pyramid. Their word for the vertical height of a pyramid was *per-em-us*. The Greeks may have turned this into the word *pyramis*. Alternatively they may have taken the word *pyramis* from their own language, in which it means 'wheaten cake', and applied it to the similarly-shaped monuments. The Greek *pyramis* gives the modern word 'pyramid'. Present-day mystics claim that the word has secret meanings, that *Pyr* is the ancient Egyptian name for Cheops and denotes 'The Light', that the whole word refers to 'The

Ten Parts of the Fiery Ecliptic of the Zodiac or Solar Wheel'.

Despite the millenia that separate us from the pyramid builders, we can still know something of their concerns. Archaeologists tell us of their history, of their gods, their wars and dynastic successions. They stress the absolute importance of the annual inundation by the Nile. If the river failed to rise, the fields remained dry, the crops perished, people starved and the desert crept closer. If the river rose too high, the problems were almost as great; one ancient account pictured a disconsolate king wading through a flooded temple hall at Karnak. They tell us, too, of gentler matters, of the Egyptians' delight in getting tipsy or walking in a shady garden. One excavator, digging into a vast tomb at Abydos, slipped back five thousand years when he found the sand still saturated with poured-out ointments: the strong and heady scent filled the tomb. (We can also feel for the archaeologists themselves. Another excavator, working through a tomb in which bodies lay heaped on the floor, reported that an extraordinary plague of fleas, multiplying in the warm, still air, rendered the place intolerable to the stoutest workman.)

Strangest of all, we can actually confront these ancient Egyptians; their mummies lie in museums around the world. Scientists probe and X-ray,

revealing that Amenophis III had dental abscesses or that Ramesses II suffered cold feet caused by degeneration of the arteries, and suggesting family relationships, or the lack of them, between various pharaohs. But anyone who travels to Egypt can visit the Egyptian Museum in Cairo and climb the stairs to Room No. 52 on the upper floor. In this light and airy chamber, royal mummies from the time of the New Kingdom, between the sixteenth and twelfth centuries BC, lie in simple wooden coffins set in file upon file of glass cases. As you pass slowly along the gangways you look down on the features of men who once thought themselves gods.

Here is Amenophis I, still well wrapped, a mask covers his head and shoulders, its polished artifi-cial eyes, black on white gaze up serenely; Tuth-mosis II, his wrappings long since gone, has his eyes closed, his mouth slightly open showing the teeth, and just a little hair curling round the back of his head; Seti I has his arms crossed over his breast, the still-bandaged fingers poke from beneath the linen sheet that covers him. Against the wall, a smaller case holds the well-preserved head of an anonymous mummy, from a village near Luxor, mounted like a portrait bust. Bend for-ward a little to put yourself on the same level and you can suddenly feel that its eyes have met yours.

With such an encounter still possible, it is hardly any wonder that people dream of magic, of re-discovering the secret wisdom of the ancients. Some look to the Egyptian gods, claiming direct

awareness of arcane knowledge gained from occult rituals. Others hope for a message of salvation in the pyramids themselves, believing that they reveal the will of God and demonstrate a true mathematical relationship between the growth of life and the universe as a whole. They explain that marks in the passage-ways of the Great Pyramid provide an almanac of past and future and state that the original apex of the Great Pyramid consisted of a pyramid of solid gold about 5 centimetres (2 in.) high. This perfect model of the pyramid, small enough to fit in the palm of a hand, could be geometrically projected through successive stages that illustrated the abstract perfection of the system. Others, still, have found that models of the Great Pyramid concentrate strange forms of energy that can be harnessed as pyramid power.

Ancient Egypt still spins a fascinating aura round its mysteries, its mummies, its magic – and its pyramids. Murtada ibn al Khafif, a thirteenth-century Arab writer, summed up the attraction: 'Some make a description of Egypt, saying that it is a land wherein there are famous places, whose river is clear and its waters sweet, where diseases are dispelled and hope crowned with effect. All those who have any affection for it find there how to employ themselves about what they like best.'

Sir Edward Poynter painted Israel in Egypt *in 1867. Although sometimes called 'Joseph's granaries', the pyramids were built long before the Israelites' tribulations.*

Chapter 1

The World of the Pharaohs

EGYPT ALWAYS WAS THE NILE, the fertile river valley running from somewhere south of Aswan northwards to the Mediterranean, with the eastern and western deserts stretching away on either side. For more than 1000 kilometres (650 miles) the river, a kilometre (half a mile) wide and more, flows through a shallow canyon that spreads into a plain 20 to 50 kilometres (12 to 30 miles) across. On either side cliffs rise 100 metres (330 ft.) high and higher. For about the last 150 kilometres (100 miles) the cliffs drop away and the river fans out into the marshy channels of the Delta.

Every year, from the earliest historical times down through the great days of the Egyptian empire and on, the Nile flooded across the valley floor during the four months from July to October. This inundation, brought about by heavy seasonal rainfalls further south in the Ethiopian highlands, spread rich black silt across the land. Indeed, the ancient Egyptians called the area of cultivation the Black Land, in contrast to the Red Land of the surrounding desert. The river made a highway, too, as boats drifted downstream or sailed up before the wind. The Nile brought life and movement to the land of Egypt while the desert and the Delta frustrated invaders.

Nomadic peoples had long roamed across all of northern Africa, living by hunting antelope and other animals. Gradually, as the climate changed and as the ice-age glaciers withdrew from Europe, as less and less rain fell, the grasslands shrank away, turning to desert, and the wandering nomads settled by the only source of water, the Nile. Here among the spreading

David Roberts drew this view of the entrance to the temple of Amun at Luxor after a visit in 1838. Amenophis III built the main court in the fourteenth century BC; Ramesses II added the gateway with its colossal statues and obelisks.

swamps and thickly-growing reeds and bushes, they found animals and birds to hunt and domesticate, fish to catch, and patches of land where crops could be grown. As agriculture developed, impermanent settlements became villages: by about 4000 BC the people of the Nile valley probably lived in clusters of reed huts, they made pottery jars and utensils for cooking and use in the community, and they fashioned tools and weapons from flints.

Over the next few hundred years, as the Nile valley people learned to co-operate in larger groups for the seasonal work required to reap the benefits of the inundation and its harvest, as they

came into contact with other civilizations in Asia, the separate villages combined into districts and the districts into kingdoms. By about 3200 BC Egypt was on the verge of becoming a nation, a political entity that mirrored a cultural unity. The Nile people had advanced to using copper tools and building their houses of mud brick. They

Egypt always was the Nile. . . . This view shows the river at Aswan. The Nile was both a highway for travel throughout the land and the bringer of life: the annual inundation that flooded the fields each summer was the miracle that 'supplies all people with nourishment and food'. A year when the Nile rose high was a year free from want. To the ancient Egyptians, this source of life and great arterial route by which everything travelled was sacred.

The Narmer palette, about 60 centimetres (2 ft.) high, provides a record of King Narmer, possibly the legendary King Menes who united Egypt around 3100 BC. On this side, the reverse, Narmer, wearing the white crown of Upper Egypt, strikes down a captive.

traded amongst themselves and with other peoples, they had a common language and a method of writing it down in hieroglyphs, they shared similar beliefs about religion and the nature of the gods, and they saw themselves as part of the twin countries of Upper and Lower Egypt. Lower Egypt, or the land of the Delta, downriver and northwards, was the more influenced by the civilizations of the Mediterranean; Upper Egypt, the long Nile valley itself, upriver and southwards, looked to itself and its northern neighbour. Upper Egypt was probably already a united kingdom, with its capital at Hierakonpolis far to the south; Lower Egypt may have had a king of its own at Buto, a town in the north-west of the Delta. Within the next hundred years or so the kings of Upper Egypt conquered Lower Egypt, forming the unified kingdom of the Two Lands.

Who actually led this conquest is not known. Tradition gave the name Menes to the first great king, but this has never been found among early records. It could, perhaps, be a second name or title of one of the two or three kings who probably consolidated a series of temporary victories into conquest. Any or all of them could have been Menes. The first was known as Scorpion. The second, Narmer, bursts into vivid political reality because a ceremonial palette, about 60 centimetres (2 ft.) high, commemorating his successes still exists today. Stone palettes, used for grinding cosmetics, were often decorated with carvings. In this case the king's name occurs at the top of each side of the palette, set between two cow's heads which probably represented the goddess Hathor, the great mother. Narmer, too, appears on both sides. On the front, he inspects the corpses of his enemies. He wears the Red Crown of Lower Egypt and has about him priests and standard bearers. Lower down, a great bull, a representation of the king, breaks into a walled town and tramples over an adversary. On the back, he wears the White Crown of Upper Egypt as he grasps a kneeling captive by the hair before clubbing him down. The third of these conquering kings was called Aha. Around this time, a new capital city, Memphis, sprang into being on the west bank of the Nile just south of present-day Cairo. Later generations of Egyptians believed that the legendary King Menes diverted the Nile to clear a site for the new city at a spot which dominated both the Nile Valley and the Delta. At this point Egypt became a single country.

As a convenient way of dividing up the thousands of years of Egyptian history from roughly 3000 BC to 300 BC and later, Egyptologists refer to dynasties of kings. Manetho, an Egyptian priest living in one of the Delta towns at the beginning of the third century BC, used this arrangement in drawing up a list of kings and his system, amplified by information from earlier king-lists found in tombs and temples, provided a useful base. These dynasties fall into groups corresponding to the major periods of Egyptian history. At times all is confusion, with kings from different dynasties battling for supremacy, with dynasties changing quickly and apparently arbitrarily, with each individual king little more than an unfamiliar name. At other times famous and powerful monarchs follow each other with measured and awe-inspiring majesty.

During the four hundred years of the Early Dynastic or Archaic Period that began with Scorpion and Narmer, the kings of the First and Second Dynasties consolidated their power and extended the influence of Egypt in the ancient world. The Old Kingdom of the Third to Sixth Dynasties, from 2686 to 2181 BC, produced the giant monuments of the pyramid age, visible memorials to political stability. In the following First Intermediate Period of the Seventh to Eleventh Dynasties, lasting until around 2050 BC, Egypt broke into smaller units once again. Then the kings of the Eleventh and Twelfth Dynasties re-established central government and founded the Middle Kingdom which continued to 1786 BC. Next came a spate of native and foreign rulers in the Thirteenth to Seventeenth Dynasties which made up the Second Intermediate Period, lasting until shortly before 1550 BC.

Once the disjointed times of the Second Intermediate Period had passed, the New Kingdom of the Eighteenth, Nineteenth and Twentieth Dynasties, which continued for roughly five hundred years, saw Egypt reach the height of its power and prosperity. The royal will was paramount and these kings, drawing upon the resources of an extensive and biddable empire, built temples and memorials of monumental splendour. The title 'Pharaoh' for the ruler came into use for the first time during the Eighteenth Dynasty, derived from a phrase meaning 'the great house', or 'the palace of the king'. Then, following the end of the New Kingdom around 1080 BC, came the later dynasties from the Twenty-first onwards to the Thirtieth and after. The empire shivered apart under the impact of continuous political disputes; in 525 BC Egypt fell to the Persian king, Cambyses; Alexander the Great and his armies passed through in

332 BC; and then the Ptolemies took the throne in 306 BC. With the death of Cleopatra, last of the Ptolemies, in 30 BC, Egypt became little more than the private estate of the Emperor of Rome.

It is difficult for us to imagine the might of the kings of Egypt. As monarchs they were more than absolute. Egypt ran on the simple principle that whatever the man at the top ordered was done; and Egypt was a power in the ancient world. But the nation-state of Egypt had limitations as well as strengths.

At the beginning of the dynastic period Egypt had a population of some million people, all that the land could support. As irrigation improved the population increased, rising to nearly three million people by the end of the New Kingdom around 1080 BC. Yet many of these people were probably undernourished and suffered from parasitic diseases such as schistosomiasis.

In one of the greatest feats of ancient hydraulic engineering, the ancient Egyptians built canals and sluices that controlled water periodically flooding from the Nile into the great depression of the Fayum, west of Memphis. Regulating the level of the Fayum lake in this way, and using it as a reservoir, brought a large area of new land under cultivation. But the Egyptians never had the capacity to control the flow of the Nile itself, which would have vastly increased their agricultural production and the size of population it could support.

One of Egypt's greatest strengths lay in the way the land was administered, a system which probably originated as a response to the inundation. In some sense the king owned Egypt; the land was his, although much of it eventually passed to the temples and hereditary nobles. After the yearly flood receded someone had to mark out the boundaries of the fields, allocate leases and so on. Local officials supervised cultivation, perhaps even deciding who grew what crops and where, and also settled arguments between villagers. These local officials developed very quickly into a network of bureaucrats and scribes organized into as many as 42 nomes (or districts) and ultimately answerable to the vizier, the chief official of the kingdom, and the king himself. The system's chief task consisted of assessing and collecting taxes due from farmers. They paid in kind, corn for corn, animals for animals, so a survey to calculate the cultivated area had to be made each year and a census of animals taken every second year. The bureaucrats administered estates, superintended courts of law and kept track of such matters as the civil calendar. The Egyptians valued the ability to read and write

because life as a scribe was far preferable to working in the fields, as scribes themselves were quick to point out to their children when encouraging them to do their schoolwork.

Egypt's effective bureaucracy was the real secret behind the building of the pyramids. It provided the workers – perhaps as many as a hundred thousand at a time – to transport the stone for the construction of the Great Pyramid of Giza built by the Fourth Dynasty king Cheops in the twenty-sixth century BC. The population around Memphis was far too small to provide this many men, even during the months of the inundation when no one worked the land; they had to come from half of Egypt or more. The bureaucracy controlled the work, keeping track of literally millions of stones, and it fed, housed and clothed the workers.

In later times, after the pyramid age ended, the bureaucracy organized the expeditions that brought back immense granite obelisks and stone for other monuments. An inscription from the time of the Nineteenth Dynasty king Seti I, at the beginning of the thirteenth century BC, records that he sent a thousand men to transport a monument and provided them with two kilograms (4 pounds) of bread and two bundles of vegetables every day and two linen garments every month. Under the Twentieth Dynasty king, Ramesses IV in the twelfth century BC, the bureaucracy equipped a stone-fetching expedition consisting of the Director of Works, who was the High Priest of Amun, 9 civil and military officers of rank, 362 subordinate officers, 10 trained artificers and artists, 130 quarrymen and stonecutters, 50 policemen, 2000 slaves, 5000 soldiers, and 800 men from Ayan; a total, excluding 900 men who died, of 8362.

But this efficiency had another side: it discouraged change. A new idea might be adopted quickly and extensively: just before the dynastic period, the Egyptians rapidly grasped the principle of writing, the basis of bureaucracy itself, following contacts with foreigners in Egypt. They were equally quick to build chariots when they came across that foreign invention around the beginning of the Eighteenth Dynasty in the middle of the sixteenth century BC – the kings enjoyed the new hobby of chariot driving as well as seeing the military possibilities. However, a method that was seen to work would fossilize as quickly as it was taken up and might then persist for centuries without alteration.

Egypt could be conservative to the point of stasis. In building, once a few hundred men had shown they could haul a monumental statue into place then that was the way for all future monuments. In art, the Egyptians early on decided that paintings had to show what was known to be rather than what could be seen. Consequently, people were drawn with the head in profile but the eye as from the front, the top of the body turned sideways

Previous spread: *The papyrus thickets of the Nile provided rich hunting grounds. This fifteenth-century BC tomb painting shows a noble killing birds with a throw stick.*

Below: *This carving, from 2650 BC, shows the king, in the white crown of Upper Egypt, striking down a captive. On the right he wears the red crown of Lower Egypt.*

to display both arms, and the legs in profile but apart, as though walking, to reveal both legs and both feet. King Narmer appeared like this and so did kings who reigned 2000 years later. In religion, what change there was occurred slowly and was of one particular kind: nothing was ever discarded, so each new god, new belief or new rite added itself to what was already there, infiltrating a matrix so complex that a single prayer jumbled together half a dozen traditions.

In Egyptian society everything centred on the king. He took personal command of the army and led them in battle. Sekenenre II, one of the kings of the Seventeenth Dynasty at Thebes, far to the south in the Nile valley, probably died fighting a northern-based king during the internal struggles of the Second Intermediate Period, although he may have been assassinated. His mummy, its face still contorted with pain, shows that blows from an axe or club smashed in his skull. The Eighteenth Dynasty king Tuthmosis III, whose conquests made Egypt the dominant power in the ancient world, laid out the battle plan before attacking the city of Megiddo in Palestine. His generals advised against an approach through a narrow valley with its threat of ambush. Tuthmosis III insisted, saying: 'I am loved by the god Re and by my father the god Amun. I will take this road. Let those who will take other roads; let those who will follow my

Above: A census of cattle, as shown in this fifteenth-century BC tomb painting, was important in the calculation of taxes.

Opposite: A high official had himself depicted in the admired role of scribe in this statue from around 2500 BC.

Majesty'. The army followed him to victory.

In ancient Egypt, the king took the final decisions in matters of foreign policy and internal planning; he settled legal disputes that the courts could not handle satisfactorily. He travelled constantly on tours of inspection, journeying up and down the river to check on local conditions and district officials – and where he went the court went too, because the king was Egypt. He controlled the working of precious metals; he endowed temples with the lands that provided for their upkeep; and he authorized the construction of the royal tombs (houses of eternity), the pyramids (castles of eternity), the mortuary temples (mansions of millions of years), and other major temples (abodes of the gods). At foundation ceremonies he 'stretched the cord', the surveyor's measure, calling on Thoth, scribe of the gods, to witness that he laid out the dimensions correctly, even if symbolically: 'I make its length good, its breadth exact, all its measurements right, all its sanctuaries to be in the place where they should be, and its halls to resemble the sky.'

Concentrated power of this kind, with its close control of government and its potentially quick response to national problems worked well when the king himself possessed the will to rule effectively; when the king was weak or confused Egypt fell apart. The longest reign of all dynastic times was almost certainly that of Pepi II, virtually the last of the Old Kingdom rulers, during the twenty-third century BC. He occupied the throne for 94 years! An ageing king might well let the reins of government slacken, allowing subordinates to grow stronger yet taking care that none should become the only contender for the throne. Why tempt assassination? The death of such a king might easily lead to internal dissension and the disintegration of the state. Whatever the explanation, after Pepi II, Egypt drifted helplessly into the First Intermediate Period.

These monarchs, who embodied the state as well as ruling it, had to be wary of the conspirator in the shadows. Intrigue might be anywhere, when a single thrust with a dagger and a single step on to the throne-room dais could make over an empire. Each new king usually built himself a new palace. This, rather than being a single building, consisted of a walled compound up to half a kilometre (a quarter of a mile) square containing government offices, stores, barracks for guards, halls where the king gave audiences, and living quarters for the royal family and the court. The palace was constructed of mud brick coated with white plaster; only pyramids and temples warranted the permanence of stone. These kings may have built anew solely for convenience; during the Old Kingdom each king probably set his new palace close to the site where he planned to construct the royal pyramid. They may have moved just to get away from accumulated filth and rubbish. They may have wanted to outdo their predecessors in magnificence. But quite probably they moved simply to make certain that the previous king's harem and palace officials no longer influenced affairs: each king wanted about him men and women who were his alone.

Somehow, despite all the hieratic trappings, these Egyptian kings lived in a strangely fragile world. The life of Ammenemes I, founder of the Twelfth Dynasty, one of the greatest dynasties of all Egyptian history, was typical of this fragility. He started with hardly a claim to the throne at all, as vizier and commander of the army. In these roles he led an expedition into the Wady Hammamat, a valley east of Thebes, to fetch special stone for his predecessor's sarcophagus. When the

time came he powered his way on to the throne himself. Next, he moved the royal residence from Thebes to It-tawi, which was probably about 25 kilometres (16 miles) south of Memphis. He went on to build a pyramid nearby at Lisht. He was undoubtedly a capable ruler but his life ended amid palace intrigues. In a treatise called *The Teaching of King Ammenemes I to His Son Sesostris I*, Ammenemes I apparently told how he survived an attempt on his life. More probably, he actually was assassinated and Sesostris I arranged for the writing of the text to show that the new king would 'trust no brother, know no friend, make no intimates'.

Ammenemes I could not imagine his own servants turning against him, nor the women of the harem giving them aid, and yet, while Sesostris I was away on an expedition, this was exactly what happened. 'Men I fed and trusted rose against me', he supposedly wrote. 'After the evening meal, when night had fallen, I lay down on my bed for an hour and fell asleep. Then weapons were being brandished and men were shouting all around me. I became like a snake of the desert when I woke to the fighting. I was on my own. I found the guard in combat. If I had snatched up weapons myself I might have driven the traitors back. But who is brave at night? And who can fight alone?'

All that is missing from the saga of the rise and fall of Ammenemes I is any claim that he tried to legitimize his position by marrying a royal heiress.

During most of Egyptian history, the throne descended through the women of the royal family. Each queen was the heiress of the previous queen, her mother. The king by right was the man who married this heiress-queen, the 'Lady of the Two Lands', rather than the man who was just the son of the previous king. In Old Kingdom statues of royal couples the queen places her arm around her husband's waist as though to press him forward and present him as the rightful king. Later on, in the New Kingdom and after, the priests played some part in choosing the new king and the eldest son of the queen may have had a particular claim to the throne, but marriage to the heiress-queen was still important right down to Roman times.

In practice, a king might pick out his successor, a son by the heiress-queen who was the 'Great Wife of the King', or by some other wife, and marry him to the next heiress. Again in practice, the son of a king who wished to be king himself would marry his sister, or his mother, or his daughter, or even all three at once: taking all the possible heiresses to wife discouraged rivals. The man who usurped the throne, by force, or cunning, or simply because he was willing to rule in troubled times, would quickly marry an heiress if he could – or dispose of her in some other way.

One episode involving such a queen followed the death at the age of 18 of Tutankhamun, the Eighteenth Dynasty king whose gold-packed tomb revealed the riches of the Egyptian rulers. His young widow, Ankhesenamun, wrote to the king of a neighbouring country: 'My husband is dead and

At its greatest extent, during the New Kingdom between the sixteenth and twelfth centuries BC, the Egyptian empire dominated the lands of the eastern Mediterranean and stretched far up the Nile into Nubia where the Egyptians built towns and temples that mirrored the cities and sanctuaries of their own country. In this fourteenth-century BC wall painting from the tomb of Huy, governor of Ethiopia under Tutankhamun, the princes of Nubia bring tribute, 'the choicest of all the southern countries', to the king of Egypt.

I have no son. Send one of your sons that he may be my husband.' The king delayed and Ankhesenamun wrote again: 'My husband is dead and I have no son. Should I take a servant of mine and make him my husband? Send one of your sons and he shall be my husband and king of Egypt.' A

26

royal prince did set out in quest of power and romance but was ambushed on the way. Ankhesenamun may have been murdered, she may have committed suicide: she certainly disappeared from the scene. One of her own high officials, the priest Ay, made himself king.

Once a king became king he rose far higher than being a man among men. He was a god. He was shrouded with divinity. In temple rituals he spoke to other gods as an equal on behalf of Egypt. At every ceremony, whether he was present or not, the priest proclaimed that the king himself made the offering, 'he and none other'. Through his gifts of land and goods the king actually did provide the offerings laid before the statues of the gods (and consumed by the priests): the animals to sacrifice, the choice hind quarters of oxen, geese, all sorts of fruit, loaves, jars of beer, fine linen, pleasing ointments.

As deities, these kings accepted their obligations towards their fellow gods. One Tenth Dynasty king set down a series of *Precepts* for his son Merikare: 'Build monuments to the gods, for it keeps your name alive. Do everything for the good of your soul, including regular service as a priest. Give riches to the temple, be discreet about the mysteries, enter into the sanctuary and eat of the temple bread, give generously to the upkeep of the altars, swell the temple revenues, add to the daily offerings; for it will profit you to do so.'

Amenophis III, a powerful Eighteenth Dynasty king at the beginning of the fourteenth century BC, gloried in the construction of a new gateway in the temple of Amun at Karnak. He placed on it the inscription 'King of Upper and Lower Egypt, Ruler of Thebes, Amenophis, who seeks to do what is useful, has built another monument for Amun, making for him a great doorway sheathed with gold. The Divine Shadow, in the form of a ram, is inlaid with lapis lazuli wrought with gold and many costly stones; nothing like it has been done before. The paving is adorned with silver. Graven tablets of lazuli are set up, one on each side. Its pylon towers reach heaven like the four pillars supporting heaven; its flagstaffs, sheathed with electrum (an alloy of gold and silver), shine more brightly than the heavens.'

In return the gods cared for their representative on earth. They appeared to him in dreams, to foretell the future, to help him lay his plans for battle, to forbid him from risking his own life in the fighting, or to call on him to restore a crumbling monument. A granite slab between the paws of the Sphinx, the giant human-headed lion at Giza,

carries an inscription telling how the royal prince who became the Eighteenth Dynasty king, Tuthmosis IV rested in the shadow of the Sphinx while hunting. As he slept he dreamed that the Sphinx, the embodiment of the Sun-god Harmachis, told him to clear away the sand from its body if he wished to be certain of gaining the crown.

Sometimes the gods acted more directly. Amenophis III, who built so magnificently at Karnak and who was the son of Tuthmosis IV, recorded promises made to him by Amun: 'When I turn my face to the south, I work a wonder for you; I cause the chiefs of Kush, the wretched, to turn to you, bearing all their tribute on their backs. When I turn my face to the north, I work a wonder for you; I cause the countries of the ends of Asia to come to you, bearing all their tributes on their backs.'

As gods, the kings prayed to gods reserved to them alone, gods who were greater than the local deities called on by the common people. In turn, the gods associated with the kings grew relatively more powerful because of the association. Re of Heliopolis, a town on the east bank of the Nile just north of Memphis called by the ancient Egyptians On or Yun, became chief among the gods. At times Ptah of Memphis, a god described as first creating himself and then the world, appeared almost as important as Re. During the Middle and New Kingdoms, when kings from Thebes dominated Egypt, Amun, a god linked with Thebes, rose high, eventually merging with Re as Amun-Re.

Essentially the living kings of Egypt, terrible in their glorious power, worshipped the sun, which burnt so fiercely in the heavens, in the form of Re, and also as Horakhti the rising sun, and Atum the setting sun, and Aten the actual disc of the sun. The earliest manifest representation of Re was as the sacred *benben* stone set in the sanctuary of the temple at Heliopolis. The *benben* was probably conical or pyramid-shaped and may have provided the model for the pyramids themselves.

In death, the kings expected to join Re, travelling with him in his 'Boat of Millions of Years' and joining with the other gods to fight off dangers as they voyaged through the perilous darkness of the underworld by night. During the Early Dynastic Period and the Old Kingdom, only the king looked forward to the full enjoyment of this eternal life, although his followers expected to continue serving him in death. This was the era when the kings built themselves great tombs at Saqqara and Abydos, palaces for the after-life that were stocked with the food and goods that a king would need. This was the era that developed first the step pyramids and then the true pyramids, which reached their full glory in the three giants of Giza built during the Fourth Dynasty.

In another version of resurrection in eternity, the living king was the god Osiris, the source of fertility. Carvings and statues of the kings showed them wearing the curved and braided, artificial Osirian beard. After death, the king fused with Osiris, lord of the other world, and so lived on in heaven. The Osiris myth belonged to all, so the idea of eternal life, the building of tombs, the making of mummies and the writing out of spells that guaranteed the dead person entry to the other world, spread throughout Egyptian society.

As a final touch that mixed divinity with practicality, the kings claimed they were begotten by the gods. They emphasized it among their titles: 'I am his son who came forth from him; he beautified all my forms, in this my name, Son of Re'. Some went further, detailing how a specific god had taken human form to visit the queen. The son of a divine father and the heiress-queen must rightfully be a divine king. Perhaps the reality consisted of the previous king, the husband of the heiress-queen, wearing the regalia of the god to go in to see his wife, although the description put it more lyrically. During the Eighteenth Dynasty, a princess, Hatshepsut, who was the daughter of Tuthmosis I and

his queen Ahmes, made herself the female king of Egypt. She then insisted that her true father had been the god Amun who made his form like that of Tuthmosis I and went into the palace where he found Ahmes asleep: 'The sweet fragrance of the god awakened her and she laughed with joy. He came to her immediately. He gave his heart to her and let her see his divine form. This god, in his majesty, did all that he desired with her. . . . Then Amun said "The name of this daughter I have planted in your body shall be Hatshepsut." '

Everything about these kings seemed god-like to the people of Egypt. The king was set apart, surrounded by splendour. To the common folk, his existence at the centre of the court, holding audience in the palace or officiating in the temple, was probably just as unimaginable as the activities of the gods in heaven. Even many of the nobles beheld his majesty only from a distance. Everything he did was notable, everything he said was recorded, everything he touched became sacred. When he sat on his golden throne, raised on a dais in the

Egyptian goldsmiths, as those shown with other craftsmen in this fifteenth-century BC wall painting, produced a wide variety of highly finished artifacts ranging from delicate jewellery, examples of which have survived the depredations of looters, to the solid gold inner coffin of Tutankhamun.

high-ceilinged hall of audience, enshrined by screens that preserved his mystery, he was as much a god as any statue in a temple sanctuary. The petitioner who approached this 'good god' threw himself to the ground in awe, he 'smelt the earth' in homage.

In private the king could afford to be a little more indulgent, although even in his own private rooms within the palace he never altogether laid aside his grandeur. He could make royal pleasantries or dispense with rigid protocol: Pepi I, of the Sixth Dynasty, granted one of his officials the privilege of wearing his sandals within the palace. He could laugh and drink: indeed, the Egyptians apparently liked the prospect of getting a little drunk. He could call for singers and dancers or the more robust entertainment of a display of wrestling by the palace guards. He could dally with his wives or play with his children. Paintings at El-Amarna, the new capital built by the Eighteenth Dynasty king, Akhenaten when he broke away from the priests and the worship of Amun, showed the king in lively domestic scenes with his wife, Nefertiti, and his daughters. The queen has her arms around his waist or sits on his lap, the children play around.

In public, however, all was pomp and display. The royal festivals, the coronation and its anniversary each year, the annual rites to bless the work of cultivation and guarantee the land's fertility, called for ritual and magnificence. The most significant festival was the *heb-sed*, celebrated after a king had reigned for some years. In the *heb-sed* he magically re-invigorated himself and, in doing so, breathed new life into Egypt itself.

As part of these festivals the king showed himself in all his glory to his court and favoured visitors. Each palace, the main residence and the smaller residences that were part of every temple the king visited on his travels, had a 'Window of Appearances' sensational in itself. The privileged crowd entered the temple through a doorway set in gate towers 21 metres (70 ft.) high to find themselves packed into a courtyard. High on the walls carved groups of captives, dominated by the figure of the king, turned their gaze towards the back face of the gateway pylons. This vast sweep of stone carried great carved reliefs of the king as the god, nine metres (30 ft.) high and painted to look life-like. Above and between them was the 'Window of Appearances' itself.

All was agleam with light. The painted façade glowed with bright reds, blues, greens and yellows. The window surround was set about with brilliant tiles, glass and polished stones which flashed in the sun. Beneath the window more carved captives waited for the king to tread on their bowed heads. Within this dazzling frame the king presented himself, crowned, carrying the emblems of state, wearing a magnificent pectoral suspended on his chest by a jewelled necklace. Truly, the king was a god.

Gods and men, these kings ruled Egypt for three thousand years. Even today their names roll on, their reputations persist. It is a kind of immortality.

Scorpion, Narmer and Aha, any one or all of whom may have been the legendary Menes, united the two lands of Egypt. Later rulers always called themselves 'King of Upper and Lower Egypt' and wore the double crown that combined the crowns of the two countries. They built Memphis, the city that became the capital although it may have started as a strategically-positioned fortress town. The other First Dynasty kings consolidated the union, sent trading and military expeditions into neighbouring countries, and constructed great tombs that prefigured the pyramids. Fables were told about these kings, that Menes was devoured by a crocodile, that during the reign of another the Nile flowed with honey for fifteen days, that another wrote a book on anatomy and medicine, that yet another discovered the central chapter of the *Book of the Dead* revealing the secrets of everlasting life. As to historical fact, however, very little is known. During the middle of the Second Dynasty an uprising may have taken place in the north, linked with the rule of a king named Peribsen, but Egypt continued strong and was certainly reunified by the reign of the last king of the dynasty, Khasekhemui.

Although the Third Dynasty is, on the whole, equally obscure, with hardly anything known about the kings themselves, it did produce the first monument of the pyramid age, the Step Pyramid of King Zoser. This stone-built structure, which reached its final form only after a series of developments from the original single-stage tomb, became a place of wonder and pilgrimage. The Fourth Dynasty brought the great true pyramids, in particular the three pyramids at Giza (slightly to the north of Memphis) built by Cheops, Chephren and Mycerinus.

Peace and power marked out the Fourth and the following Fifth Dynasties with a strong Egypt growing wealthy from agriculture and trade. Manuscripts dating from the Middle Kingdom provide a series of *Instructions* apparently drawn together by an Old Kingdom official, Ptah-hotep, which reveal a concern for stability: 'If you are a man of standing, you should set up a household and love your wife at home, as is fitting. If you are a man of standing in the councils of his lord, fix your heart on what is wise; be silent; speak only of what you know. Bow down before your superior in the king's service and your house will benefit; do not resist authority. Be of cheerful countenance. Hear these things and all your plans will prosper.' The Sixth Dynasty saw more pyramid building and further military campaigns. Songs of triumph record that the army returned safely after destroying the land of the Sand-dwellers, after slaying tens of thousands of soldiers. But Egypt faltered as the long reign of the ageing Pepi II weakened the monarchy, as endowments to build and maintain the pyramids and temples ate away the revenues as local princes grew bolder, and the country slid towards the divided confusion of the First Intermediate Period. A mess of kings struggled for power.

Around the middle of the twenty-first century BC, one of the Eleventh Dynasty kings from Thebes, Mentuhotep II, reunited the Two Lands. Thebes now became the capital of Egypt, the kings built their temples there and its local god, Amun, gained influence. Mentuhotep IV, last king of the Eleventh Dynasty, gave way to his own Chief of Works who, as Ammenemes I founded the Twelfth Dynasty about the beginning of the twentieth century BC. He moved the capital north, re-established the king's dominion over district governors and took to pyramid building once more. Sesostris I, his son, reorganized the army and carried Egypt to new significance in the ancient world by conquering the countries to the south. Ammenemes II, Sesostris II and III, and Ammenemes III continued as vigorously: setting up trade with Asia, working the copper mines in Sinai, opening a canal through the first cataract on the Nile near Aswan, and controlling the level of the lake in the Fayum depression. They also carried on building pyramids.

Once again, however, the smooth succession of powerful kings broke down and, around the beginning of the eighteenth century BC, Egypt drifted into the Second Intermediate Period. The Two Lands separated. One dynasty established itself at Thebes, ruling Upper Egypt; Lower Egypt split further, with an independent line of kings ruling the western Delta while Asiatic intruders pushed in from the east. With Egypt divided against itself these foreign groups entered the country as infiltrators rather than military invaders. They controlled the eastern Delta and, for a while, their kings ruled from Memphis itself. These foreign kings allowed the local administration to continue much as before, they adopted classical Egyptian styles for their monuments, they made improvements to weapons and household tools, and they brought the horse and chariot to Egypt. They were called the Hyksos, a Greek form of the Egyptian description 'rulers from foreign lands'. Manetho, in his account, gave a different interpretation of the name as well as anguishing over their supposed cruelty.

'It came to pass,' he wrote, 'I know not why, that God was displeased with us and men came from eastern lands who invaded our country and easily subdued it without a battle. Once they had our rulers in their power they burned down our cities, and demolished the temples of the gods, and used every barbarity against the inhabitants; some they slew, and led their wives and children into slavery. At length they made one of themselves king, and he lived at Memphis. . . . All this nation was called Hyksos, that is "Shepherd Kings"; for *hyk* denotes a king, and *sos* a shepherd.'

Eventually, around the middle of the sixteenth century BC, the Theban kings felt strong enough to confront the Hyksos. At least a couple of them died in the fighting but they did push the foreigners northwards. King Ahmose, first king of the Eighteenth Dynasty which began the glittering era of the New Kingdom, finally laid siege to the last great Hyksos stronghold at Avaris, then drove them out of Egypt altogether and chased them into Palestine. One officer, an admiral also named Ahmose, recorded that after an early battle he was awarded a hand cut from the body of a dead foe as a sign of valour and that when Avaris fell he 'carried off as captive slaves one man and three women, four heads in all'.

With the Hyksos on the retreat, Ahmose turned southwards, striking down Tety the Handsome who 'had gathered rebels about him': the Egyptians labelled as rebels anyone who stood against them. He also took the time to build a new, pyramid-shaped memorial for the grandmother he and his wife shared. Ahmose's son and successor, Amenophis I, continued campaigning north and south as he rebuilt Egypt into a single state. His own name reflects the new importance of the Theban god Amun now that Thebes was firmly established as the capital city of the kings of Egypt. All the New Kingdom dynasties provided vast endowments for the temple of Amun at Karnak and built on a lavish scale, with splendid courts, halls and gateways.

Next came Tuthmosis I, a warrior-king who ranged even further abroad. He fought his way to the banks of the river Euphrates in the north, setting Palestine as a barrier between Egypt and the newly-active states to the north-east. He adventured southwards, reaching the Third Cataract on the Nile and beyond. The excellent admiral Ahmose declared that 'his Majesty raged like a panther in the south, his Majesty threw his spear which stuck fast in the body of the enemy chief'. Tuthmosis I set two granite obelisks in the Karnak temple in gratitude to Amun; he also became the first ruler to cut a secret tomb in the hidden Valley of the Kings near Thebes.

Tuthmosis II came to the throne by marrying the heiress-queen, his half-sister Hatshepsut. Like all other kings of Egypt he quickly led military expeditions into neighbouring countries to stifle any thoughts of rebellion against an inexperienced ruler. Then he died. His young son, who eventually ruled as Tuthmosis III, found his accession was delayed, however, by some twenty years or more. Hatshepsut first appointed herself Regent on his behalf (he was, after all, very young) and then, in an unprecedented step, she took the throne herself. Although the dynastic lists contain the names of two or three previous female rulers, the Egyptian system was disturbed by the idea: even the title of Queen implied daughter of the previous king, great wife of the present king rather than a ruler by right. Hatshepsut claimed that Amun himself had come from his temple, saying: 'Welcome, my sweet daughter, my favourite, the King of Upper and Lower Egypt, Son of the Sun.' She had statues carved showing her as king, wearing the short, masculine kilt, the royal head-dress and the artificial beard of Osiris.

Hatshepsut concentrated on trade and raising monuments instead of military conquests. With her chief official, Senenmut, she built a beautiful temple set beneath towering cliffs at Deir el-Bahari, near Thebes, and erected a pair of magnificent obelisks at Karnak. She sent a trading expedition far down the Red Sea to the Land of Punt, probably somewhere on the east African coast. The people of Punt sent back gold, ivory, precious stones, myrrh trees, ebony, hounds, apes and more.

Though for much of its history Ancient Egypt was under centralized rule, there were regional subdivisions, nomes, with as many as forty-two local districts. In these, such officials as the one depicted in this nineteenth-century BC granite statue played an important administrative role.

Eventually, Tuthmosis III did reach the throne. Possibly he conspired to hasten Hatshepsut's end. He certainly erased her name from inscriptions on her monuments, substituting his own or his father's or grandfather's, and he dated his reign from his father's death: Hatshepsut had no official being. Tuthmosis III copied her, however, in calling Amun his father. He also claimed that, when he was a child serving as a priest in the temple, the statue of Amun bowed down before him as it was carried in procession, declaring him to be the true king. 'This is not a lie,' he stated. 'There is no untruth. The god went round the pillared hall. He recognized me and halted. I stretched myself on the ground before him.'

As king, Tuthmosis III campaigned vigorously, moving swiftly and fighting strongly. In his first venture, northwards into Palestine, he took the fortified city of Megiddo, defeating the prince of Kadesh, chief among the northern states. Further expeditions strengthened the Egyptian hold on a spreading empire and, year by year, vassal states sent rich tribute to the great king: when Tuthmosis III inscribed his conquests on the gateway pylons of the Karnak temple the list included no less than 360 places.

While Tuthmosis III bestrode the ancient world, his chief official, the vizier Rekhmire, handled all the affairs of Egypt. Rekhmire's tomb, a hall 34 metres (111 ft.) long driven into the hillside above Thebes, contains, among the wall paintings, the instructions given him by the king. These precepts encapsulated the Egyptian idea of justice, summed up in the word *ma'at*. *Ma'at* was personified as a goddess; *ma'at* was the feather balanced against the heart of a dead person to check that the candidate for entry to heaven could truly claim to be free of evil; *ma'at* was in the judgements of the king as a living god; *ma'at* was a sense of order, of rightness, of proper behaviour towards others; *ma'at* was a pragmatic approach to moral life. 'Look to the office of vizier,' said Tuthmosis III. 'It sustains the land. . . . When a petitioner comes from Upper or Lower Egypt see that everything done conforms to the custom of the law. A petitioner should not say "My right has been denied me." The god hates partiality; treat the person you know equally with the person you do not. . . . Let men fear you because you offer justice. . . . This is laid upon you.'

Amenophis II shared the throne for a short while with his father, Tuthmosis III, before the older king died, a recurrent Egyptian method for easing the transfer from one autocratic monarch to the next. He, too, and his son in his turn, Tuth-mosis IV, kept the borders of Egypt secure and increased its glory so that their successor, Ameno-phis III, has been called 'the Magnificent'. When he came to the throne he was able to count on alliances with kings far across Asia.

Amenophis III built a temple at Karnak, another at Luxor, yet another on the west bank of the Nile near Thebes. In front of this third temple he set two vast statues of himself, about 20 metres (66 ft.) high yet cut from single blocks of stone. The Greeks and Romans called them the Colossi of Memnon. He made a lake and sailed across it in his barge, hunted lions, killing over a hundred, and left records of these feats inscribed on large scarabs. Scarabs were beetle-shaped amulets, in this case carved from the soft stone steatite. One of these inscriptions announced his marriage to his wife, Tiye: 'The name of her father is Yuya, the name of her mother is Tuya. She is the wife of the mighty king.' She was not, apparently, the

Tutankhamun, shown here as a young boy, came to the throne when he was ten years old and died at eighteen. The riches from his tomb, one of the smallest in the Valley of the Kings, revealed the splendours of the royal burials.

royal daughter of a king.

Amenophis III ruled for some forty years. During the last few years of his reign, which ended between 1375 and 1365 BC, he probably shared the throne with his son, Amenophis IV. The latter began by building great jubilee temples at Karnak. The new king really did regard himself as the 'Son of the Sun', so much so that he honoured only that one god. He went further than any other king, rejecting the compromise between the Sun-god Re and the local god Amun which produced the composite god Amun-Re, rejecting even those aspects of the Sun-god represented in human or animal form. The new king worshipped the Sun-god at its most abstract, as the Aten, the light-giving disc of the sun. In temples he built at Karnak the image appeared again and again: wall carvings showed the king and his queen, Nefertiti, making offerings to the simple disc of the sun which sent out rays ending as human hands bringing life to the royal family. Amenophis IV decreed that all temple revenues should now go to the new cult; he changed his name to Akhenaten, 'He who serves the Aten'; and he moved his capital to a new city, Akhetaten, the 'Horizon of Aten', about 240 kilometres (150 miles) north of Thebes at a place now called El-Amarna. He had temples, palaces and luxurious villas built from scratch for the officials who had to follow him from Thebes.

Akhenaten's intention, in part at least, could have been to limit the political power of the priests of Amun: the new city certainly reduced their wealth by cutting off the rich flow of tribute sent up the Nile from Lower Egypt and Asia. However, something more was involved. Akhenaten immured himself in his isolated capital, devoting himself to his religion, encouraging a more naturalistic artistic style, showering gold on his officials as a mark of favour. When he honoured his adviser Ay, who later became king himself, the royal family, the king, the queen, and the young princesses, literally threw down necklets, bracelets and chains of gold from the palace balcony. Akhenaten refused to leave the city, although the kings normally travelled through the country to make their authority known. He never went on a military campaign. He welcomed foreign envoys to the jubilee to celebrate the twelfth year of his reign but his policy, if it was as positive as a policy, was to let the states on the fringes of the empire battle among themselves without Egyptian involvement.

Sometime after the jubilee, Akhenaten raised up as his co-ruler a young man, Smenkhkare, who may have been his brother. Then Akhenaten died. Smenkhkare died soon after and the throne then passed to his ten-year-old brother, Tutankhaten. The latter soon left the city of Akhetaten and changed his name to Tutankhamun: Amun had come back to favour. Tutankhamun died at the age of eighteen; the treasures that astound the world today were those of a king who hardly figured in the dynastic history of Egypt. Ay then ruled for a few years and was succeeded by the general Horemheb, who thought so little of the previous kings that he dated his reign from the death of Amenophis III. Akhetaten became a ghost city; the Aten temples at Karnak were cast down and their stones used in later construction; the Eighteenth Dynasty passed away.

Another general and high official now took the throne as Ramesses I, founding the Nineteenth Dynasty: the Nineteenth and Twentieth Dynasties, running from roughly 1300 BC to somewhat after 1100 BC, are called the Ramessides. Ramesses I died very shortly after and his son, Seti I, became king, moving his capital to a city in the north-eastern Delta. Seti I carried out all the traditional kingly duties. He restored monuments and built a temple at Abydos dedicated to the glory of the dead kings of Egypt in their form as the living god Osiris. He cut an extensive and finely decorated tomb in the Valley of the Kings. He made a well on the route between the Nile and the gold mines of the eastern desert, for of those who went to fetch gold half might die on the way, together with their donkeys: ' "How does the thirsty man cool his throat?" his Majesty said. "I will care for them." His Majesty travelled through the mountains seeking a fitting place and the god guided him. Then stone-masons were brought to dig a well and the water overflowed abundantly.'

Seti I campaigned widely. He and his son, Ramesses II, who ruled for over 60 years, faced the same problem: the Hittites in Syria had become strong enough to resist Egyptian dominion. Most Egyptian campaigns had brought easy successes as the Egyptian forces quickly dominated smaller armies, but now the warfare drifted on. In addition, Ramesses II and his son, Merenptah, faced the possibility of losing the Delta region to foreign settlers and Libyan invaders. In the end, Ramesses II made a treaty with the Hittites and Merenptah broke the Libyans in a day-long battle that left 6000 dead.

All these Nineteenth Dynasty kings gave the impression that they enjoyed a good battle; perhaps they found stimulation in manoeuvring

Horemheb, last of the Eighteenth Dynasty kings around the end of the fourteenth century BC, shown here being decked with jewellery, followed Amenophis IV or Akhenaten and Tutankhamun. Akhenaten had made the Aten, the disc of the sun, the main god of the pharaoh and built a new capital Akhetaten; Tutankhamun returned the god of Thebes to pre-eminence. Later generations sometimes ignored these kings and regarded Horemheb as succeeding Amenophis III directly.

against a near-equal opponent. One officer noted his king's reaction to news that the Arabs were gathering for war: 'His Majesty rejoiced. For the good god exults when he begins the fight, he is joyful when he has to cross the frontier, and is content when he sees blood. He cuts off the heads of his enemies, and an hour of fighting gives him more delight than a day of pleasure.' Another high-ranking officer, however, recorded his own misgivings: 'Let me tell you how the soldier travels to Syria, marching through the upland country bearing his food and water like a donkey. This makes his neck stiff and breaks his back. He drinks dirty water. When he faces the enemy he feels like a bird in a snare. If he reaches his home in Egypt he is like worm-eaten wood. He is ill. They have to bring him home on a donkey while his clothes are stolen and his servants run away.'

Both Seti I and Ramesses II blazoned their exploits across huge wall-carvings. In virtually every carving, Ramesses II proclaimed that his personal valour alone had brought the army through one tactically-disastrous encounter. The Egyptians planned to attack Kadesh in northern Syria and Ramesses II was close by the city with four divisions of the army. Two Arabs came to see him, pretending that they and their tribes wished to join him as allies, and said that the Hittite army was still far to the north. They lied, but Ramesses II believed them and, with one division and his bodyguard, advanced quickly towards Kadesh. The Hittites, however, were very, close and fell upon the second division as they came up to join Ramesses II. The Egyptians fled, the panic spread to the first division and Ramesses II and his bodyguard faced the Hittite might alone.

Ramesses II set himself at the head of his tiny band of troops and drove his chariot furiously at the encircling horde. The wall-carvings show the king fighting by himself, raining arrows on the enemy who fly in wild confusion. 'When his Majesty saw them he became like a lion. He put on his armour, he hastened to his horses and stormed forwards – he was quite alone. He broke through the ranks of the army of the prince of the Hittites. He made havoc of them and threw them into the waters of the river.' A third Egyptian division now appeared and helped stand the Hittites off until, two or three hours later, another division came up to attack them from the rear. At the end of the day both armies withdrew. This was just one indecisive battle in a 20-year war but Ramesses II boasted of his role: 'I defied the armies of all nations when I was alone and my infantry and my

chariot squadrons had forsaken me; not one of them stood still or returned. I swear that I myself truly did all that I have said.'

Ramesses II went on to build on a scale greater than almost any other king, constructing temple after temple, raising statues of himself and inscribing his name everywhere. His monuments marched down the Nile, from his new capital in the Delta, to the rock-cut temple at Abu Simbel far to the south. Merenptah, too, built temples and so did Ramesses III, one of the earlier kings of the Twentieth Dynasty around 1200 BC. The age of the great kings was passing, however, and Ramesses III was the last ruler to dominate Egypt and wage wars beyond its frontiers. Even so he died ignominiously as the victim of a conspiracy hatched within his own harem, although he lived long enough after the attack made upon him to arrange a secret trial of the queens, princes and court officials involved. The conspirators probably hoped to place a prince named Pentuere on the throne and he, and others, were condemned to death: 'He was brought before the court because he joined with his mother Ty when she conspired with the women of the harem, and because he acted with hostility against his lord. He was brought before the judges that they might question him. They found him guilty; they dismissed him to his house; he took his own life.' But the judges themselves turned out to be frail creatures. Three of the six held drunken revels with some of the accused women of the harem: 'Their punishment was fulfilled by the cutting off of their noses and ears.'

Somehow the fabric of Egyptian society was wearing thin as the kings dissipated their authority. Local officials became almost openly corrupt. One accusation records that a supervisor named Panebe forced his workmen to labour on his private projects, that he stole tools and blocks of stone from construction sites and more. 'He went down into the tomb of the workman Nachtim and stole the couch on which he lay. He also took the objects provided for the deceased and stole them.'

In an even more extensive case, the governor of eastern Thebes, named Paser, virtually accused the governor of western Thebes of condoning tomb-robbery in the necropolis. High officials found one royal tomb broken open, that of the Theban king, Sebekemsaf; they took eight suspects into custody and beat them on the hands and feet until they confessed. 'We found the noble mummy of the king with a long chain of golden amulets and ornaments around his neck; the head was covered with gold. The noble mummy of the king was entirely overlaid with gold, and his coffin covered both inside and out with gold and adorned with precious jewels. We tore off the gold, which we found on the noble mummy of this god, as well as the amulets and ornaments from round the neck and the bandages in which the mummy was wrapped. We found the royal consort equipped in like manner, and we tore off all that we found upon her. We then divided between us all the gold which we found with this god.' Paser continued with his charges but the affair drifted towards an inconclusive close. Quite probably the reality consisted of a governor and his officials taking bribes from robbers, who then despoiled the tombs without hindrance. The investigators conspired to conceal the spread of corruption.

At some point an heiress-queen from this dynasty married one of the High Priests of Amun at Thebes. As a result, the dynasties split. The Twenty-First Dynasty continued in the Delta region but in Upper Egypt the High Priests ruled. These priestly kings probably established the exacting daily rituals recalled in the history of Egypt written by Diodorus Siculus in the first century BC. The life of the kings of Egypt was, apparently, not like that of other monarchs who were irresponsible and might do just what they chose; on the contrary, everything was fixed for them by law, not only their official duties but even the details of their daily life. The hours both of day and night were arranged at which the king had to do not what he pleased but what was prescribed for him. For not only were the times appointed at which he should transact public business or sit in judgement, but the very hours for his walking and bathing, for sleeping with his wife, and for performing every act of life were all settled. Custom enjoined a very simple diet; the only flesh he might eat was veal and goose, and he might drink only a prescribed quantity of wine.

As these dynasties petered out, around 950 BC, Egypt fell further into disarray while various kings, from Nubia and Libya as well as Egypt, held sway in different parts of the country. Around 660 BC an Egyptian king, Psammetichus, succeeded in re-uniting the country under the Twenty-sixth Dynasty and, for a while, Egypt found a new confidence. Then, in 525 BC, the Persians invaded, setting up their own line of kings. Although a rebellion did put some Egyptian kings on the throne for a few years, Persian rule ended only when Alexander the Great conquered Egypt in 332 BC. Alexander made himself pharaoh but,

after his death in 323 BC, the governor he had appointed, Ptolemy Lagus, took power and eventually declared himself king. The line of Ptolemies, the Greek kings of Egypt, ended only with Cleopatra's death in 30 BC.

Egyptian glory stretched out over twenty-five centuries and more. When the last Egyptian pharaohs contemplated the works of even greater, earlier kings they looked on monuments that were already twice as old as London's Westminster Abbey is today. For hundreds of years the Egyptians had accepted their kings as living gods, as beings laid around with splendour. Yet they also told each other stories that revealed deep suspicions about the behaviour of their illustrious monarchs, suspicions that were far worse than anything that can actually have happened.

Herodotus, the Greek historian of the fifth century BC, collected one of these tales, a cry of protest against the king who built the Great Pyramid 2000 years before – and perhaps against the demands of kings in general. Cheops apparently came to such a pitch of wickedness that, being in want of money, he caused his own daughter to set herself in a brothel and ordered her to obtain from those who came a certain amount of money. She not only obtained the sum appointed by her father but also decided privately to leave behind her a memorial. She requested each man who came into her to give her one stone: and of these stones she built the middle pyramid of the three which stand in front of the Great Pyramid, each side being 46 metres (150 ft.) in length.

During the confusion of the First Intermediate Period, the wise man Ipuwer stood before the court and looked back to the days of the ideal monarch, the Sun-god who first ruled Egypt: 'He brings cooling to the flame. He is the shepherd of all people. There is no evil in his heart. Though his herds are small he spends the day gathering them together. . . . Where is he today? Does he sleep? His might is no longer seen.' In the world of the pharaohs the Sun-god always was king.

Ramesses II, a Nineteenth Dynasty king who ruled during the thirteenth century BC, built monument after monument to his own power. He campaigned through Syria for twenty years in all, although the final peace treaties recognized that Egypt could not dominate the area. He founded a new capital in the Delta, he completed the great hall in the temple at Karnak, added a court and pylon gateway at Luxor, raised the Ramesseum funerary temple on the other bank of the Nile and cut temples into the solid rock at Abu Simbel. The shattered but monumental statue of him in the Ramesseum inspired Shelley's famous poem 'Ozymandias'.

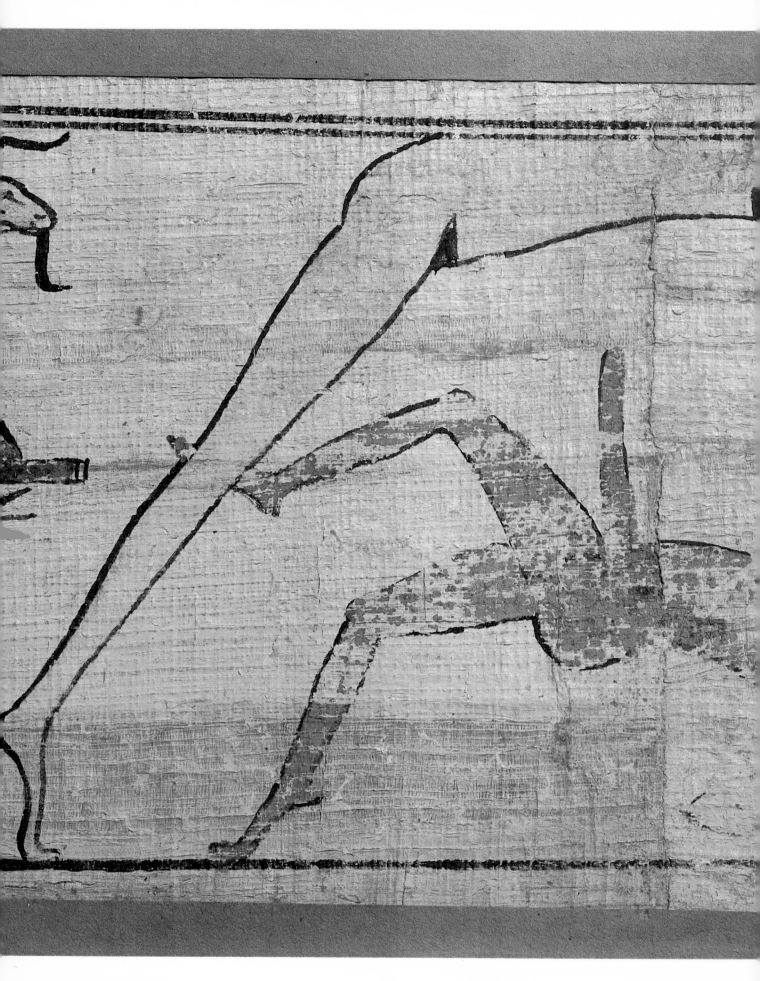

Chapter 2

Religion of the Kings

ULTS AND RITUALS, gods and goddesses, sacraments and mysteries: ancient Egypt had them all and more. Religion flourished throughout the thousands of years of Egyptian history as though nourished by the fertile waters of the Nile itself. Districts and cities had their local deities, jolly gods who amused the populace, goddesses who protected them, beings who answered their prayers; greater gods figured in myths about creation and rebirth in the other world; the king communed with deities that were his alone; the Sun-god shone in differing ways; and always their religion grew more complicated. Egypt was a land of faiths.

Local gods lived on from pre-dynastic times when each settlement had its totem, in many cases an animal-headed god or goddess. As Egypt coalesced into districts and, eventually, a kingdom these godlings merged and fought and married and arranged themselves in hierarchies. They accepted new gods as they appeared and even drew in gods from outside Egypt itself. Some were raised up to become the gods of the kings with the well-being of Egypt in their care; others continued as the refuge of the common people. Some remained as purely local influences while others were taken up by all.

Indeed, one of the oldest of the Egyptian deities, Thoeris or Ta-urt, the great one, goddess of pregnancy and birth, had no particular locality and no limitation on who could worship her. Any woman in Egypt might pray to her statue or wear one of the amulets that showed her as a hippopotamus standing on its hind legs.

In the beginning, after the first stirrings of creation from water and darkness, the goddess Nut lay with her husband, the god Geb. However, she agreed to raise up the Sun-god Re, who was weary of life among the peoples of the world, upon her back, holding him suspended above the earth. So Nut became the sky above and Geb the earth below.

41

Local gods were honoured with their own shrines. This double shrine, built in Ptolemaic times, honours the god Horus and a local crocodile god.

Later, the god Bes became husband to Thoeris and he, too, appeared as friend to all. The bandy-legged Bes took a lowly place in the pantheon of gods, he entertained the other gods with his singing and dancing, but people could approach a lowly god more easily. They sought his protection against demons for Bes was a warrior who destroyed evil spirits and strangled lions and serpents. Statues show him as squat and ugly, half-man, half-animal, with two short horns sprouting above a hideous face. Yet Bes was the god of the family and his fearsome appearance, his fighting powers and his whirling dances all served to keep a mother and her new-born child safe from harm.

Amun of Thebes was by far the most important of local gods. During the early dynasties, when Thebes was a minor town far to the south of the capital, Memphis, Amun appeared as insignificant as his provincial worshippers. After the kings of Thebes conquered the entire country, however, Amun gained authority until he became supreme among the gods of Egypt, the father of the kings themselves. He gave these kings their victories in battle and they returned to him their allegiance. In gratitude they raised and extended the magnificent temples of Karnak and Luxor and endowed them with almost unbelievable riches. 'I am his son,' pronounced Tuthmosis III, the Theban king who consolidated Egypt's position in the ancient world. 'I have built his house as an eternal work in order that I might extend the throne of him who made me, that I might supply with food his altars upon earth.' And the offerings flowed in: golden crowns with lapis lazuli rosettes, gold seal rings, gold vases and drinking vessels, basins of silver trimmed with gold, harps made from ebony embellished with gold and silver, ceremonial barges of new cedar, shrines of gold and silver and clothing of fine, white linen. Eventually so much passed to Amun that his High Priest at Thebes became more important than the Pharoah himself.

Curiously enough, hardly anything is known about this god who was honoured as the one, the only one, maker of all that is, the maker of existences. Few stories were told about him and he hardly figured in the myths of creation and rebirth. Even his bodily representation differed disconcertingly: he sometimes took the form of a ram or a ram-headed man marked by curving horns; he appeared in human form but in doing so wore two goose feathers on his head as a vestige of some earlier existence as a goose. He was the great Cackler that laid the egg which produced the earth. One of the lesser gods, Geb, claimed: 'I protect the egg of the great divine Cackler. If I thrive it thrives, if I live it lives.' Amun existed from the beginning and persisted to the end of the religious life of ancient Egypt.

At the other extreme, many local gods remained just that, spirits of a certain place with limited, though useful, powers. One example was Meritseger, goddess of the necropolis at Thebes. She dwelt among the mountain peaks above and so was called the western summit. One necropolis worker left an inscription that told how he fell ill because he offended Merit-seger but, when he prayed to her, she relented: 'I was a man without knowledge and knew not what is good and what is evil. I sinned against the mountain summit and she chastised me. I say beware of the western summit who pursues him who sins against her. But when I called to my mistress I found she came to me with sweet breath and she was gracious to me. She caused me to forget my illness which had befallen me. Truly, the western summit is gracious.'

Like other peoples, the Egyptians incorporated into their religious system many of their ideas about the creation of the world and about their own history. These appear in the form of myths and legends apparently telling of the acts of gods. Perhaps their dependence on the Nile led them to believe the world sprang from a watery abyss. Perhaps their earliest experiences of the cycle of agricultural growth, harvest, sowing and regrowth gave rise to the notion of the sacred king who forfeited his life to regenerate the land. In turn this led to the concept of a god who died and was reborn, Osiris. Perhaps wars between different groups who tried to dominate the Nile valley produced the tales of gods fighting each other, of Osiris slain by Seth. Perhaps their desire to unite

Egypt lay behind the urge to have the gods and goddesses arrange themselves in families. Perhaps their curiosity about the universe itself, about the reasons why night followed day, coalesced with their fears and hopes for the after-life when they described the abode of the gods. And perhaps the circumstances of their own king influenced the descriptions of the god he identified as being particularly his, the Sun-god Re.

As the final touch, their religious system soaked up everything and squeezed out nothing. Whatever was said about a god went into the mix whether it blended easily with other concepts or not. If two gods had similar attributes the Egyptians might make them one. If one god had different aspects the Egyptians could honour them all at the same time. If two accounts gave different versions of the actions of the gods, the Egyptians

Animal gods featured largely in Egyptian religion. Ta-urt, goddess of pregnancy and birth, features as a hippopotamus in a star chart of the northern sky.

43

would accept them both. Religion, as always, did not have to be consistent and perhaps even the Egyptians failed to understand all that they believed.

Creation began with nothing except water and darkness. Several different traditions grew up explaining how this watery waste produced heavenly and worldly life. In general terms, the water contained the germ of everything that would be and from it developed the primeval matter that became all things. The primeval mound thrusting itself out of the waters may have been the model for the heap of gravel piled over the first simple tombs and, later, for the pyramids themselves. The water also brought forth the gods, and in particular Re, the shining Sun-god. Re appeared in a number of different forms: the priests of Heliopolis identified Re with Atum; he could be Harmachis; he could be Khepri. The name Khepri means existence and in this form his symbol was the scarabaeus beetle. This creature lays its eggs in balls of dung which it rolls from animal droppings, or even in the dead body of another scarabaeus beetle. When the Egyptians saw the young beetles emerging from these forms of waste and destruction they took the scarab as a symbol of resurrection. The name Khepri also means to roll; each morning the scarab rolled the rising sun into the sky.

Around the company of gods brought into being by the creation the Egyptians wove legends setting up family relationships and accounting for the world as it appeared day by day. Here is the creator-god, now under the name of Nu, still acting to complete the imperfect universe that resulted from the earliest efforts. And here is Re, now known as king and father of the other gods.

In those ancient times Re ruled the people of the earth, as well as the gods, but he grew old. 'Look,' said his peoples, 'we see him age. His bones are like silver, his flesh like gold and his hair like lapis lazuli.' So Re, too weary to remain with ungrateful mankind, sought to withdraw from the world. He turned towards Nu and asked him to make a place where he could not be reached. 'My limbs,' he said, 'are tired.'

Nu called upon the goddess Nut, who had been in the primeval waters with the god Geb, who became her husband, and said 'Daughter Nut, place Re upon your back and hold him suspended

above the earth.' Nut and Geb lay close together but she consented to leave her husband. Then Nu called upon the god Shu, who also came from the primeval waters, and asked him to raise up Nut. Obediently, Shu placed himself between Nut and Geb and supported her. So Nut, who sometimes took the form of a cow, became the sky, Geb the earth and Shu the air.

Re, from time to time, had to leave the sky to go down into the underworld, which he also ruled, so he called into being the stars and the moon to appear in his place. In this way the Egyptians explained the creation of the firmament and the reason why night followed day.

Buried within this particular myth are hints that, in the earliest stages of Egyptian religious development, human sacrifices and even ritual cannibalism occurred. At the point when Re finally separated himself from mankind he agreed to accept the sacrifice of his enemies as expiation of the wrongs he had been done; from then on he had no wish that his children should be killed and settled for the offering up of beasts instead. One nineteenth-century commentator on Egyptian religion, Charles H. S. Davis, quoted a text which told how a pre-historic king consumed the men and loaves of the gods and went on to explain how the men who served as food for his majesty were captured by certain officers of the king. Then they were examined, bound, their throats cut and their entrails taken out. Finally they were hewn in pieces and roasted in pairs or baked in ovens. The meals of the king took place three times a day and consisted of the juicy parts of the 'poor captives'. The 'horrid rite' was intended to bestow upon the one that devoured the flesh of the victims all the intellectual and magical tributes which resided within them, and thus to increase his own capacities and powers.

With Re in his heaven – and he did organize a whole new world upon Nut's back – the next generation of gods came to rule the earth. For some reason Re was jealous of the love between Nut and Geb and, in revenge, decreed that she could not give birth on any of the 360 days in the Egyptian year. But, by trickery, she gained an extra five days to become the mother of the gods Osiris and Seth and of the goddesses Isis and Nephthys. Osiris and Isis then became the father and mother of the god Horus. According to one legend, Osiris and Nephthys, whose husband was supposed to be Seth, became the father and mother of Anubis, the god of death. Osiris himself became the most important god of all, as the god of fertility and even creation, and as the god of resurrection and everlasting life in the other world.

At this time, before men ruled mankind, Osiris was king of Egypt, monarch of the two lands, Upper and Lower. He was good and bountiful. He set himself to civilize the Egyptians, taught them to till the fields and cultivate the fields, gave them law and religion and instructed them in every useful art. Indeed, he travelled throughout the world persuading people to turn away from barbarism.

However, his brother Seth was overcome with jealousy of his goodness and decided to kill him. When Osiris returned to Egypt, Seth laid his plans. First he secretly obtained the measurements of Osiris's body and called in joiners to make a chest of exactly that size, so beautifully ornamented that anyone would want it. Then he invited Osiris to a great banquet, displayed the chest to all his guests and casually announced he would give it away to anyone of them that fitted exactly into it. One by one they climbed in, and one by one they had to admit it was not for them. But when Osiris stepped into the chest and lay down, he fitted perfectly. Seth dashed forward, slammed the lid down, nailed it shut and poured molten lead on as a seal. Then he threw the chest into the river.

When Isis heard what had happened she cut off a lock of her hair as a sign of mourning and wandered the country asking everyone she met if they had seen the chest. She even asked children playing in the countryside. In the end, some of these children were able to tell her which branch of the Nile the chest had floated down and this is why the prattle of children as they play became a form of divination. Even as she searched, Isis discovered that her sister Nephthys had tricked her husband Osiris into making love to her and had borne his child. Isis herself went looking for the baby and brought it up. When grown, he became her constant guard and took the name Anubis.

At length, Isis heard that the chest had floated to the sea and been carried by the waves to Byblos, which some say is on the Syrian coast and some in the Nile delta. Here, cast up on the shore, it lodged in the branches of a tamarisk tree. In time, the tree-trunk grew around the chest, hiding it completely. So fine was this tree that the king of Byblos had it cut down and fashioned into a pillar to support the roof of his palace.

Isis, hearing this, went to Byblos and sat sadly by the side of a well, speaking only to some of the queen's women who happened to be there. She plaited their hair for them and breathed on them the fragrance that came from her own body. When the queen heard of this she called her to the palace and made her nurse to one of her sons. Isis fed the child by letting him suck her finger instead of the breast and every night she laid him in the fire to burn away his mortal part. Meanwhile, she turned herself into a swallow and flew around the pillar, lamenting. One night the queen stood watching and, seeing the child all aflame, cried out, destroying his chance of becoming immortal. Isis explained who she was, asked for the pillar to be given her, cut out the chest and returned the outer wood wrapped in fine linen and covered in perfumed oil. In the morning she set sail upon the river.

Soon Isis arrived at a desert place where she thought she could be alone. She opened up the chest, laid her face against her dead husband's, embraced his corpse and wept bitterly over his lifeless limbs. Then she hid the chest in a remote and secret spot and, according to some stories, went to visit her son Horus. That night Seth was hunting by the light of the moon and, by accident, came across the chest. He opened it up and, recognizing Osiris, hacked the body into fourteen or sixteen pieces which he scattered through Egypt.

Isis set out once more to look for her husband. Some stories say that as she found each part she held a funeral ceremony and buried it where it lay. Others suggest that she set up the many shrines to Osiris to mislead the furious and malicious Seth. The most important shrine was at Abydos and for this reason all Egyptians hoped to voyage there to be united with Osiris in death. Other stories say that Isis collected the parts of Osiris's body together and bound them up with bandages, making the first mummy. She then breathed life into him again and, according to some stories, conceived his child, Horus.

Now eventually, Horus came to battle against Seth to avenge his father, to free his mother from Seth's domination and to take the throne himself. In some stories Horus and Seth contended in law before the court of the gods. Isis trapped Seth into conceding Horus's claims but Seth then challenged Horus to fight him in the water after they had both turned themselves into hippopotamuses. In other stories Horus and Seth led armies against each other. Osiris returned from the other world to teach Horus the use of arms then asked him what was the most glorious action a man

Osiris, shown here as a wooden statue, could be worshipped by all as the god of fertility, creation, resurrection and everlasting life in the other world.

could undertake. 'To revenge injuries offered to his father and his mother,' answered Horus.

In all the stories Horus prevailed over Seth. Seth, however, had one more trick. He appealed to Isis as his sister and she allowed him to go free. Horus was so incensed by his mother's act that he struck off her head. But the god Thoth, 'ibis-headed Thoth, scribe of the gods, the god of learning and of magic', gave her another head, a cow's head. Horus renewed the struggle with Seth but eventually they were reconciled and Horus took his father's throne.

Osiris became all things to the Egyptians. A memorial tablet left by Ramesses IV at Abydos told of his knowledge of the god: 'Your nature, Osiris, is more secret than other gods. You are the moon in heaven. You rejuvenate yourself at your own desire, you become young according to your own wish. You appear in order to dispel darkness, anointed and clothed, for the gods and magic came into existence to illuminate your majesty and bring your enemies to shambles. Truly, you are the Nile, great upon the banks at the time of the beginning of the season; man and gods live by the moisture which comes from you. I also know your majesty as king of the under-world.'

As god of the inundation, Osiris made the country fertile and was sometimes identified with the creator-god. As ruler of the under-world, the king of the dead, he could allow or refuse entry to the realms of bliss, judging the deeds of all who had run their time on earth. As the god who had risen from the dead he was the resurrection, the life that began again after death, symbolized by the yearly miracle of crops springing from the ground: mourners left figures of Osiris in tombs, wooden silhouettes filled with earth and sprinkled with seed that sprouted greenly into life. As the one-time ruler of Egypt, he provided the living model for his successors. Each king became Osiris here and in the life here-after.

God and man, the king was both. As a boy he was Horus the child, the son of Osiris and Isis. As an adult he became Horus the protector, whose emblem was the falcon and who had himself been one of the original gods of Egypt. Some of the legends of the contendings between Horus and Seth hint at this double origin. As Horus, the king had a Horus name. During the Early Dynastic Period this was written inside a *serekh*, an upright rectangle symbolizing the façade of the palace, which was topped by the Horus falcon. Later it appeared within a cartouche, an elongated ring. As Horus, the king occupied the Horus-throne.

And as the occupier of the throne he was Osiris and would continue as Osiris into death. Statues of the king set about his mortuary temple as insurance against the destruction of his body after death showed him as Osiris, carrying the emblems of Osiris and wearing the narrow, outward-curving Osirian beard.

As a divinity, the god-king stood in a special relationship to the other gods. His subjects saw him as the actual god they worshipped, the embodiment of their local deities. But the king himself worshipped another god, a god who was his alone, a god above the other gods in the way that the king was above the other people of his kingdom. That god was the Sun-god Re.

Re, the father of the gods, had his principal temple at On or Heliopolis, close to the Cairo of today. This temple held his sacred symbol, the *benben*, which was probably a conical or pyramid-shaped stone. Set on a stone shaft, the *benben* became an obelisk: it could even have been the model for the pyramids themselves. As the king's own god, Re's influence spread across the nation and other gods joined with him in compromise rather than struggle. So Amun of Thebes became Amun-Re and the priests of Ptah of Memphis explained that Re was his father and he, in turn, was the father of the other gods. Re himself had different forms. His emblem was the sun itself, the source of heat. When he rose into the sky in the morning he was Horus in the horizon, Harmachis or Horakhti, who, as a falcon, could fly high in the sky. He was Re at midday and in the evening he became Re-Atum, the setting sun.

Each king called himself the 'Son of Re', the 'Son of the Sun'. Pepi I, a Sixth Dynasty king around 2250 BC, made this claim: 'Pepi is the son of Re who loves him; and he goes forth and raises himself up to heaven. Re has begotten Pepi. Re has conceived Pepi. Re has given birth to Pepi; and he goes forth and raises himself up to heaven.' Ultimately, after death, the king hoped to join the Sun-god in his daily journey across the sky, for this is what the Egyptians thought Re actually did.

Re travelled through the sky by boat, the natural way to a people whose highway was the Nile. His route by day was obvious enough but what happened by night, in the darkness, aroused conjecture. According to one account, the sky-goddess Nut swallowed the sun, which passed through her

Isis, wife of Osiris, sought his dead body after he had been killed by the god Seth. Her cult, as the divine mother, was taken up by the Roman empire.

48

body to be re-born at dawn. In another, more complex account, the Sun-god's boat moved on through the other world. This other world, the Duat or Det, was divided by gates into twelve sections corresponding to the hours of the night. The gods and goddesses who filled the boat, and the kings who had gone to join them, protected Re against the hazards of the journey. Each night these guardians had to fight against such enemies of the sun as the terrible serpent Apophis. Even though they won the battle on any particular night the serpent would still be waiting next time the boat passed by . . . and they might always lose. The Egyptians could not be certain that the sun would rise. Towards the end of this night-time journey the boat even had to pass across a sandy desert, turning itself into a snake to do so. When, at last, it completed its voyage through the other world, the soul of Re could reunite with Khepri and the sun could appear in the morning sky.

And yet, even though Re was the king's own god and chief of the gods, the Egyptians could still tell stories about him that suggested he had weaknesses. In one of these stories, Re had once been king of Egypt. As king, he travelled through the land, much as the Sun-god travelled through the other world by night. He listened to men small and great, settled their quarrels, taught them spells against snakes and wild beasts, pitied their sufferings and gave them aid. So great was his bounty that, eventually, he was left with only one resource, his name. This was the name his father and mother had given him at birth, a name that he alone knew and which he kept concealed because of its magic power.

In time, Re grew old, his body bent, his mouth quivered, he drivelled and his saliva dropped upon the ground. Isis, a woman as clever as the gods and equal to the spirits to whom nothing was unknown, wanted to become a goddess and realized she could do so if she knew the secret name of Re. She took some of the mud formed where Re's saliva fell upon the earth and moulded it into a snake which she hid in the dust of the road. When Re passed by, the snake bit him and he cried out. 'What is it?' called the other gods. 'What is the matter?' But Re could not answer because his lips trembled and his limbs shook as the venom took hold.

The falcon, an early emblem of Egyptian royalty, symbolized Horus, one of the original gods of Egypt. This Horus displays a winged scarab, symbol of resurrection, rolling the disc of the sun into the sky.

At last Re was able to speak: 'Something painful has stung me. I have never experienced suffering like it.' The gods came together, bringing their books of magic, but only Isis offered comfort: 'What is it, father of the gods? Has a snake bitten you? Surely we can destroy this creature with the proper incantations. He will retreat at the sight of your rays.' So Re explained what had happened. 'I travelled through the land of Egypt to look upon what I had made and I was bitten by a snake I never saw. Now I feel hotter than fire and colder than water. My body runs with sweat although I am shivering. I can hardly see. My face streams with perspiration.'

At that point Isis sprang her trap. 'Tell me your name,' she said, 'and I can cure you'.

But Re prevaricated, reeling out a list of his achievements and his titles instead of revealing the name that was his alone. 'I am the creator of heaven and earth,' he said. 'In the morning I am Khepri; at noon I am Re; and in the evening I am Atum.' Still the poison ran through his body. 'You have not told me your true name,' said Isis. 'Only when you tell me your name can I remove the poison. Tell me your name and you will live.'

Re said 'My name is hidden in my body. Let it pass from my heart to your heart.' So Isis had her wish and, knowing the magic name, drove the poison from Re's body. He could, it seems, be blackmailed.

One king went far beyond all others in establishing a personal relationship with a god that was his alone. This king was Amenophis IV, one of the Theban kings of the Eighteenth Dynasty around 1360 BC. In his worship of the Sun-god he concentrated on one aspect, the Aten, the actual disc of the sun which sends out rays of light. Soon after the beginning of his reign, Amenophis IV turned against the local and national god Amun. Perhaps the priests of Amun, who had been gathering increasing power into their hands, found themselves on the wrong side of some political schism. Whatever the reason, when Amenophis IV rejected Amun he moved his capital from Thebes northwards to a new city he called Akhetaten which he built on the east bank of the Nile. Today the area is known as El-Amarna. He also changed his name from Amenophis, which means 'Amun is content', to Akhenaten, 'He who serves the Aten'.

Akhenaten immured himself in his new city, vowing not to leave it, and devoted himself to the worship of the sun. Those who joined him, his wife Queen Nefertiti, his officials and the court, discovered that they had no god but the king.

All other gods were virtually banned and the Aten, as the royal god, could be approached only through the king. A long hymn to Aten, possibly written by the king, spelled out the new beliefs required by this commitment to a single god. Everything is Aten without any mention of the magic and majesty, the journeys through the other world, the crowns and sceptres and sacred cities that are part of the glory of other gods:

'You dawn in glory in the horizon of the heavens, you living Aten, source of light. When you rise on the eastern horizon you fill the earth with light. From high above, your dazzling rays enfold the lands that you have made. You are god, everything is yours, bound to you by love. Although you are far away your beams search out the earth.

'When you set in the western horizon the earth is in darkness as though dead. . . . Lions come from their dens, reptiles from their holes, to seek their prey. The world is dark and silent because he who made it rests in the horizon.

'Early in the morning you rise in the horizon and shine as the sun by day. Darkness flies before your rays. Egypt rejoices: people wake and stand upon their feet because you have raised yourself. They wash their bodies and put on their clothes. They lift up their arms to praise you. Then the whole world sets to work. . . .

'How much you have done, and more than we can know. You, and you alone, created the heavens and the earth and everything that is on the earth. You created mankind, cattle and all kinds of beasts that go on foot, and creatures of the air that fly with wings. . . . Every eye can see you when you come as the sun of day over the earth.'

However, Akhenaten's aim of making Aten preeminent in Egypt faded away with his own death and the company of gods continued as before.

This great emphasis on religion made Egypt a land of temples. Each temple was the actual home of a god, in the same way as a tomb was an eternal home for its dead occupant. On a very large scale, it was laid out like a house: from the imposing pylon or gateway a pathway ran down the centre of the temple leading through courts and pillared halls, the equivalent of the garden and rooms of an ordinary house, to the sanctuary, or bedroom, of the god. At every stage the floor level rose a few steps and the rooms became smaller and dimmer so that the sanctuary was a place of mystery.

In the sanctuary, the 'great place' as it was called, stood the statue or emblem of the god that, to the Egyptians, was the god itself. This statue was probably quite small so that it could be taken out and carried around in its shrine. Every day the officiating priests performed a series of ceremonies involving the statue, matching everything they did to long recitations based on the histories of the gods. In this high-flown language the simple act of entering the sanctuary became, symbolically, the opening of the gates of heaven, the undoing of the gates of earth. Then the priests burnt incense, sprinkled the statue with water, dressed it up, anointed it and set out offerings of food and drink. At festivals the god might be carried round the temple and through the town: ordinary people were never allowed inside the inner temple and the sanctuary. Worshippers sang and shouted, danced and leapt about ecstatically, beat their breasts with clenched fists and rattled musical instruments. The offerings piled high, thousands of loaves, hundreds of jugs of beer, and the excitement climaxed with a feast for all.

Providing for this kind of festivity brought the temples firmly into the economic life of Egypt. Theoretically the king owned all the land, but much of it was made over to the temples who used the crops to support themselves and supply the festival goods. In a way they became part of the administration of Egypt. Each temple, with its offices, stores for grain, a small palace for the king when he came visiting and a high surrounding wall, was virtually a self-contained township and might become the centre of a larger town. People whose livelihood depended on the temple packed into the houses crowded higgledy-piggledy about its geometrical rectangularity: officials, scribes, teachers, stablemasters, guards, cultivators and herdsmen, craftsmen and workers in precious metals. In addition, the temple gates and outer courts provided the setting for every sort of transaction between pilgrims coming to worship the god or consult the oracles and the dream-interpreters, magicians, exorcists and writers of petitions who thronged around.

And temples meant priests. The priesthood was rigidly hierarchical, with candidates for the higher offices moving upward through a series of lesser positions. The principal priests had close links with local officials and could themselves become politically powerful. At lower levels, as well as carrying out their sacred duties, priests might be involved with teaching in the schools for scribes, with the civil and criminal courts that drew upon the close presence of the gods for their authority and with answering the continuous prayers for help and guidance. Gaston Maspero, Director of the Antiquities Service in Egypt in the late

nineteenth century, thought that petitioners who approached one of the oracles of ancient Egypt, the miraculous statues that considered every plea, must have known that the priests answered for the god. According to him, when these idols were addressed, they replied either by gesture or by voice. They would speak and utter the right verdict on any particular question. They moved their arms and shook their head to an invariable rhythm. 'And as they assuredly did nothing of all this by themselves, someone had to do it for them. Indeed, there were priests in the temples whose business it was to attend to these things. Their functions, being anything but secret, were carried out openly, in the sight and to the knowledge of all. They had their appointed places in ceremonies, in processions and the sacerdotal hierarchy; each individual knew that they were the voice or the hand of the god, and that they pulled the string to set his head wagging at the right moment.' Consequently, Maspero believed, this was not one of those pious frauds that people today might suspect; no one was ignorant that the divine consultation was brought about by this purely human agency.

Priestliness demanded purity and purity meant cleanliness. Herodotus noted that the priests shaved their heads and recorded other requirements of cleanliness for both priests and populace.

Offerings to the gods and to the dead played a central part in the religious system. This fifteenth-century BC relief carving shows animals being led to sacrifice.

They wore garments of linen always newly washed. They circumcised themselves for the sake of cleanliness, 'preferring to be clean than comely'. The priests shaved themselves all over their body every other day, so that no lice or any other foul thing might come to be upon them when they ministered to the gods. The priests wore only garments of linen and sandals of papyrus. They washed themselves in cold water twice in the day and twice again in the night; and they performed other religious services almost without number.

Purity quite possibly involved more than bodily cleanliness, spreading into dietary and social taboos. Georg Ebers, a nineteenth-century German Egyptologist, produced a series of romantic novels set in ancient times, complete with footnotes to vouch for their historical authenticity. In one of these, *Uarda*, he told of the princess Bent-Anat, daughter of Ramesses II, driving over a girl in her chariot and, full of remorse, carrying her to her family's house. The girl's father, it turned out, was an embalmer, one who opened the bodies of the dead, and in crossing the threshold of such a man Bent-Anat, according to Georg Ebers, knowingly defiled herself. The maiden princess – tall, fair, barely eighteen, her blue eyes kind and frank, her profile noble but sharply cut – drove to the temple to seek purification.

The great doors of the pylon were wide open, Georg Ebers continued, and 'afforded a view into the forecourt of the sanctuary, paved with polished squares of stone, and surrounded on three sides with colonnades. The walls and architraves, the pillars and the fluted cornice, which slightly curved in over the court, were gorgeous with many-coloured figures and painted decorations. In the middle stood a great sacrificial altar on which burned logs of cedar wood, whilst fragrant balls of incense were consumed by the flames, filling the wide space with their heavy perfume. Around, in semi-circular array, stood more than a hundred white-robed priests, who all turned to face the approaching princess and sang heart-rending songs of lamentation.

'Many of the inhabitants of the Necropolis had collected on either side of the lines of sphinxes, between which the princess drove up to the Sanctuary. "Hail to the child of Ramesses! All hail to the daughter of the Sun!" rang from a thousand throats; and the assembled multitude bowed almost to the earth at the approach of the royal maiden.

'At the pylon, the princess descended from her chariot, and preceded by the chief soothsayer, who had gravely and silently greeted her, passed on to the door of the temple. But on the threshold of the door, the High Priest Ameni, in full pontifical robes, stood before her, his crozier extended as though to forbid entrance.

' "The advent of the daughter of Ramesses in her purity," he cried in loud and passionate tones, "augurs blessing to this sanctuary; but this abode of the Gods closes its portals on the unclean, be they slaves or princes. In the name of the Immortals, from whom thou art descended, I ask thee, Bent-Anat, art thou clean, or hast thou, through the touch of the unclean, defiled thyself and contaminated thy royal hand?"

'Deep scarlet flushed the maiden's cheek, there was a rushing sound in her ears as of a stormy sea surging close beside her, and her bosom rose and fell in passionate emotion. Already her lips were parted in vehement protest against the priestly assumption that so deeply stirred her to rebellion, when Ameni, who had placed himself directly in front of the princess, raised his eyes, and turned them full upon her with all the depth of their indwelling earnestness. A nameless anguish seized

her soul and she sank slowly down before him, saying in low tones: "I have sinned and defiled myself; thou has said it. Restore me to cleanness Ameni, for I am unclean."

'Like a flame that is crushed out by a hand, so the fire in the High Priest's eye was extinguished. Graciously, almost lovingly, he looked down upon the princess, blessed her and conducted her before the holy of holies, there had clouds of incense wafted around her, anointed her with the nine holy oils and commanded her to return to the royal palace.'

In descriptions such as this, Georg Ebers revealed a nineteenth-century consciousness as well as a scholarly knowledge of ancient Egypt. But the idea of purity did have strange ramifications. The pig was a particular case. Pigs were sacred to Osiris, no one might harm a pig. This prohibition developed into the tougher proposition that any contact with a pig was a breach of purity. As a result, pigs and the people who tended them became untouchables. The effects were the same, pigs remained protected beasts except for the annual sacrifice, but the implications were different. It is also true, as a practical matter, that when the temperature rises, pigs will cover themselves with their own filth if they have no mud or water to wallow in. Herodotus, realizing that the pig was accounted by the Egyptians as an abominable animal, noted that if any of them in passing by should touch a pig he went into the river and dipped himself in the water together with his garments. 'Then, too, swineherds, though they were native Egyptians, unlike all others did not enter any of the temples in Egypt; nor was anyone willing to give his daughter in marriage to one of them or to take a wife from among them, but the swineherds both gave in marriage to one another and took from one another.'

Animals became a central part of the religious system. To some extent they were symbols of the gods. Some of them featured as sacrificial victims, eventually offered up and eaten by the priests and other devotees. Some were worshipped for themselves. Even the royal emblems of Egypt were animals. The vulture goddess, Nekhbet, of the south or Upper Egypt, sheltered the king with her wings; the cobra goddess, Wadjet, of the north or Lower Egypt, spread her hood ready to spit poison in his defence. The king wore the symbols of these protective goddesses on the front of the double crown of Egypt and other crowns.

Sometimes living animals became more than representations of a god: they were the god itself.

The Apis bull at Memphis was one of the most important of these animal gods. The Egyptians worshipped him for himself, as a representation of Hapi, the god of the Nile, and as an incarnation of Osiris. When an Apis died they preserved his remains in a vast underground mausoleum and sought out the new Apis, a calf born at the right time to which the soul of the god migrated. The mother of Apis, so the Egyptians said, conceived by a flash of light coming down from heaven and after bearing the god was not permitted to produce more offspring. The priests recognized the new Apis by these signs: it was black, with a white square on its forehead and the figure of an eagle on its back; it had double hairs in its tail; and a beetle-shaped mark on its tongue. Finding the new Apis was the signal for a festive holiday.

Some of the main gods appeared as animals. Hathor, as one of the earliest goddesses of Egypt, developed a many-sided identity as she and other goddesses, such as Isis, became confused with each other; sometimes Hathor was a frightening avenger, slaughtering Re's enemies without pity; sometimes she was a gentle nurse, suckling Horus when Isis had to leave him; sometimes she was the goddess who helped people enter the other world. She made her home in the western mountains and took the form of a cow: all cows were sacred to Hathor.

Archaeologists who excavated an Eleventh Dynasty temple at Deir el-Bahari near Thebes found that the kings of the Eighteenth Dynasty had added a cave-like shrine to Hathor, placing in it a full-size representation of her cow form. The archaeologists pointed out that, Hathor being a goddess who comes out of a mountain, it was necessary to have a cave about three metres (10 ft.) long and 2.4 metres (8 ft.) wide hewn from the rock and painted. The cow was of sandstone, cut from an enormous piece the full thickness of the animal and sufficiently high to reach the top of the plumes on its head. She was natural size and in shape was a perfect likeness of the cows of the present day. Her colour was a reddish brown, with spots which looked like a four-leaved clover. Probably this was a sign that such cows were the incarnation of the goddess. The head, neck and horns of this cow were originally covered with gold, but the gold must have been very thin, so thin that the sculpture was made with the same care as if the coating did not exist. The cow wore between her horns the lunar disc, above which were two feathers. This is the usual representation of Hathor. She is the goddess of the mountains; she comes out of her cave and goes towards the river to the marshes, where she was supposed to have suckled Horus.

God-like animals required god-like treatments. Charles H. S. Davis described the lives of the oxen, dogs, cats, ibises and hawks held in reverence throughout the land. He thought that curators were appointed whose duty it was to care for the sacred animals, and whose office descended by inheritance. Land was assigned for their maintenance. Parents made vows to the gods, to whom the animals were sacred, for the health of their children if they were sick. The vow was discharged by spending on food for the sacred animals a weight of silver equal to that of the children's hair. Warm baths were prepared for the sacred animals, they were anointed with the choicest unguents and perfumed with the most fragrant odours. Rich carpets and ornamental furniture were provided for them, and every care was taken to consult their natural habits. Females of their own species were kept for them, and fed with the utmost delicacy and expense; those selected being remarkable for their beauty. When any died, the grief of the people could only be equalled by that felt at the loss of a child. Mourners often shaved their eyebrows on the death of a cat, and their whole body for the loss of a dog; all the provisions which happened to be in the house at the time were looked upon as unlawful food, which could not be eaten.

Even in death, however, the sacred animals had a role. Whether they were sacrificed to a god or allowed to die naturally, the dead animals were mummified and laid in huge pits. An early-nineteenth-century investigator, Colonel Howard Vyse, described the catacombs at Saqqara, near Memphis, recording that the mummies were deposited in galleries irregularly excavated in the rock. He thought the material which was removed was ground up and employed in the manufacture of the coarse vases which contained the birds. They were of a conical shape, rounded at the ends, and usually contained the mummy of an ibis, wrapped up in various ways; some being merely tied up in a linen rag, while others were carefully bandaged. The vases, of which there were an immense number, were laid in rows, with the large and small ends in alternate directions, forming a solid mass. Other galleries held mummified cats and dogs; earthenware jars containing eggs, beetles, and, in a few cases, embalmed snakes were buried under heaps of sand near the main entry shafts.

Greeks and Romans visiting Egypt were happy enough to respect most of the Egyptian gods whom they identified with their own: they recognized

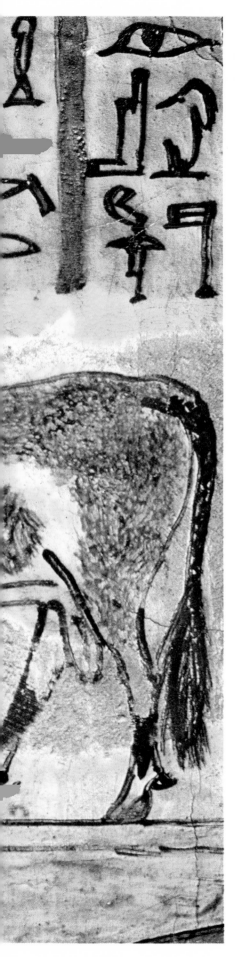

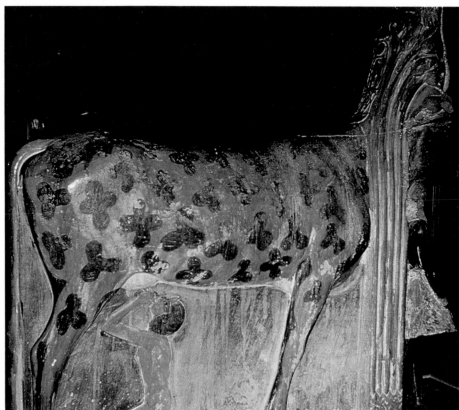

Left: *The Apis bull, shown here in a drawing from the coffin of a tenth-century BC priest, was worshipped for himself, as a representation of the Nile and as an incarnation of Osiris.*

Above: *The goddess Hathor sometimes took the form of a cow. She had once suckled Horus when his mother, Isis, had to leave him. This life-size statue comes from a fifteenth-century BC shrine at Deir el-Bahari.*

Right: *Cats enjoyed status as domestic and sacred animals. This bronze dates from the sixth century BC.*

57

Osiris as the fertility god and the cult of Isis spread throughout the Roman Empire. But they baulked at the animal gods. Clemens Alexandrinus, a Greek living in Egypt at the end of the second century AD, summed up the attitudes of these sophisticates: 'In Egyptian temples the porticoes, vestibules and graves are constructed with great splendour; the halls are adorned with numerous columns; the walls are perfectly splendid with rare stones and brilliancy of colour; the sanctuary shines with gold, silver, and amber, and with a variety of glittering stones from India and Ethiopia, and the secret shrine is hung with curtains of gold tissue. If you enter the circuit of the holy place, and hastening to behold what is most worthy of your search, you seek the statue of the deity, one of the priests who perform the rites steps forward to introduce you to the object of his worship, looking upward with a grave and reverent face, as he chants the hymn in his native tongue. But no sooner does he draw aside a portion of the veil, as if to show a god, than you find ample reason for smiling at the mysterious deity. For the god you sought is not there; but a cat, or a crocodile, or a native serpent, or some such animal, which is more suited to a cave than a temple; and you behold an Egyptian god in a beast lying before you on a purple carpet.'

A large part of Egyptian religion was to do with life and living in this world, providing myths that would explain, and rites that could influence, an otherwise arbitrary creation, but great emphasis was always given to death and the shape of the world to come. The Egyptians liked the idea of a long life, wishing each other the gift of 110 years in the here and now, and yet they had to die. So, in compensation, they believed in an existence after death that was virtually a continuation of life, they described this other world that resembled a gloriously fertile and transcendentally beautiful version of Egypt itself, and they laid out formal protocols expected to guarantee entry to these realms of bliss.

All the many strands of the Egyptian religious system contributed something towards these beliefs about survival after death and they are therefore just as complicated as the accounts of the creation and the connections between the gods. The ultimate, and apparently straightforward, hope of the Egyptians was that, some time after death, all aspects of a person's being were reunited in Osiris: the dead person did not actually become the god but lived on through him. However, their notions about this everlasting life, about the steps that led to it and the spiritual entities involved, produced an uneasy bundle of ideas that was difficult to shape into a coherent whole.

As a first step towards life hereafter, the Egyptians tried to preserve the body. Mummification, by drying the body and wrapping it in linen bandages, produced a permanent remembrance of the dead person. They also carved statues of the deceased and placed these in the tomb in case the mummified body should be destroyed. Both the mummy itself and any duplicating statues remained an earthly focus for the spiritual parts of the dead person. The Egyptians did not hope for the physical resurrection of the body itself, but they did feel that the spiritual entities that made up a living person needed an identifiable image to cluster about in death. Some part of the spirit went forward to the realms of bliss but another part stayed close to the scenes of life on earth.

In order to make sure that the spirit knew what to expect, the Egyptians compiled a guidebook setting down exactly what should happen on the road to heaven. This *Book of the Dead*, supposedly written by the scribe of the gods, the god Thoth, allayed every worry the dead (and, by implication, those yet to die) might have. A person's name was an essential part of the immortal identity, someone without a name vanished from existence, so the *Book of the Dead* gave a spell to make certain the spirit remembered its name. The dead person had to face the judgement of the gods, so the *Book of the Dead* laid down the responses the spirit must make: so long as the dead person gave these responses correctly, judgement had to be favourable. To reach the realms of bliss, the spirit had to pass through dangers: so the *Book of the Dead* listed spells for protection. Once in heaven, the spirit might want to return to earth from time to time: so the *Book of the Dead* provided spells that allowed the spirit to venture out and this was why the ancient Egyptians called it the *Book of Coming Forth by Day*.

During the later dynasties these accounts of how to act on the journey to the other world were written on papyrus and placed in the coffin or even bound up in the mummy wrappings. At an earlier stage, and this continued into later times, they were painted on the coffin. The earliest record of these texts was the appearance of some of them carved on the walls of the burial chamber of the pyramid of King Unas, last of the Fifth Dynasty kings, around 2350 BC. Whatever form the *Book of the Dead* took the message was clear: 'Whoever knows these texts is one who, in the day of resurrection in the other world, arises and enters in.'

In the simplest version of entry into the other world, the dead person's shadowy double, the *ka*, left the body it had accompanied in life and headed west, into the desert. The *ka* was roughly equivalent to an individual's immortal spirit and, in paintings of events in the other world, looked just like the living person. Soon the *ka* reached a great sycamore tree growing in the desert. The goddess Hathor, mother of all, leaned down from its branches to offer fruit, bread and water. By accepting these the *ka* crossed the border from the land of the living to the other world.

Although the journey had its hazards, the well-instructed *ka* could bring a battery of spells to bear backed with all the awesome powers of the gods. What crocodile could stand against this curse? 'Back, beast of the water, when Osiris passes you. O dweller in the water, Re shall close your mouth, Thoth shall cut out your tongue, the god of magic shall blind your eyes, this day.' The *ka* that knew how to ask might even persuade Hathor or Thoth to carry it direct to the realms of bliss.

Some texts suggested that, following death, the spirit went straight to heaven. 'He goes to heaven like the hawks. He kisses heaven like the falcon. He flies away from you; he is no more upon the earth, he is in heaven.' Here the sky-goddess Nut placed the vaulting spirit in the night-time firmament as an imperishable star. This may have referred to another aspect of the immortal being, the *ba*, which was a kind of external soul represented with a human head and a hawk's body.

In the more complex versions of the journey through Amenti, the Egyptian name for the other world, the spirit trying to enter heaven had to face the judgement of the gods. This was a very real ordeal. The spirit found pure and cleansed from all stain of evil passed on, to be welcomed into the heavenly fields of peace and rest. The spirit revealed as an enemy of Re was cast into the outer darkness of the underworld among pits of fire, snakes and scorpions, and torments worse than anything yet encountered. For this reason the *Book of the Dead* detailed with particular care the responses the spirit must make to ensure a favourable decision.

Examination of the spirit of the dead person, and the giving of judgement, took place before 42 subsidiary gods in the Hall of the Two Truths, represented by the goddesses Isis and Nephthys who personified integrity and straight dealing. Osiris waited to learn the result enthroned in a chapel set beyond the Hall. As the spirit, anointed and

Akhenaten encouraged naturalism in the arts, as these busts of himself (right) and his daughter (left) illustrate.

clothed in new linen, entered the Hall of the Two Truths it cried out: 'Hail, great god, lord of the two truths. I come before you to behold your splendour. I know you, I know your name, I know the names of these 42 gods with you in the Hall of the Two Truths, who live to watch for evil doers and who drink their blood on the day of reckoning. I come before you to bring you truth and set aside evil.'

Continuing the prayer, the spirit made its claim for judgement by denying all possible charges of wrongdoing even before they could be made: 'I did not do any harm to anyone. I did not make my relatives nor my companions unhappy. I did not do any vile act in the Abode of Truth. I had no acquaintance with evil. I did not do evil. I did not make anyone work beyond their capabilities. I did not cause anyone to suffer nor to be fearful, poor, or wretched. I did not do what the gods hate. I did not cause the slave to be misused by his master. I did not cause anyone to be hungry. I did not cause anyone to weep. I did not kill. I did not command anyone to kill treacherously. I did not lie to anyone. I did not plunder the supplies in the temples. I did not take the bread of the gods. I did not steal any offerings to the dead. I did not fornicate. I did not commit any shameful act with a priest. I

Following page: Entry in to the joys of the other world depended on a favourable judgement in the Hall of the Two Truths.

did not overcharge nor defraud by lessening the supplies. I did not alter the weights of the balance. I did not tamper with the balance itself. I did not steal milk from the mouth of the child. I did not steal cattle from their pasture. I did not snare birds sacred to the gods. I did not take fish from their lakes. I did not hinder the waters of the inundation. I did not divert water running in a canal. I did not blow out the offering flame before its time. I did not deprive the gods of their choice offerings. I did not injure the cattle belonging to the gods. I did not defy any god. I am pure, pure, pure.'

By this denial of sin, or negative confession, repeated step by step but in slightly different form before the forum of the 42 gods, the spirit showed that it was fit to enter heaven. But the gods had one more test to make, the trial of the dead person's heart by weighing it in the balance. The heart inspired every emotion, it could bear witness that the spirit was 'true of voice', that the dead person was blameless. For this reason the embalmers left it in place when preparing the mummy.

In the Hall of the Two Truths the dead person's spirit looked on as the gods proceeded with the weighing. One pan of the balance held the heart, the other a single feather that was the symbol of *ma'at*, the combination of justice and truth. The jackal-headed god Anubis, god of the dead, supervised the weighing and checked that heart and truth balanced equally; Thoth, as scribe of the gods, recorded the result; the dreadful beast Amemt waited to devour the heart found wanting. At this awesome moment, with fate literally hanging in the balance, the spirit entreated the heart to speak truly. This prayer was so important that it was often engraved on a stone scarab placed on the dead person's chest and bound up in the mummy wrappings.

'My heart from my mother! My heart from my mother! My heart necessary to my transformations! Do not rise against me, do not bear witness against me, do not oppose me among the circle of the gods and do not part with me before the keeper of the scales. You are my personality in my bosom, divine partner, protecting my flesh. If you go out towards the place of happiness, carry us there. Do not let people rise against me in the good dwelling. Let shouts of joy be heard there when my words are weighed; do not let anything be said against me before the great god; may I be protected by everyone who is there.'

With the weighing done, and the spirit justified, Thoth announced to the other gods 'The heart of this Osiris has been weighed and his spirit has stood as a witness for him. He has not sinned.' At this point the dead person became identified with Osiris. The god Horus then led the spirit forward into the presence of Osiris himself, the judge and ruler of the dead.

In the kingdom of Osiris, the dead person enjoyed for ever all that was best about life on earth. Scenes in tomb paintings and in papyrus copies of the *Book of the Dead* showed the spirit eating and drinking the food of the gods, inspecting the fertile farmlands, taking stock of rich harvests and finding pleasure in the thousands of good and pure things given to its memory. Indeed, to make this everlasting life as comfortable as possible, the spirit called upon the magical aids and implements provided in its earthly tomb. These facilities even included model figures, *ushabtis*, that could act as substitutes if the gods called for workers in the fields. The stone or pottery figurines carried the inscription 'O *ushabti*, when I am called to do any kind of work, to till the fields, to irrigate the banks, or to carry sand from the east to the west, then you shall say, "Here I am." '

Yet even though the other world possessed every attraction, the spirit still wanted more: it wanted to go out from heaven by day, to return to its earthly haunts. So the *Book of the Dead* gave a spell that allowed the spirit to go in and out. 'I go across heaven. I pass through its wall and make light in it. I fly away to illuminate the shades. I open and I close; that is granted to me by the good lord and I go across!' This chapter hinted that the ancient Egyptians believed in a kind of reincarnation because the spirit that knew this spell was able to take all the forms of the living.

For the spirit coming forth by day the tomb provided an earthly base. This idea coalesced with another belief that the *ka* remained on earth and required the tomb as its home for eternity. In some way the *ka* emanated from the imperishable mummy that remained in the tomb: the burial ritual included ceremonies symbolically opening the mouth, eyes and ears of the mummy, loosing its arms and legs, and restoring breath to the throat and movement to the heart so that the *ka* might live. The tomb was actually laid out like a house. The burial chamber was equivalent to a bedroom; the entrance and antechambers provided a hallway and living space; the larger tombs had kitchens, bathrooms and even lavatories.

Most important of all, the relatives of the dead person, and priests appointed to the task, brought offerings of food and drink to the tomb. The *ka* had to eat. As time went by, the ancient Egyptians

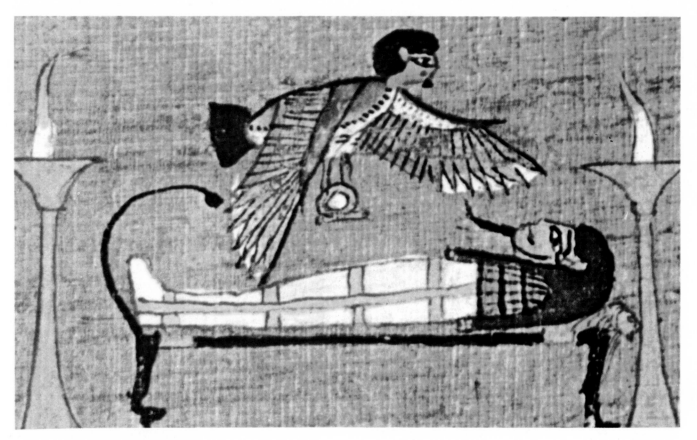

Part of a person's spirit appeared as the ba, *thought to hover around the mummy as a human-headed bird.*

realized that the living tended to neglect the dead, that no one could rely on offerings of real food and drink, and so they substituted prayers and rituals guaranteeing an endless supply of incorporeal provisions. The final safeguard became a formula carved on the tomb for anyone to read and so release the bounty of the gods. This inscription appeared on the sepulchre of a Theban prince: 'You who still exist upon this earth, whether you be private individuals, priests, scribes or ministers entering into this tomb, if you love life and do not know death, if you wish to be in favour with the gods of your cities and to avoid the terrors of the other world, if you wish in the end to be buried in your own tombs and to transmit your dignities to your children, you must, if you be scribes, recite the words inscribed upon this stone, or if not you must listen to their recital: pray to Amun, master of Karnak, that he may give thousands of loaves of bread, thousands of jars of beer, thousands of oxen, thousands of geese, thousands of garments, thousands of all good and pure things to the *ka* of the Prince Intef.'

However, a bleaker vision always overrode this indulgent conception of death as the gateway to the everlasting enjoyment of all good things. Death was never preferable to life. In a composition called *The Dispute Between A Man And His Soul*, an unhappy man, resigned to misery, thought about taking his own life. He tried to persuade his soul, or *ba*, that the release of death was but the last elusive pleasure:

'I look on death today as when a once-sick man feels well again, as when someone goes out after an illness.

I look on death today like the smell of myrrh, like sitting in the shadow of a sail on a breezy day.

I look on death today like the scent of lotuses, like feeling tipsy.

I look on death today like a fresh-washed path, like a man returning home from war.

I look on death today like the clearing of the sky, as when a man learns what he had not known before.

I look on death today as a man longs to see his home after years in exile.'

Yet despite this subtle appeal, and despite the further plea to the soul to accept what will be, the piece as a whole still seems to say cling on to life, death comes as an end soon enough. It is the simplest of principles to find embedded in the mysteries of a people who, according to Herodotus, were religious excessively beyond all others.

Chapter 3

From Graves to Pyramids

IN THE EARLY MORNING, before the sun reaches its full heat, a young boy wanders through the humps and hollows of an ancient desert burial place scuffing at the drifted sand. He finds a softer patch and calls a couple of men across to help him shift the underlying gravel. Quickly they dig down about half a metre (2 ft.) then stop when they find signs of a burial. They have located another ancient grave.

Now a more experienced worker takes over. He scrapes carefully away at the gravel, cleaning the skeleton of earth but leaving everything in place. After the grave is cleared one of the archaeologists makes a drawing of the burial and records all the objects before they are taken away. These graves are older than almost anything else in Egypt, dating from before the first kings, from before Egypt was properly Egypt, and everything they contain reveals something more about these people who lived six thousand years ago.

At El-Badari in Middle Egypt, one of the earliest cemeteries excavated, people had already settled as farmers by around 4000 BC although a fair proportion of their food still came from hunting and fishing. They probably lived in small, insubstantial huts that were little more than tents made from wood and reeds but they buried their dead with care. This included animals, too. Dogs or jackals and even cows and sheep had their graves. The cemetery was slightly separate from the village itself, set out on agriculturally-worthless desert ground where it would escape the annual inundation by the Nile: it would continue in use right down to Roman times.

Even at this early stage the Badarians placed everyday objects in each grave, possibly for

The girdle wall around the Step Pyramid of King Zoser – this is a reconstructed section – may have been modelled on the walls of the palace or the city of Memphis itself.

remembrance but more probably because they felt the dead person would need these clothes, cosmetics, tools and magical amulets in some sort of after-life. A pattern had been set that led on to the huge monuments and hoards of gold and goods that accompanied the Pharaohs into death.

Each grave was a circular or oval pit about 1.5 metres (5 ft.) across and a metre (3 ft.) deep, large enough for a single body wrapped in matting to lie on its side with the legs drawn up towards the chest. The hot sun working on the shallow gravel filling of the grave quickly dried out the body tissues, preserving skin, bone, hair and scraps of clothing. The Badarians buried their dead in their finest clothes. They wore a kilt or short skirt of linen or animal skins and sometimes a shirt or longer robe. They liked decorative belts made from strings of cylindrical blue-glazed beads, necklaces of shells, stones and coral, bracelets of ivory or horn and they pinned their hair in place with combs carved to look like birds. Some of them wore tiny amulets, hunting charms maybe, which showed hippopotamuses or antelopes. As a final touch they painted their faces and bodies with green malachite, which they ground to powder on a slate palette then mixed to a paste with fat or oil pressed from castor seeds.

Fine-walled bowls and pots placed in niches in the graves could have been used for storage or cooking; bone needles, found only in the men's graves, were for sewing skins or linen; knives and arrowheads had been chipped out of flint and spoons carved in ivory; small ivory vases probably held cosmetics. To these practical materials the Badarians sometimes added small statuettes of women, perhaps in the hope of companionship and a continued family life in the hereafter.

Soon after these graves were first excavated, one of the research officers of the Egypt Exploration Fund, Professor Edouard Naville, told a meeting in London that the typical prehistoric tomb was a square or oval pit of a very small depth. The body was generally lying on the left side, there was no mummification such as occurred later. The body was contracted, with the knees drawn up against the chest, and the hands clasping the knees or held before the mouth. This position had been called 'embryonic'; but Edouard Naville preferred the explanation drawn from African peoples who buried their dead in a sitting posture. 'When we speak of men sitting,' said Professor Naville, 'we must not think of men sitting on chairs, or even stools; chairs do not belong to the furniture of the desert. We must think of men sit-ting on their heels, as even now do most of the Orientals, and as we see in a considerable number of Egyptian statues, even of men who do not belong to the poorer classes. A dead body in that position would fall naturally on the left side, the side of the heart. This sitting posture is that of everyday life, it is that which the hunter assumes when he returns to his tent or hut to rest after his labour. Now place beside the dead man some jars and vessels containing grain or other food, and the tomb will become the picture of the hut where he sat or crouched with his primitive furniture around him.'

At Naqada, further south into Upper Egypt, another cemetery revealed some of the changes that took place over the next thousand years or so. During the early Naqada period burials continued much as before, a shallow pit with a single crouched body wrapped in matting or placed in a wicker basket, although some graves held up to seven bodies of adults and children. The larger graves and those with the most goods tended to be for women.

By now people were probably living in small circular huts built of reed walls on a mud base. They made black and red pots in many different shapes and decorated them with patterns and paintings of animals in white. Their flint-workers provided high-grade stone tools and one or two graves contained beautifully-made knife blades, up to 35 centimetres (14 in.) long, where the flint had been thinned down and then flaked off from both sides to give a finely serrated edge. Small statuettes found in some of the graves ranged from naturalistic animals to stylized figures of men and women and some vases bore a symbol, a human head between the horns of a cow, that might be the image of a fertility goddess, the first of the cows, the great mother.

In the later Naqada period, as the population grew, as agriculture improved, as the first attempts at artificial irrigation took place and as the scattered communities moved towards unification under one king, their houses, their possessions, and the graves which chanced to preserve the record all became more elaborate, reflecting a higher standard of living. The poorer people were still buried in their circular pits, as they would be throughout Egyptian history, but the better-off were laid to rest in rectangular graves lined either with the wooden planks that were the fore-runner of the coffin or with the sun-dried mud-bricks they were now using to build their homes. By the end of the Naqada period some graves were on the way to becoming chambered tombs: the body lay in a recess to one side of the main pit which held the funerary goods for the dead person. All these early desert graves were probably marked out by a pile of sand and gravel which, while it lasted, showed the living where to bring their offerings.

One grave from this period contained a pottery model of a house showing it had a single rectangular room with a small courtyard. Highly-decorated bowls and vases depicted birds and animals, hunters, dancers, desert scenes and, as a constant background, the Nile with boats passing to and fro. The people still used flint tools, but they had discovered copper for making adzes and axes and had fashioned daggers, knives and decorative figures of silver. They knew of gold, too. One grave produced a block of gold, a few centimetres long, wrapped in silver foil. Indeed, the ancient name for Naqada meant gold. By now, too, some of the gods had been given physical shape: the jackal that was lord of the necropolis and god of the dead; the falcon that was Horus.

Around 3200 BC great changes took place. The Egyptians discovered the art of writing so there is some sort of intermittent record (although it is difficult to interpret) of what was going on. Much of what is known, however, still has to be deduced from objects found in tombs. Inscribed mace-heads and ceremonial powder-grinding palettes from what may have been a royal tomb at Hierakonpolis suggest that Upper Egypt was then united under one king. Lower Egypt, too, was

The Step Pyramid of Zoser, constructed around the twenty-seventh century BC, was the first pyramid and also the first major edifice the Egyptians built in stone.

probably a single kingdom, but at this point Upper Egypt set out to conquer it. As a result the Kingdom of the Two Lands came into being under one of the three kings Scorpion, Narmer and Aha, any or all of whom could have been the legendary Menes. And now, with the kings of the first dynasty firmly on the throne of a united Egypt, the royal tombs began their march to splendour.

As a slightly confusing start, these First Dynasty kings built at least two tombs each, one at Saqqara close by the new capital city of Memphis and the other at Abydos, in Upper Egypt, which always had been a place of burial. The tombs at Saqqara are the larger and more impressive and this is probably where the kings themselves were buried: those at Abydos are probably cenotaphs, empty memorials. The ancient Egyptians thought that, after death, some part of the spirit remained in close touch with the pattern of ordinary life and the double tombs may have given the dead king another resting place if his spirit wished to journey through the kingdom. In line with this idea, the tombs themselves took on the form of miniature palaces providing the accommodation the dead king would require: the burial chamber itself was a bedroom.

Even the settings are impressive. At Abydos the cemetery is a wild and silent place on the west bank of the Nile, with hills rising high behind and the river valley and the eastern cliffs stretching out before. At Saqqara the line of tombs runs along the very edge of the steep escarpment to the west of the river. These royal tombs are huge, in some cases more than 125 metres by 30 (410 by 100 ft.), built on a rectangular plan with the longer side aligned with the Nile.

At first the grave itself was a pit about three or four metres (10 ft.) deep covering almost the entire area of the tomb. Thick mud-brick walls divided the pit into a burial chamber plus a couple of dozen or more storerooms that held the supplies necessary for life in the after-world. Although the grave was designed as a house for the dead, doors and passages could be left out because the Egyptians thought the spirit passed directly through the walls. Above ground the tomb consisted of a flat-topped mud-brick mound two or three metres (8 ft.) high. This mound gave these tombs their name of *mastabas*. *Mastaba* is the Arabic word for the low, mud-brick benches that are part of every village home.

In some cases extra storage rooms within the superstructure held more funereal equipment but, as time went by, it was more often filled completely with sand and rubble. Within the superstructure of the earlier *mastabas*, at least, a walled-in mound of sand directly above the burial chamber represented the piled-up gravel that had once marked the simpler pit-graves. In every aspect of their religion and their funerary cults the Egyptians tended to add new ideas without discarding what had once been meaningful.

Each royal tomb became the nucleus of an array of smaller *mastabas*, for queens, princes, nobles, priests and servants. People who had been close to the king in life wanted the association to continue in death. Some of these subsidiary *mastabas* were separate tombs, graves arranged around a focus, others were virtually standardized body-holders, long trenches divided by brick partitions into individual sections which were roofed over piecemeal after each burial. With one or two of the earliest tombs these mass graves were actually beneath the superstructure of the royal *mastaba*: the implication is that, up to and into the beginning of the First Dynasty, after the king died his courtiers and servants took poison and were buried with him.

One of the largest of the Saqqara tombs belonged to Uadji, a mid-First Dynasty king who reigned around 3000 BC. The archaeologists who discovered it labelled it Tomb No. 3504, which shows how many tombs they had to deal with, and took two full months to clear it of sand and work their way through the inner chambers. In one of the underground storerooms they found remnants from the time of the original burial: fragments of elaborately-carved ivory and wooden furniture which had once been overlaid with gold; copper tools; a collection of ivory gaming-pieces made up of a set of seven tall pieces, seven low ones, six lions, eleven dice rods and thirty-five limestone marbles for marking the score; and a red-and-black-painted label that listed the offerings. Virtually everything else had fallen to tomb-robbers.

In this particular tomb robbers had tried to cover their traces by setting fire to the burial chamber and other underground rooms. In the airless tomb the wooden roofing smouldered for weeks until it finally collapsed, bringing much of the superstructure with it. The robbers struck so soon after the original burial that the damaged tomb was cleared and repaired by Ka'a, the last of the First Dynasty kings.

Robbery had a strong influence on tomb development. Everything about the Egyptian conception of the after-world, of the connection between the living and the dead, of the particular role of the king as a beneficent source of protection in life and death, urged them to mark out each tomb prominently and bury with the deceased as rich a selection of funerary goods as possible. But the growing wealth associated with these burials made them increasingly attractive to the tomb robbers who could dig through the mud-brick structures with little difficulty. The Egyptians put their faith in two solutions, the first an excursion into magic, the second an attempt at bank-vault security.

Magically, the Egyptians decided that the representation of a thing was as good as the thing itself. To some extent this may have lightened the burden of the original funeral, too. Early burials involved real provisions for the after-life, real servants buried around the tomb, real wheat piled in the storerooms for making real bread, real ointment for the skin stored in real jars. In stages this gave way to models of the household at work, to lists of offerings that could do duty for the offerings themselves, to jars of 'ointment' that were actually solid clay. Statues and painted reliefs kept the tomb-owner's spirit in being if thieves plundered everything else.

However, the tomb robbers still broke in. They would even tear the body apart to get at its last ornaments: workmen clearing a burial chamber at Abydos which belonged to the queen of a First Dynasty king, Zer, found part of an arm lying in a hole in the wall of the tomb. Robbers had probably stuffed it there as a temporary hiding place but never returned for it. The arm still had on it the four bracelets of gold and jewellery that the thieves had been after. The most impressive of the bracelets consisted of alternating plaques of gold and turquoise in the oblong shape of a *serekh*, the symbol derived from the huge doors and the brick-built facade of the royal palace, each topped by the figure of a hawk. The workmen who turned up the bracelets were paid in gold sovereigns to encourage others to report their finds.

Practically, the Egyptians tried to find ways to keep the robbers out. Thieves just dug their way through the sand filling and brick walls of the early graves and *mastabas*, taking what they found. Guards and custodians could be bribed or threatened and, in any case, probably became less watchful over the years. Protection for these early tombs depended on their frightening darkness and the thought of vengeance from beyond the grave, but the robbers were always able to screw their courage high enough to face these terrors. So the Egyptians dug deep, driving into the rock that lay beneath the surface sand and gravel, looking for impregnability.

Early in the First Dynasty, when the royal *mastabas* were little more than the superstructure with a smaller, shallow basement, most of the goods were in storerooms or magazines only a few layers of mud brick away from the opportunist robber. By the end of the First Dynasty the emphasis was firmly on the subterranean, with the dead person's house burrowed deeper in its pit and all the valuable goods down there too; during the Second Dynasty the superstructure became completely solid while the underground part might be a vast lay-out, up to 125 metres (410 ft.) long, with dozens of rooms; by the Third Dynasty the tomb itself had gone deeper still and, because of the effort involved in hacking out rock, might be just a single compartment with a recess for a coffin.

In the earlier graves the body was placed directly in the burial chamber, the wooden roof constructed and the *mastaba* overhead completed. There never was a way in, a way out. In the later tombs the builders sank a vertical shaft 20 or 30 metres (65 or 100 ft.) into the rock and cut the burial chamber to one side. From the shaft they ran a staircase up to the northern end of the *mastaba* so the body could be carried down. Once the funeral was over, a heavy slab of stone dropped down to block the doorway of the burial chamber like a portcullis. The builders then filled the shaft and staircase with rubble and bricked over the entrance.

But the funeral was only a beginning. As well as being a house for the dead the *mastaba* was a place of offering to which members of the family and their paid priesthood continued to bring gifts to delight the dead person's spirit. Because the *mastaba* was a house they decorated it brightly. When the royal tombs were first built they looked like palaces. The mud-brick walls of the *mastaba* were built on the same pattern of rectangular niches as the panelled façade of the king's palace and were covered with the same shining white plaster: the close-by capital, Memphis, was actually called the city of the white walls. On this white background the builders painted multi-coloured patterns, perhaps to imitate woven reed hangings, and they may have planted trees round about: the Egyptians liked shady gardens. Today, however, these *mastabas*, and some of the smaller pyramids built nearby, are crumbling piles of rubble. A nineteenth-century Scottish traveller, James Bruce, described the scene: 'The traveller is lost in the immense expanse of desert, which he sees full of pyramids before him; is struck with terror at the unusual scene of vastness and shrinks from attempting any discovery amidst the moving sands of Saqqara.'

Offerings were a significant part of the after-life almost from the moment of death: Uadji's tomb – *mastaba* No. 3504 – had a low mud-brick bench around it topped by a row of full-size bulls' heads modelled in clay but fitted with real horns, which probably came from a herd of cattle slaughtered at the funeral. Because offerings were so important the builders, from the Second Dynasty onwards, added a small temple to the *mastaba* where people could bring their gifts. This temple usually contained a statue of the tomb owner and a carved stone slab, called a stele, which listed the needs of the dead person and so magically compensated for any neglect by the living.

And then, during the Third Dynasty, came the first pyramid, the Step Pyramid of Zoser.

Zoser's Step Pyramid dominates the Saqqara skyline. Imagine its impact when first built, when the citizens of Memphis raised their eyes to the hills that marked the beginning of the desert and saw, as high again or higher, this memorial to their dead king. The west bank of the Nile Valley slopes quickly up to between 30 and 75 metres (100 and 250 ft.), a thin band between water and sky. Along the top of the escarpment, the 10 metre high (33 ft.) wall that surrounded the pyramid enclosure marked out a sharply-defined horizontal section, an artificial plateau running for about 550 metres (1800 ft.). From the centre of this apparent base the six levels of the pyramid rose up 60 metres (200 ft.).

Early in the morning the citizens of Memphis would see the Step Pyramid glow pinkly as it caught the very first rays of the sun while the valley itself was still in shadow. During the day it would gleam out white against the blue expanse of the sky, trembling with the movement of the burning desert air. Late in the afternoon it would turn to a black silhouette before the reds and yellows of the setting sun. It was, and is, a noticeable presence.

Amelia Edwards, a late-nineteenth-century English traveller and novelist who became fascinated by Egypt, described the effect a trip to Saqqara had on her. As she came up on to the barren plateau she saw, for the first time in one unbroken panoramic line, the solemn company of pyramids: those of Saqqara straight before, those of Dashur to the left, those of Abusir to the right, and the great

The mastaba of the First Dynasty king Uadji, built at Saqqara around 3000 BC, provides a fine illustration of the size and complexity of these early royal tombs. As well as the burial chamber, they had dozens of storerooms for the goods the dead king would need.

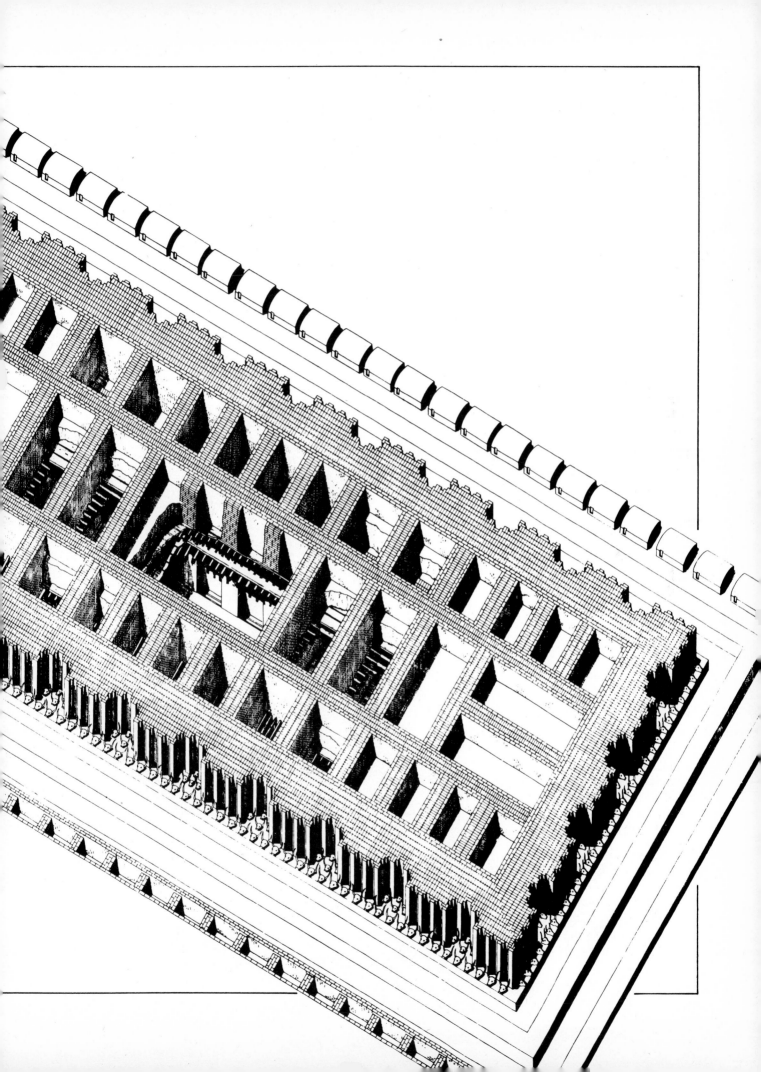

pyramids of Giza always in the remote distance.

She told those who thought there would be some monotony in such a scene, and but little beauty, that, on the contrary, there was beauty of a most subtle and exquisite kind – transcendent beauty of colour, and atmosphere, and sentiment: and no monotony either in the landscape or in the forms of the pyramids. One, the Step Pyramid, was particularly marked out as built in a succession of platforms gradually decreasing towards the top.

'The colouring,' she exclaimed. 'Colouring not to be matched with any pigment yet invented. The rocks, like rusty gold – the paler hue of the driven sand-slopes – the warm maize of the nearer pyramids which, seen from this distance, takes on a tender hint of rose, like the red bloom on an apricot – the delicate tone of these objects against the sky – the infinite gradation of that sky, soft and pearly towards the horizon, blue and burning towards the zenith – the opalescent shadows, pale blue, and violet, and greenish-grey, that nestle in the hollows of the rock and the curves of the sand-drifts – all this is beautiful. It is a long and shelterless ride from the palms to the desert; but we come to the end of it at last. The edge of the plateau here rises from the plain in one long range

The ancient Egyptians gradually shed the burden of providing real food, real drink and real goods for the use of the dead by placing models of these things in the tomb. This wooden model from about 2000 BC shows butchers with a slaughtered ox.

of perpendicular cliffs pierced with the dark mouths of rock-cut sepulchres, while the sand-slope by which we are climbing pours down through a break in the rock. . . . As for the pyramid in platforms, its position is so fine, its architectural style so exceptional, its age so immense, one's imagination recoils upon the brink of such a gulf of time. . . .'

Seen from a distance Zoser's Step Pyramid is impressive. Close to it becomes even more astounding; the Step Pyramid, this first pyramid, and all the temples and courtyards that surround it are built of stone. The Egyptians had already made some tentative use of stone, a granite floor in one tomb at Abydos, a hewn limestone chamber in another and perhaps even some complete buildings such as a long-lost temple they named *The Goddess*

Endures. Mud bricks eventually crumble under the onslaught of sun, wind and rain – rain in Egypt, though rare, is heavy when it comes – and when the Egyptians realized they had the techniques and organization to build in stone they threw themselves wholeheartedly into deciding how to use this more permanent material as the guardian of eternity. As they went on they changed their minds and developed their ideas so that the Step Pyramid is a record of experiment in stone.

First they built a solid *mastaba*, about 8 metres (26 ft.) high and 65 metres (210 ft.) long, of local stone. They completed it with a smoothly-finished layer of finer limestone from quarries at Tura near Cairo. Next they extended each side of the *mastaba* by about 4 metres (14 ft.) and again faced it with dressed limestone: either of these *mastabas* could have been a finished building. Then they set to building a further extension but before they completed it they had the idea that sparked off the pyramid age: they added three more layers to make a four-step pyramid. Even so they had not finished. They extended the base still further, added two more steps, making it over 60 metres (200 ft.) high on a base about 125 by 110 metres (410 by 360 ft.), and faced the entire edifice in Tura limestone.

And that is virtually how the pyramid appears today, although later generations filched the outer casing because it was such a convenient source of high-grade stone. When the Step Pyramid was first built, when the newly-dressed limestone shone white in the sunlight, it must have seemed both monumental and yet ethereal. One of the oldest fragments of Egyptian writing may refer to this pyramid when it says: 'A Staircase to Heaven is laid for him that he may ascend it to the sky.'

Down below, the convoluted passages beneath the Step Pyramid reflect the changes which had happened above ground. The main shaft, driven vertically beneath the original *mastaba*, is about seven metres (22 ft.) square and eventually reached a depth of nearly 30 metres (100 ft.). A pink granite tomb chamber sits at the bottom of this shaft. The original entrances to this shaft and others sunk around the first *mastaba* were buried under the later extensions and the builders had to dig a new passage from the northern face of the Step Pyramid to give access to the subterranean maze of shafts, corridors, galleries and chambers.

One of the first people to explore the warren seriously in modern times was a nineteenth-century surveyor John Shae Perring. His patron, Colonel Howard Vyse, recorded what they found beneath the pyramid they knew by the Arab name, *Haram el Modarrggeh*, the Pyramid of Degrees, pointing out that it differed from the rest in the form and mode of building, in the number and complexity of passages, in having four entrances, and also a variety of small excavated chambers upon the walls of two of which were hieroglyphs and peculiar ornaments. Perring also discovered the main shaft, which he called the large apartment. It had a timber ceiling and contained a great quantity of fragments of marble, of alabaster vases and of sarcophagi. Altogether the passages gave the edifice the character of an extensive catacomb.

According to Perring, the entrance, which was in a pit about 16 metres (52 ft.) from the building and 3 metres (10 ft.) west of the centre of the northern front, was generally closed up by the sands of the desert or, indeed, by the Arabs who wanted money from strangers wishing to visit it. The pit opens into a passage which is nearly horizontal for 37 metres (120 ft.) and then descends, 'in circuitous and irregular manner', to the lower part of the main shaft. Perring thought this had been intended to provide a secret communication with the large apartment and also with the small chambers and lower passages. He also found a passage running from the main shaft towards the south side of the pyramid. The southern end of the gallery was stopped up with sand but in the 49 metres (160 ft.) that was open he discovered some 30 mummies, apparently undisturbed. When he tried to examine them, they crumbled to pieces. He inspected the ceiling of the main shaft, with the help of flaring torches made of greased rags, and found it consisted of planks supported by cross-bearers and two principal beams. One of these beams had fallen, bringing with it a quantity of masonry. Perring reported that the sides of the shaft were blackened by the smoke of torches.

Later excavators worked their way more thoroughly through the various chambers, although tomb robbers had always been before and may even have dug some of the tunnels themselves.

These robbers worked hard, taking any risk in their search for gold, but they, too, were often disappointed. In one part of the pyramid enclosure they put a lot of effort into driving a mole-hole, just large enough for a person to crawl along, deep into a pit that turned out to be full of nothing but rubbish. Despite the robbers, the tombs still contained many thousands of beautiful pots and dishes, two alabaster coffins, one still holding the skeleton of a child, and in the burial chamber itself a few pieces of an early mummy, the left foot, still in its bandages with the toes padded out with linen, and the right shoulder. These could be the last remains of Zoser himself.

Ordinary tourists, too, felt the lure. An archaeologist working on the pyramid structures between the two World Wars noticed a dog waiting outside the door they had put across one of the passages leading into the pyramid. 'Someone may have climbed in,' he thought and went off to fetch lights and keys. He penetrated well into the maze of passages before he came upon two young people sitting in the dark. They had found their way in by striking matches but each thought the other had some spare to light the way back. They were lucky. 'You might have waited a long time,' the archaeologist told them. 'We come in here about once a year.'

Yet what these archaeologists and tourists are looking at as they wander through the complex of buildings around the pyramid is still a mystery. The Step Pyramid itself contains the riddle of all the pyramids: is it a tomb marker, an emblem of the after-world, a house for the dead, a stairway to the stars? Do the buildings around it represent Zoser's palace in Memphis, or even Memphis itself contained within a city wall? Were the buildings and courtyards the scene of some ceremony while Zoser was still alive, the haunt of priests and pilgrims who kept his cult in being after his death, or even the arena where the dead king's spirit could work its magic?

Zoser certainly participated in one festival, the *heb-sed*, while he was still alive. The *heb-sed* was a kind of jubilee, a celebration which magically re-invigorated the king. In earlier times the old king may actually have been put to death so that a younger man might replace him. As part of the ceremony the priests ritually laid the king to rest and raised him again, they restaged his coronation and finally, as though to confirm his new-found energy, they ran with him around the special *heb-sed* court. Carved reliefs in chambers deep beneath some of the buildings around the Step

Pyramid show Zoser running the *heb-sed* course, vigorous for five thousand years and more.

Zoser has the continuing glory of being the first king commemorated by a pyramid built in stone. Everything about the Step Pyramid and its enclosure suggests transition. This new material excited and inspired the builders yet, at the same time, they drew on what they already knew. They leapt forward technologically. The Step Pyramid may look like six *mastabas* piled separately on top of each other; in fact internal buttress walls run near-vertically up through the entire structure. This development, together with inward-inclining layers of stone, provided stability. They could build high with safety. Yet they worked with smaller blocks of stone than the later pyramid builders would use, blocks less than a third of a metre (1 ft.) high. This meant extra work cutting more edges but they were able to handle them easily, treating them almost like mud bricks.

In the buildings around the Step Pyramid the same tentative jump into the unknown shows up again and again. They built the walls up solid, then cut out panels as though carving a statue. They planned colonnades, but set the columns into the walls because they did not know if a free-standing stone pillar would support itself. They decorated underground chambers with blue tiles patterned to look like reed hangings. Everywhere they duplicated in stone the wooden fitments and bundles of papyrus stems they were used to seeing in their mud-constructed homes and palaces. In places they even carved stone replicas of wooden doors standing half-open and equally carefully they cut holes in the door jambs for bolts that would never slide home.

Pilgrims who came to visit Zoser's tomb thought the result a wonder. They came up the dusty incline from Memphis, disappeared into the single entrance in the enclosure wall, walked through the long corridor that decanted them into the central courtyard and marvelled at their first full sight of the Step Pyramid. They even scribbled their praise on the buildings. 'The temple of Zoser seems to have heaven within it and the sun rises from it,' wrote one, although another added that these ugly scrawls sickened his heart.

In a way Zoser actually has achieved immortality. Tucked against the northern face of the pyramid that keeps his name in being is a small, cellar-like chapel, called a *serdab*. Here, walled up in virtually total darkness, a life-size statue of the king sat and waited through the ages. He wears a leather or linen head-dress and the long, white robe of his perpetual *heb-sed* festival. The eyes, probably made from rock crystal, have been chipped away and bits of the painted limestone have flaked off but hieroglyphs carved on the base still proclaim his royal titles and one of the names by which he was known, Neterikhet.

Fate preserved another set of hieroglyphs which link Zoser with his architect, Imhotep. This man who masterminded the raising of the first stone pyramid was Chancellor of the King of Lower Egypt, Chief One under the King of Upper Egypt, Administrator of the King's Great Mansion, Hereditary Noble and High Priest of Heliopolis. He went on to become Vizier, the highest of all officials, the king's representative in all things. Imhotep rose high in his own lifetime and almost certainly some of the overseers and masons who worked for this self-made man belonged to the royal family itself: later generations raised him higher still. They called him first among the scribes; they made him into a magician and healer; and they prayed to him as a god. The Greeks thought he must be one and the same with their own god of healing, Asclepius.

Some, however, called upon the name of Imhotep because of self-seeking vanity. The priests of Khnum told a fable in which a mythical Zoser asked Imhotep what to do when famine stalked the land and the Nile failed to rise. According to the greedy priests, Imhotep answered 'Give riches to the priests of Khnum.' Others made gentler requests. A young wife recorded that she and her husband prayed to the Lord God Imhotep for a son: 'And he answered our prayer, as he does for those who pray to him.'

Zoser and Imhotep brought off a triumph but the kings who followed ran out of time, their architects went beyond their capabilities and the next few pyramids are poor in comparison. Zoser's successor, Sekhemkhet, who reigned for just six years, began a second pyramid at Saqqara that was intended to be higher than Zoser's own. Today only two layers survive. Archaeologists who excavated its underground chambers discovered a sealed sarcophagus and, for a short while, hoped they had found a royal burial. It turned out to be empty. The body, if ever there was one, had long since gone. A couple more enclosures at Saqqara, some ruins at Zawaiyet el Aryan, near Giza, and four small step pyramids spread far up the Nile are all that remain of these early projects.

Still, the kings persevered and the next attempt, the pyramid at Meidum, about 65 kilometres (40

miles) south of Memphis, marked the shift from step to true pyramid. Meidum started as a step pyramid of seven layers. Once this was complete the builders extended the base, raised each step and added an eighth layer. Although both the seven- and eight-layer pyramids could have been final versions the builders went on to pack out the steps and face the edifice with Tura limestone in one continuous slope.

Meidum set the pattern for the later pyramids, including the main group at Giza. The standard Pyramid Complex included the pyramid itself, a Mortuary Temple or offering place built against its eastern face and a Causeway that sloped down to a Valley Building on the edge of the cultivated plain. The actual construction consisted of an internal step pyramid built around a core of walls rising at an angle of about 75 degrees and faced off on a slope of about 52 degrees.

Meidum, today, is a ruin. The central core remains, rising about 75 metres (250 ft.) above the desert. It seems to stand on a small hill but that is actually a mound of rubble that was once part of the pyramid itself. Its builders cut so many corners that it collapsed, possibly even before it reached completion. The buildings around were never finished. Those pyramids that still stand today were founded on rock or a bed of limestone: at Meidum they built on sand.

John Shae Perring visited the pyramid but did not know quite what to make of it. He sailed to Meidum on October 29, 1837, but was delayed by his boat going aground on the ruins of a bridge, where the water ran with great force. The boat could not be got afloat without taking everything out of it. Luckily a number of Arabs were on the spot, but 'their assistance could not be procured till a remuneration had been regularly settled.'

Once he reached the pyramid, however, he noted that it is near the limits of the cultivated ground and about three kilometres (2 miles) to the north-west of the village from which it takes its name. It was called the False Pyramid because the base was supposed to have been formed out of a knoll of rock and it certainly seemed to him to have that appearance. He made two excavations, one at the north-eastern angle and the other on the west side, but did not reach the underlying rock.

King Zoser's Step Pyramid, a 'staircase to Heaven', was a wonder to the inhabitants of ancient Egypt. Pilgrims visited it and marvelled at the sight. 'The temple of Zoser seems to have heaven within it,' wrote one.

The base, about 160 metres (530 ft.) square, was cluttered with rubbish. The superstructure appeared to be in three steps, each having the form of a truncated pyramid.

Perring found that the pyramid is made from blocks of compact limestone which are about 60 centimetres (2 ft.) thick: 'They are laid at right angles to the external face, and have been worked and put together with great skill; indeed, the excavation made by the removal of the stone for a bridge shows that the masonry is of a superior description, and that it has been continued into the mound, upon which the edifice is built.'

No one else built pyramids at Meidum and archaeologists are still uncertain whether the pyramid belonged to Huni, last king of the Third Dynasty, or Sneferu, first of the Fourth, or whether one started and the other finished it. A few members of the court, however, did make their tombs nearby and from one of these half-ruined *mastabas* came a pair of statues, the seated figures of Prince Rahotep, commander of the army, and his wife Nofret, which preserve the early liveliness of Egyptian sculpture. Gaston Maspero, Director of the Antiquities Service in Egypt in the late nineteenth century, described their effect on him:

'The statues of Rahotep and of the lady Nofret have fortunately reached us without having suffered the least damage, almost without losing anything of their original freshness; they appear just as they were when they left the hands of the workman. Rahotep was the son of a king: but in spite of his high origin I find something humble and retiring in his physiognomy. Nofret, on the contrary, has an imposing appearance: an indescribable air of resolution and command invests her whole person, and the sculptor has cleverly given expression to it. She is represented in a robe with a pointed opening in the front: the shoulders, bosom, waist and hips are shown under the dress with purity and delicate grace. The wig, secured on the forehead by a richly embroidered band, frames with its somewhat heavy masses the firm and rather plump face: the eyes are alive, the nostrils breathe, the mouth smiles and is about to speak.'

Sneferu went on to build *two* pyramids at Dashur, slightly south of Saqqara. Indeed, the variety of pyramids, and the riches that they promised, made Dashur particularly attractive to later treasure hunters. Medieval books of magic explained what to do: 'Go to the mosque in the village of Dashur and dig under the threshold

to the depth of a man's full height. You will find a tomb and a princess buried within. Remove the body and under her head you will discover a box which contains three rings: choose any ring and rub hard upon the stone set in it. The spirit of the ring will appear before you and follow your instructions. Before you leave, put the body back into its place and cover the tomb once more.'

Sneferu came down through Egyptian history with a reputation as a gentle king: later generations called him *mnh*, which means beneficent, and told how he addressed his courtiers as 'Comrades' and his chief priest and magician, Zazamankh, as 'My brother'. Hundreds of years after Sneferu died they recorded, in a papyrus telling of the feats of magicians from the past, the story of how he was supposed to have whiled away a day.

King Sneferu was bored. He wandered through his palace seeking amusement but none of the courtiers could think of anything that might lift his mood. So he said 'Bring before me the chief ritualist and spell-binder, the scribe Zazamankh.' They did so and the king said to him 'I have looked for entertainment and found nothing.'

And Zazamankh said 'Let your Majesty go down beside the palace lake; and let there be made ready a boat, with all the fairest women from the harem of the palace as crew. Your Majesty's heart will rejoice to see them rowing up and down while you look around at the trees set about the lake

A nearly life-size statue of King Zoser gazes from the small chapel (serdab) beside the Step Pyramid through two small holes designed to give him a view of the world for eternity.

and the marshy ponds where the birds eat. Your heart will be lightened.'

And the king said 'I will do it. Bring me 20 oars, ebony inlaid with gold. And call 20 of the prettiest women from the harem, those with shapely breasts and beautiful hair, virgins who have not yet had children. Bring fishing nets, too, and give them to the women to wear after they have taken off their clothes.'

And the women rowed up and down and the king enjoyed watching them row. But then one of the women knocked a turquoise slide out of her hair and it fell into the water. She stopped rowing; and so all the other women stopped rowing too. And the king said to her 'Why have you stopped?' And she said 'Because my turquoise slide has fallen into the water.' Then the king said to her 'I will give you another just like it.' But she said 'I want my own, not a copy.'

And the king said 'Bring before me the chief ritualist, Zazamankh.' And as soon as he came the king said 'Zazamankh, my brother, I did as you said and my heart did rejoice to see the women rowing up and down. But one of the women knocked her turquoise hair-slide into the water and stopped rowing. I said to her "Why aren't you rowing?" And she said to me "Because my turquoise slide has fallen into the water." So I said to her "Row on and I will give you another." But she said to me "I want my own, not a copy." '

So the chief ritualist Zazamankh cast a magic spell; and he piled one half of the waters of the lake up upon the other half; and he found the hair-slide and picked it up and gave it back to the woman who had dropped it. Then he cast another magic spell and returned the waters of the lake to their proper place. And the king, and all the royal household, spent the rest of the day enjoying themselves and he rewarded the chief ritualist Zazamankh with many good things.

The change in gradient of the Bent Pyramid at Dashur may have stemmed from a feeling that the gentler slope would be more stable or, possibly, a need to finish the structure quickly.

Sneferu's first Dashur pyramid, the Southern Pyramid, attracts attention because it is an ungainly looking edifice. It changes slope about half-way up and so is known as the Bent Pyramid. The builders may have wanted to finish it more quickly or maybe they worried about stability as they rose higher and changed to the gentler slope. John Shae Perring, in investigating the structure, stumbled upon one of the mysteries that are still to be solved. Are there secret chambers within the pyramids, or burrowed in the ground beneath them, that are yet to be discovered? And do these hidden chambers, as the treasure hunters hope, hold the concealed riches of the pharaohs?

Perring reported that the Bent Pyramid was built in two inclinations so that the lower part is a truncated pyramid with a perfect pyramid on top of it. The lower part slopes at about 54 degrees and the upper at about 43 degrees. The beds of the casing stones incline downwards towards the interior: this, he thought, produced greater stability and saved materials, as less of the external faces of the stones thus laid would require to be planed away to complete the exterior of the building. The casing stones of the lower part are very large, some of the courses being 1.4 metres (5 ft.) in height. The courses in the upper part are seldom more than 60 centimetres (2 ft.) in height.

He began to clear the passages on September 20, 1837, starting with the one which was then open in the centre of the north face. It had evidently been closed up intentionally because it was full of large stones like those found in the desert around. The work could be carried on only at intervals 'in consequence of the want of air'. By October 15, operations had nearly been abandoned when a rush of fresh air down the passage after breaking into the interior apartments enabled the men to complete the job in a few minutes. This current of air continued for two days, almost blowing out the lights, which suggests there could be some still undiscovered connection with the outside.

Both the Bent Pyramid and Sneferu's second pyramid, the Northern Pyramid, are internally straightforward compared to Zoser's Step Pyramid. The passage from the north face of the Bent Pyramid runs down to a lofty chamber some 17 metres (57 ft.) cut in the underlying rock. The passage from the west face runs down to an equivalent chamber within the body of the pyramid. A roughly-fashioned passage, apparently hacked through the stonework almost as an afterthought, connects the two chambers. In the

A corner of the Bent Pyramid shows the layers of roughly-squared blocks that make up the core and the facing of well-finished casing stones.

Northern Pyramid an entrance in the north face leads to a series of three chambers at ground level. The designers of the Northern Pyramid settled for the same lesser angle of about 43 degrees as the upper part of the Bent Pyramid.

Both pyramids, the Bent Pyramid at a height of about 103 metres (335 ft.) and the Northern Pyramid at 105 metres (340 ft.), were larger than anything that had come before. But they seem low by comparison with those that followed. The pyramid builders had worked out their techniques at Saqqara, Meidum and Dashur. Now they could raise the giant monuments of Giza with confidence.

Chapter 4

The Pyramids of Giza

FROM A LONG WAY off the pyramids of Giza look like mountains as they rise sharply from the desert plateau. Closer to, by some strange paradox, they appear less impressive, no longer mountains, not even hills, just rough-faced piles of stone. At some point even nearer, however, these piles of stone become marvels and their size suddenly hits. They are enormous. The base of each one stretches away to left and right and the summit soars into the sky. Even the individual stones are big: each single course rises more than half the height of a person.

Cheops, second king of the Fourth Dynasty and successor to Sneferu, built the first and largest of the Giza pyramids, the north-easternmost of the three. His successor, Djedefre, went 8 kilometres (5 miles) north to Abu Roash to build but the following king, Chephren, returned to Giza and erected the middle pyramid. His successor, Mycerinus, built the smallest one to the south-west of the other two. The last king of the Fourth Dynasty, Shepseskaf, probably finished details of Mycerinus' Pyramid Complex but built his own tomb at Saqqara. In a little over a century, from 2613 BC to 2494 BC, these kings of the Fourth Dynasty, from Sneferu to Shepseskaf, built the largest and finest of the pyramids and the greatest of all were Cheops' and Chephren's, 'breasts on the bosom of Egypt'.

Marvel at the dimensions for a start. The base of the Great Pyramid of Cheops measures just over 230 metres (756 ft.) along each side. Originally it stood about 147 metres (481 ft.) high but some of the topmost stones have gone and its height today is 137 metres (450 ft.). For comparison, the

Like all the pyramids, those at Giza stand on the west bank of the Nile, between the inhabited valley and the setting sun: Cheops' is to the right, Chephren's in the centre.

spire of Salisbury Cathedral, the highest in England, rises 123 metres (404 ft.) and the Washington Monument, in Washington D.C., is 169 metres (555 ft.) high. Chephren's pyramid is slightly smaller, although it sometimes seems larger because it stands on higher ground. The base of the pyramid is 215 metres (706 ft.) square. Today it is just over 136 metres (448 ft.) high but when first built was somewhere between 140 metres (458 ft.) and 144 metres (472 ft.). Mycerinus' pyramid is much smaller: only about 66 metres (215 ft.) high on a base of 105 metres (346 ft.). Three subsidiary pyramids to the south of Mycerinus' range in height between 21 metres (70 ft.) and 28 metres (92 ft.) and three more, now virtual ruins, to the east of the Great Pyramid once reached around 43 metres (140 ft.).

Contemplate the sheer quantities of material. The Great Pyramid, so the estimates go, is built of some two-and-a-half million blocks of limestone of an average size about 1.3 metres by 1.3 by 0.7 (4 ft. by 4 by 2.5) and weighing about 2.5 tonnes (tons). Some blocks are much bigger and up to 15 tonnes (tons) in weight. In all, the Great Pyramid contains around 2.6 million cubic metres (90 million cu. ft.) of stone weighing a total of around six million tonnes (tons), about 20 times the weight of the Empire State Building in New York. To give an idea of the work involved, the four faces of the Great Pyramid total some 85000 square metres (925000 sq. ft.) of dressed and finished limestone: the masons who built St Paul's Cathedral, in London, reckoned they were doing well if each man finished a fifth of a square metre (2 sq. ft.) a day.

Even the quarries which supplied the fine Tura facing stone are impressive in themselves. Abd al Latif, an Arabian physician from Baghdad who travelled to Egypt at the very end of the twelfth century, observed that on the eastern bank of the Nile were a number of immense excavations, the quarries, driven deeply into the cliffs. He thought a man on horseback with his lance erect might enter them and ride for a whole day without traversing them all, so numerous and vast were they, and of such great extent.

And the pyramids themselves in their imposing setting, built on the edge of the desert escarpment overlooking Memphis, have always been marvelled at. Giovanni Belzoni, an early-nineteenth-century traveller who made a profession of finding Egyptian antiquities for European collectors and museums, spoke for virtually everyone who has seen the pyramids when he described his first visit

to Giza: 'Though my principal object was not antiquities at that time, I could not restrain myself from going to see the wonder of the world, the pyramids. We went there to sleep, that we might ascend the first pyramid early enough in the morning to see the rising of the sun; and accordingly we were on the top of it long before the dawn of day. The scene here is majestic and grand, far beyond description: a mist over the plains of Egypt formed a veil, which ascended and vanished gradually as the sun rose and unveiled to the view that beautiful land, once the site of Memphis. The distant view of the smaller pyramids on the south marked the extension of that vast capital; while the solemn, endless spectacle of the desert on the west inspired us with reverence for the all-powerful Creator. The fertile lands on the north, with the serpentine course of the Nile, descending towards the sea; the rich appearance of Cairo, and its numerous minarets, at the foot of the Mokatam mountain on the east; the beautiful plain which extends from the pyramids to that city; the Nile, which flows magnificently through the centre of the sacred valley, and the thick groves of palm trees under our eyes; all together formed a scene of which very imperfect ideas can be given by the most elaborate description. We descended to admire at some distance the astonishing pile that stood before us, composed of such an accumulation of enormous blocks of stones, that I was at a loss to conjecture how they could be brought thither. We went round the second pyramid, examined several of these mausoleums, and returned to Cairo with the satisfaction of having seen a wonder.'

But these pyramids, for the people who built them, were more than just strange and impressive piles of stone. They were tombs or, at least, tomb-like monuments. So, they contain passages and chambers corresponding to the burial places excavated beneath *mastabas*. The corridors under Chephren's and Mycerinus' pyramids, like those beneath Sneferu's at Dashur, are simple in lay-out and lead straight to a burial chamber cut into the rock beneath the centre of the pyramid.

Mycerinus' pyramid has a single entrance low down in the northern face. A passage slopes down through the core of the pyramid into the underlying rock and then runs horizontally, leading into a small group of chambers that once contained a sarcophagus. A second and incomplete passage running into the burial chambers suggests that the builders changed their plans about how big to make this pyramid while constructing it.

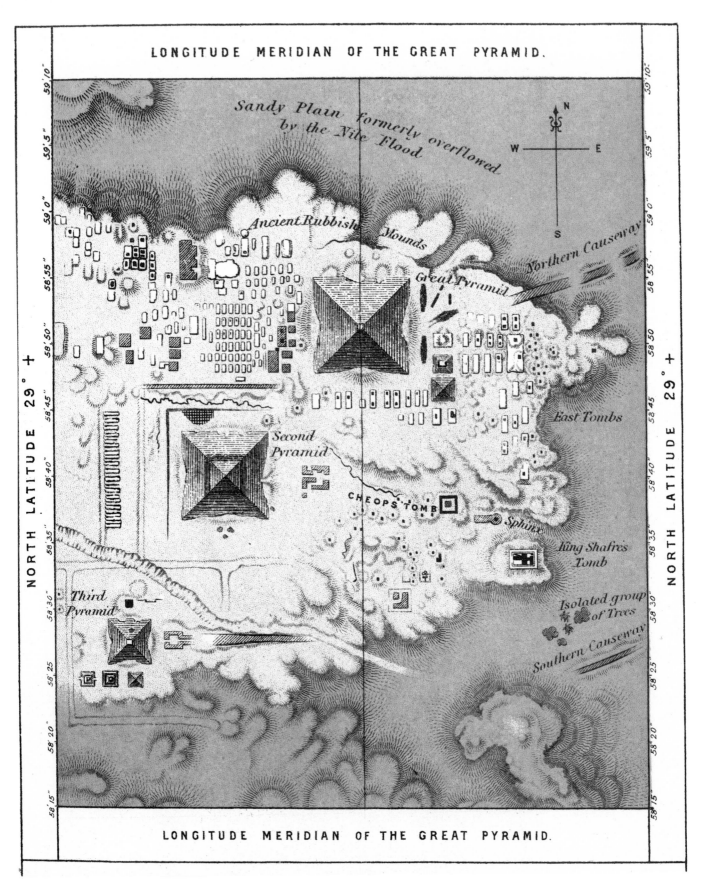

Sandy Plain formerly overflowed by the Nile Flood

N
W · E
S

Ancient Rubbish Mounds

Great Pyramid

Northern Causeway

East Tombs

Second Pyramid

CHEOPS TOMB

Sphinx

King Shafre's Tomb

Third Pyramid

Isolated group of Trees

Southern Causeway

NORTH LATITUDE 29°

NORTH LATITUDE 29°

Each main pyramid at Giza has subsidiary pyramids (for that king's queens), a Mortuary Temple and a Causeway leading down to a Valley Temple at the edge of the Nile. Tombs of members of the court who wished to be near their king cluster around. The Sphinx lies to the east of the centre pyramid, Chephren's. The pyramids, which make with these other buildings a large complex, are oriented according to the points of the compass.

Chephren's pyramid has two entrances. Both are just to the east of the mid-line of the northern face, one in the structure of the pyramid itself, about 12 metres (39 ft.) above the ground, and the other in the rock just outside its base. From the first a passage slopes down through the pyramid to the bed-rock; from the second another passage drives into the rock and then rises to join the first in a corridor running to the single burial chamber which is about 14 by 5 metres (47 by 17 ft.) and 7 metres (23 ft.) high.

An 'improved' view of the Sphinx and pyramids by David Roberts, 1838.

Giovanni Belzoni was the first modern explorer to find the way into this pyramid and his account tells of the perils of archaeology as well as the rewards. He first of all put his men to work in a false passage excavated by some previous seeker after treasures: 'To introduce many men to work in this place was dangerous, for several of the stones above our heads were on the point of falling. One of the men narrowly escaped being crushed to pieces. A large block of stone fell from the top, while the man was digging under it; but fortunately it rested on two other stones, one on each side of him, higher than himself. We had some difficulty in getting him out; yet, happily, he received no other injury than a slight bruise on his back.'

Belzoni went on to find the true entrance and then discovered that the builders had blocked off the horizontal corridor with a granite portcullis. However, he set to. The raising of it was a work of no small consideration. The passage is only 1.2 metres (4 ft.) high and 1.1 metres (3.5 ft.) wide.

When two men were in it abreast of each other they could not move, and it required several men to raise this piece of granite which was 1.8 metres (6 ft.) high, 1.5 metres (5 ft.) wide and 0.4 metres (1.3 ft.) thick. The levers could not be very long otherwise there was not space in the 1.2 metres (4 ft.) height to work with them; and if they were short he could not employ enough men to raise the portcullis. The only method was to raise it a little at a time; and, by putting some stones in the grooves on each side to support the portcullis while changing the fulcrum of the levers, it was raised high enough for a man to pass.

Giovanni Belzoni at last made the entrance large enough to squeeze himself in – he was a big man – and after 30 days exertion had the

The ancient Egyptians did not have the benefit of sophisticated technology for agricultural work or for building. As far as is known, the pyramids were built without even the simple pulley for lifting. This model of a simple plough shows one man goading the ox while another presses down the handles.

pleasure of finding himself on the way to the central chamber of one of the two great pyramids of Egypt. He observed that, after entering within the portcullis, the passages are all cut out of the solid rock. The passage leading towards the centre is 1.8 metres (6 ft.) high and 1.1 metres (3.5 ft.) wide.

'I reached the door at the centre of a large chamber,' Belzoni wrote. 'I walked slowly two or three paces and then stood still to contemplate the place where I was. I certainly considered myself in the centre of that pyramid which from time immemorial had been the subject of the obscure conjectures of many hundred travellers.'

Cheops' pyramid is altogether different internally from any other because most of the corridors and chambers are high in the structure itself rather than buried in the rock beneath. Also they are far grander than in any other pyramid. The highest, and most impressive passages were probably planned after building began, although the dimensions of the pyramid were fixed right from the start.

A single entrance in the north face, about 15 metres (50 ft.) above the ground and 7.3 metres (24 ft.) east of the centre, leads into a passage 1.2

Although Mycerinus' pyramid, shown here, is smaller than the other two at Giza, it was never fully finished, suggesting an untimely death.

metres (4 ft.) high and about a metre (3.3 ft.) wide that slopes down at an angle of about 26.5 degrees deep into the bedrock. This passage, which is about 115 metres (377 ft.) long, ends in an unfinished chamber 14 metres (46 ft.) from east to west, 8.2 metres (27 ft.) north to south and 3.5 metres (11.5 ft.) high. About 18 metres (60 ft.) in from the entrance a similar passage runs upwards from the Descending Corridor, at an angle of about 26 degrees, for about 38 metres (124 ft.). A horizontal corridor then leads off to a room about 5.5 metres (18 ft.) square with a pointed roof rising from 4.5 metres (15 ft.) to 6.2 metres (20 ft.). This room has acquired the name of the Queen's Chamber but is probably just an unfinished burial chamber. The Ascending Corridor continues past this horizontal corridor into the Grand Gallery, one of the wonders of the Great Pyramid.

Cheops' priests and ritualists may have planned some last funeral procession up this Grand Gallery; it is certainly a most impressive passageway.

The Grand Gallery is 47.5 metres (156 ft.) long, 8.5 metres (28 ft.) high and, up to a quarter of its height, 2.1 metres (7 ft.) wide. Above this, seven courses of stone step in so that the roof is just over a metre (3.3 ft.) wide. A stone ramp 0.7 metres (2 ft.) high and 0.5 metres (1.7 ft.) wide runs along the base of each wall with a channel just over a metre (3.3 ft.) wide between them.

A short, low passage leads from the top of the Grand Gallery into an antechamber and then into the King's Chamber itself, a room 10.5 metres (34 ft.) long from east to west, 5.2 metres (17 ft.) from north to south and 5.8 metres (19 ft.) high. The King's Chamber is built entirely of granite, well finished and finely jointed. Even though the walls have shifted slightly and the nine ceiling slabs, weighing a total of 400 tonnes (tons), are all cracked across the southern end, the King's Chamber still holds together. A series of five low compartments above the roof of the King's Chamber may have helped protect it. A rectangular granite sarcophagus, so large that it must have been positioned while the King's Chamber was still being assembled, stands close to the west wall.

Colonel Howard Vyse and John Shae Perring, while surveying the pyramids in 1837-38, put much of their effort into looking for further chambers but eventually decided none existed. Colonel Vyse had conjectured that the great magnitude of the building, compared with the smallness of the chambers and passages, and also the position of the entrance off-centre to the eastward in the northern face, suggested a duplicate entrance to the westward which might conduct to passages and apartments constructed in the great space between the three chambers entered from the north. 'But,' he concluded, 'this does not appear to be the case; and it is to be believed that the King's Chamber is the principal apartment, and the security of the sarcophagus within it the great object for which the Great Pyramid was erected.'

Security meant blocking off the passages and disguising the entrances. Slots in the walls of the antechamber to the King's Chamber suggest that this last entry was barred by stone portcullises. The Ascending Corridor actually starts unexpectedly in the *roof* of the Descending Corridor and was hidden behind a limestone slab that looked just like the rest of the ceiling. Three granite

Chephren's pyramid still has some of its smooth casing near the summit: originally all three pyramids at Giza were faced with well-finished blocks of the finest stone.

blocks fill the beginning of the Ascending Corridor. These plug-blocks, which are only a centimetre (0.5 in.) less all round than the size of the Ascending Corridor itself, were probably stored in the Grand Gallery until after any funeral and then manoeuvred down the Ascending Corridor and into place. The workmen who slid the plugs into position did have a way out: a floor slab at the top of the Ascending Corridor concealed the mouth of a rough, well-like passage that dropped down to join the Descending Corridor near its lower end. Another slab covered its exit. As a final touch, the original builders probably ran the limestone facing of the pyramid right across the entrance itself in the hope of making it undetectable.

Pyramid-fanciers have always titillated themselves with the thought of living people walled up within these giant edifices, whether as companions for the dead king or to preserve the last secrets of the closing of the tomb. Perhaps the discovery that the plug-blocks were positioned from above contributed to this myth: another factor has been the fact that small rectangular shafts run up from the King's Chamber to the north and south faces of the pyramid. These could have provided ventilation. Benoît de Maillet, who was the French consul in Egypt at the beginning of the eighteenth century and an advocate of the systematic exploration of its antiquities, sketched out his suggestion for the function of these shafts.

He held that, when the body of the king who built the pyramid was deposited in this sumptuous mausoleum, living persons were brought into it at the same time who were never to go out of it but to bury themselves, as it were, alive with their prince. He grounded his opinion of this 'matter of fact' upon the foundation that in the walls of the King's Chamber there were two holes 1.1 metres (3.5 ft.) above the floor. One towards the north was 30 centimetres (1 ft.) broad and 20 centimetres (8 in.) high. It went through in a straight line to the exterior of the pyramid but was stopped up with stone within 2 metres (7 ft.) of its opening. The other, which opened to the east, was perfectly round. It was large enough to thrust in two fists. It then enlarged to 30 centimetres (1 ft.) in diameter and went down to the bottom of the pyramid.

'I believe,' wrote Maillet, 'everyone will conclude that they were intended for no other use than the convenience of those that were to remain in this tomb. The first was to give them air and convey to them their food and other necessaries. They were no doubt provided with a long box proportioned to the width of the passage; to this box was fastened a long cord by the help of which they could draw in the box; another cord was left hanging to the outside of the pyramid for the people without to draw out the box. It is probable that this was the way they were supplied with necessaries as long as any of them remained alive. I suppose, at their going in, each of them had provided himself with a coffin to be laid in; and that they successively performed that pious and last duty of putting each in his coffin, except the last who failed of that succour which the rest of the company had found in him and the others. The second hole was to convey their excrement, which fell into a great pit made for that purpose.'

By the time Benoît de Maillet put forward this idea about accompanying the king into death, people had been going in and out of Cheops' pyramid for centuries. Tomb robbers probably

Opposite: *The King's Chamber, enclosing a granite sarcophagus, is one of the marvels of the Great Pyramid. This view, from around 1800, is by Luigi Mayer.*

Below: *The Great Pyramid, uniquely, has chambers high in the structure itself, as well as in the rock below. Why this should be so is one more unsolved mystery.*

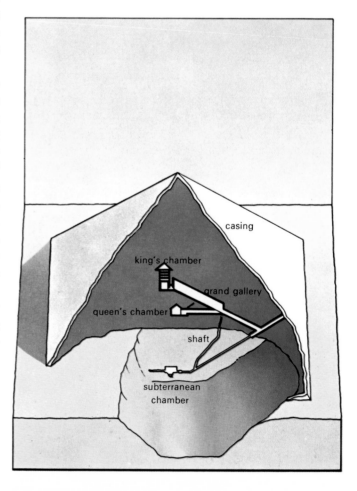

broke in; later kings may have repaired the damage; treasure hunters may have broken in again. When the Greek historian Herodotus visited Egypt, in the fifth century BC, his guides casually told him that Cheops had constructed underground chambers in the hill beneath the pyramid. They went on to produce the unlikely amplification that he led in a canal from the Nile and made his sepulchral vault on an artificial subterranean island. The entrance and passages as they are known today may have been opened up by the Caliph Mamun in the ninth century. According to tradition, he decreed 'An opening *must* be made.' His workmen excavated the chasm in the northern face, breaking the stones apart with the help of fire and vinegar, and eventually stumbled across the Descending Corridor. They burrowed their way around the granite plugs blocking the mouth of the Ascending Corridor but descriptions of what they found drifted towards the fanciful.

One of the more restrained accounts stated that the Caliph ordered the Great Pyramid to be opened and an excavation was accordingly made which disclosed an ascending narrow passage, dreadful to look at and difficult to pass. At the end of it was a quadrangular chamber, about 8 cubits (about 4 metres or 14 ft.) square, and within it a sarcophagus. The lid was forced open but nothing was discovered except some bones completely decayed by time. The Caliph declined any further examination as the expenses had been great.

Going beyond this, however, the Caliph is said to have found a hollow image of a man, made of green stone and covered with a stone like emerald, which contained a body in golden armour, a sword of inestimable value, and a ruby as large as an egg. Also, the Caliph ordered his people to climb the Great Pyramid, which they ascended in three hours and found at the summit a space sufficient for eight camels to lie down, and upon it a body wrapped up in cloths so much decomposed by time that scarcely any part of them remained except an embroidery of gold.

Also, a hall was mentioned in this pyramid from which three doors led to as many chambers. The doors were 10 cubits high and 5 broad (about 5 by 2.5 metres or 17.5 by 9 ft.), and made of marble slabs beautifully put together and inscribed with unknown characters. They are said to have resisted any effort for three days but, being at length forced open, three marble columns were discovered at the distance of 10 cubits (about 5 metres or 17.5 ft.). These columns supported the

images of three birds in flames of fire. Upon the first was that of a dove, formed of green stone; upon the second that of a hawk, of yellow stone; and upon the third the image of a cock, of red stone. Upon moving the hawk the door which was opposite moved, and upon lifting it up, the door was raised; and the same connection existed between the other images and doors.

In one of the chambers were found three couches, formed of a shining stone, and upon them three bodies; each body was shrouded in three garments and over their heads were tablets inscribed with unknown characters. Another chamber contained arches of stone and upon them chests of the same material full of arms and of other instruments. The length of one of the swords was seven spans; and the coats of mail measured twelve spans. All these things were brought out and the doors were closed, as at first, by order of the Caliph. Also, a sarcophagus is said to have been found in the pyramid, covered with a lid of stone and filled with gold.

Abd al Latif saw no such wonders when he ventured into the pyramid. He knew that the opening into the interior led to narrow passages, to deep wells, and to pits and precipices, because he was told so by those who had had the courage to explore them in search of treasures. The most frequented passage ascended to a square chamber, in the higher part of the pyramid, containing a stone sarcophagus. He knew, too, that the opening by which the pyramid was entered was not the original entrance but a hole excavated with great trouble, and directed by chance, made, it was said, by the Caliph Mamun.

'Many of my companions entered this opening and ascended to the chamber in the upper part of the Pyramid,' he wrote. 'On their return they detailed the wonderful things they had seen and told us that the passage was almost stopped up with bats and their ordure. The bats were as large as pigeons. In the upper part were openings apparently designed to let in air and light. On a second visit I myself, with several others, entered this passage and penetrated about two-thirds of its length. But, losing my senses owing to the terror I experienced in the ascent, I returned half dead.'

Even as these travellers were going in and out of the pyramids, fabulous tales proliferated. The reality of vast monuments, of mummies and tombs and broken statues scattered across the desert, provided the background for stories about treasure and danger and powerful spirits. Murtada ibn al Khafif, an Arabian writer who, it is thought, lived in the thirteenth century, collected many of these stories together into *A History of the Marvellous Things in Egypt* which was put into English by John Davies of Kidwelly in the late-seventeenth century.

Murtada wrote that after the pyramid was opened people went in out of curiosity for some years, many entering into it, and some returning without any inconvenience, others perishing in it.

'One day it happened that a company of young men (above 20 in number) swore that they would go into it, provided nothing hindered them, and force their way to the end of it. They therefore took along with them meat and drink for two months: they also took plates of iron and bars, wax-candles and lanterns, match and oil, hatchets, hooks and other sharp instruments, and entered into the pyramid.

'Most of them got down the first descent and the second, and passed along the ground of the pyramid, where they saw bats as big as black eagles, which began to beat their faces with much violence. But they generously endured that inconvenience and advanced still till they came to a narrow passage through which came an impetuous wind, extraordinary cold. They could not perceive whence it came, nor whither it went. They advanced to get into the narrow place and then their candles began to go out, which obliged them to put them into their lanterns. Then they entered, but the place seemed to be joined and closed before them: whereupon one of them said to the rest, "Tie me by the waist with a cord and I will venture to advance, conditionally that if any accident happen to me, you immediately draw me back."

'At the entrance to the narrow place there were great empty vessels made like coffins, with their lids by them; from which they inferred that those who set them there had prepared them for their death; and that to get to their treasures and wealth there was a necessity of passing through that narrow place. They bound their companion with cords, that he might venture to get through that passage; but immediately the passage closed upon him, and they heard the noise of the crushing of his bones: they drew the cords to them, but they could not get him back. Then there came to them a dreadful voice out of the cave, which startled and blinded them so that they fell down having neither motion nor sense. They came to themselves a while after and endeavoured to get out, being much at a loss what to do.

'At last after much trouble they returned, save only some of them who fell under the descent.

The entrance to the Great Pyramid, long since stripped of its casing stones, was sketched during Colonel Howard Vyse's operations at Giza in 1837.

Being come out into the plain they sat down together, all astonished at what they had seen, and reflecting on what had happened to them; whereupon the earth cleft before them and cast up their dead companion, who was at first immovable, but two hours later began to move and spoke to them in a language they understood not, for it was not *Arabian*. But some time after one of the inhabitants of Upper Egypt interpreted it to them and told them his meaning was this: *This is the reward of those who endeavour to seize what belongs to another*. After these words their companion seemed dead as before, whereupon they buried him in that place. Some of them died also in the pyramid.

'Another history related that some entered into the pyramid and came to the lowest part of it, where they turned round about. There appeared to them a hollow place, wherein there was a beaten path along which they began to go. And then they found a basin, out of which distilled fresh water, which fell into several pits which were under the basin, so as they knew not whence it came, nor whither it went. After that they found a square hall, the walls whereof were of strange stones of several colours. One of the company took a little stone and put it into his mouth, and immediately his ears were deafened. Afterwards they came to a place made like a cistern full of coined gold, like the large sort of cakes that were made; for every piece was the weight of a thousand drams. They took some of them, but could not get out of the place till they had returned them into the place whence they had taken them.

'They afterwards found another place with a great bench, such as is ordinarily before houses for people to sit on; and on the bench a figure of green stone, representing a tall ancient man sitting, having a large garment about him and little statues before him, as if they were children whom he taught: they took some of those figures, but could not get out of the place till they had left them behind them.

'They passed on along the same way and heard a dreadful noise and great hurly-burly, which they durst not approach. Then having advanced further, they found a square place, as if it were for some great assembly, where there were many statues, and among others the figure of a cock made of red gold: that figure was dreadful, enamelled with jacinths, whereof there were two great ones in both eyes, which shined like two great torches. They went near it, and immediately it crowed terribly and began to beat its two wings, and thereupon they heard several voices which came to them on all sides.

'They kept on their way, and found afterwards an idol of white stone, with the figure of a woman standing on her head, and two lions of white stone lying on each side of her, which seemed to roar and endeavour to bite. They recommended themselves to God and went on and kept on their way till they saw a light; after which going out at an open place, they perceived they were in a great sandy desert. At the passage out of that open place there were two statues of black stone, having half-pikes in their hands. They were extremely astonished, whereupon they began to return towards the east, till they came near the pyramids on the outside.'

But these are fables. The real record is in the stone itself. All around the three Pyramids of Giza are the temples and tombs that tell of their import-ance to the ancient Egyptians. In death, as in life, the nobles and officials clustered about their king while generations of priests and ritualists continued the cult of the living god. The pyramid itself was only one part, although the most obvious part, of a complex of buildings. Even at Giza some part of the complex for each individual pyramid may be missing or unfinished, but the pattern is clear.

Each pyramid had round it a levelled pavement surrounded by an enclosure wall. On the eastern side of the pyramid stood a Mortuary Temple; another temple, the Valley Building on the edge of the cultivated plain, was connected with the Mortuary Temple by a Causeway maybe 500 metres (1650 ft.) in length. The Causeway was roofed over to make a long corridor. Carvings probably covered the walls of the temples and causeways; statues of the king stood in the hall-ways of the temples as insurance against the destruction of his bodily remains, the earthly home of his spirit. Some that remain, a seated statue of Chephren from his Valley Building, some group statues of Mycerinus between two goddesses, are beautiful examples of Old Kingdom sculpture.

A small pyramid to the south of Chephren's pyramid may have been a resting place for the king's spirit; rather larger subsidiary pyramids to the east of Cheops' and the south of Mycerinus' may have belonged to these king's queens. Oval pits sunk into the rock near the pyramids held full size wooden boats – one was measured at 43.5 metres (143 ft.) long – in which the dead king could travel through his domains. Close by, a pyramid city, a small town of mud-brick buildings, housed the officials and priests who administered the construction of the pyramids, performed the funeral ceremonies and continued to celebrate the services necessary to guarantee the dead king's well-being in the after-life. They were exempt from taxes, supported by the income from grants of land.

Around the pyramids, the *mastabas* of the City of the Dead spread out. The king wished to have his entourage around him in the other world: and they, in turn, hoped to retain their privileges as servants of the king. Death, for the Egyptians, always was a continuation of life by other means.

A few titles gathered from tombs linked with Chephren's pyramid show the complexities of court organization that the king expected to recreate in the after-life: Overseer of the City of the Pyramid; Pilot of the Royal Boat; Overseer of All the Works of the King; Overseer of the

Weapons; Overseer of the Gangs of Workmen; Overseer of the Hairdressers of the Palace; Mistress of Pleasures; Assistant Priest of the Pyramid; Guardian of the Gold Ornaments; The Embalmer Priest of Anubis; Carpenter and Builder to the King; Assistant to the Cooler of the Drinks; Priest of Osiris; Judge and Book-keeper; Treasurer.

Just as Cheops' pyramid is the greatest, so the necropolis around the Great Pyramid is the most extensive. Cheops' planners laid out regular avenues of *mastabas* that reflected the hierarchies of the court, although later generations destroyed the symmetries by cramming in *mastabas* higgledy-piggledy so as to be near the lustrous pyramid. The original *mastabas* to the west of the Great Pyramid belonged mainly to officials, including Prince Hemiwn, the vizier, one of the architects of the Great Pyramid itself: the larger *mastabas* to the south and east of the Great Pyramid belonged to princes and queens of the royal blood. Selim Hassan, one of the twentieth-century archaeologists who has excavated at Giza, described the scene: 'The Great Pyramid stands amid the numerous tombs of these two necropoli, towering above them, although these *mastabas* are themselves large and impressive monuments. And thus it was that Cheops himself, the central figure of the kingdom, towered over the lesser members of his family and officials, who were themselves great men and women, the powerful lords and ladies of the ancient world.'

Here in the royal necropolis, in 1925, between the field of *mastabas* and the Causeway, American archaeologist George A. Reisner stumbled across a most exciting find: the secret tomb of Queen Hetep-heres, wife of Sneferu and mother of Cheops. The American expedition had cleared the area of sand, a photographer setting up his tripod chipped some plaster from what seemed to be solid rock and suddenly they realized they were looking at the well-concealed mouth of a shaft going straight down into the ground. Months went by as they cleared out the stone blocks that filled the 30 metre (99 ft.) shaft and pieced together the crumbling funerary equipment found in the chamber opening off its base. Restoration disclosed the beauties of the discovery: simply designed yet perfectly finished wooden chairs, a canopy frame and a bed, all partly covered with gold sheet; alabaster vessels and vases filled with ointment; gold and silver tools, a manicure set and jewellery; even a chest containing the preserved internal organs of the queen although the sarcopha-

gus where her body should have lain was empty.

George Reisner conjured up a graphic tale to explain away the missing body. Queen Hetep-heres, he suggested, was originally buried near

The goddess Hathor is flanked by a local goddess and King Mycerinus in this forceful statue – only one metre (3.3 ft.) high – from his Valley Temple. Mycerinus probably intended to have a statue representing each of the forty-two districts of Egypt.

her husband's pyramids at Dashur but thieves broke in and destroyed the body while stealing its golden ornaments. The vizier, Prince Hemiwn, hurried to inspect the despoiled tomb then decided to remove all that remained to the safer burial place beside her son's Great Pyramid. Cheops himself, by this account, never knew his mother's body had disappeared.

One last wonder stands out on the Giza plateau: the Sphinx. The Sphinx is a vast, human-headed lion cut from an outcrop of the living rock left in a small hollow to the east of Chephren's pyramid. It is about 73 metres (240 ft.) long and 20 metres (66 ft.) high. It wears the royal headdress and the face is that of Chephren who caused it to be built. Later generations believed the Sphinx was the Sun-god Harmachis protecting Giza against the encroaching sand.

Abd al Latif thought the Sphinx was the most impressive sight in Egypt: 'At little more than an arrow's flight from these pyramids is a colossal figure of a head and neck projecting from the earth. The name of this figure is Aboo' lhaul and the body to which the head pertains is said to be buried under the earth. To judge from the dimensions of the head its length must be more than 70 cubits (about 37 metres or 123 ft.). On the face is a reddish tint and a red varnish as bright as if fresh put on. The face is remarkably handsome and the mouth expresses much grace and beauty. One might fancy it smiling gracefully. A sensible man enquiring of me what of all I had seen in Egypt had most excited my admiration, I answered, the nicety of proportion in the head of this Sphinx. In fact, between the different parts of this head, the nose, for example, the eyes and the ears, the same proportion is remarked as is observed by nature in her works. Hence the wonder that in a face of such colossal size the sculptor should have been able to preserve the exact proportion of every part, seeing that nature presented him with no model of a similar colossus.'

How, Abd al Latif wanted to know, did the Egyptians carve the Sphinx without a Sphinx-size model to copy? But that is just part of a greater mystery: how did they build the pyramids themselves? Every stage produces a new query: how did they level the site and set out the plan for the pyramid; how did they ensure that the sides of the pyramid were flat and that the edges met in a point at the top; how did they quarry the stones; how did they bring them to the pyramid site; how did they shape them and raise them into place; how many men worked on each pyramid and how long did it take them to build? Virtually all the answers are conjectures based on guesses because no account of how these things were actually done has yet been found.

First they had to choose a site on the west bank of the Nile, clearing away the surface gravel down to a foundation of rock, cutting away any rise and filling any hollow. The Great Pyramid actually incorporates a small hill into its structure but the pavement that surrounds it, running under the edges, is almost perfectly flat and slopes up by less than 2 centimetres (0.8 in.) from the north-west to the south-east corner. Levelling probably depended on taking measurements from the surface of water lying in trenches or mud-banked channels: according to one suggestion the Egyptians might have flooded the entire site in order to level the base of the pyramid.

Next they set out the base oriented north, south, east and west. Perhaps this was so that one side faced the western horizon where the sun went down into the underworld and the opposite side looked towards the east where the Sun-god appeared at dawn. The Great Pyramid is laid out more accurately than any other monument: the longest side differs from the shortest by only 20 centimetres (8 in.) or so; the four corners are within one-sixteenth of a degree of a right angle; the overall orientation is within one-tenth of a degree of the present-day true north.

Some minimal evidence from these early dynasties suggests that the king himself ceremonially laid out the ground plan of the pyramid using measuring cords and observations of the stars. Although the real work was done by others, and the king's contribution was similar to laying a foundation stone, this does indicate how they probably went about it. The ancient Egyptians almost certainly did have measuring cords, and probably measuring rods, and they would have needed only the simplest of instruments for sighting stars, possibly just a notched stick and a plumb bob.

A straightforward method of setting out a line north-south or east-west depends on sighting the same star twice at the moments when, ascending and descending, it is at the same angle above the horizontal. One speculation is that the Egyptians built an artificial horizon of a circular wall levelled off with a water channel and then marked the rising and setting of a star in the northern sky. The point half-way between the two showed true north. Marking a star as it rose roughly in the east and set in the west would have given an east-west line. Once construction was underway the survey-

This view of the Giza plateau from the south shows the pyramid of Mycerinus, with its subsidiary pyramids in front, the pyramid of Chephren behind and that of Cheops in the far distance.

ors may have used sighting points set beyond the diagonals of the pyramid to keep the corners from twisting and taken measurements from plumb lines or marks set out on tall, mud-brick walls to control the slope.

Even as the builders laid out the base of the pyramid the conveyor system for quarrying stone, moving it to the pyramid site and shaping it ready for raising into place was getting under way. Stone for the pyramid core and for the causeway leading up from the edge of the Nile came from quarries in the Giza plateau itself: the Sphinx actually squats in a small quarry that supplied stone for the Great Pyramid. Finer quality facing stone came from quarries on the other bank of the Nile. Although earlier travellers, such as Herodotus and Abd al Latif, saw these pyramids in all their glory this fine, smooth facing has mainly disappeared. A few courses remain along the lower edges of the main pyramids and towards the top of Chephren's pyramid but, over the past few hundred years, the rest has vanished into other ancient projects and the bridges and buildings of Cairo. Granite for the King's Chamber and other compartments and corridors, for parts of the temples and valley buildings and for the facing on the lower courses of Mycerinus' pyramid came 800 kilometres (500 miles) down the Nile from Aswan.

In the tunnel-like limestone quarries on the east bank, workmen burrowed a working space above the next layer of blocks, chipped down the back and sides with copper chisels and split the base away with wedges. The harder granite, too, might be split out with wedges or, more laboriously, bruised out by pounding at the surrounding rock with balls of a particularly hard stone, dolerite. Rough-cut blocks might be shifted by rolling them over and over or mounting them on wooden sleds and dragging them along. In a typical scene shown in a later tomb-painting a 60 tonne (ton) statue is pulled along by 172 men while others pour out water or oil in front of the runners to grease the way. The sleds probably ran over track-ways of mud-brick, stone or baulks of timber. In some cases the stone-moving teams may have used timber rollers.

At the pyramid site masons shaped the stone. Core blocks could be left almost as quarried, and any spaces filled with mortar, but the facing blocks had to fit snugly against each other. For handling, the blocks might be shifted on to rockers, short wooden sleds with curved runners. At this stage, the masons left the front faces undressed so that they could move the stones into place without damaging them. The builders probably smoothed down the surfaces in one final sweep.

Colonel Howard Vyse recorded his impressions of the quality of the masonry although these were

*The Sphinx is one of the most intriguing images of Egypt.
Chephren, whose pyramid appears behind it in this view, had it
carved from a knoll of rock left in a small quarry that provided
stone for the core of the pyramid: the Sphinx has Chephren's
features. Later generations thought of it as the god Harmachis
protecting Giza against the encroaching sand.*

gathered under gruelling conditions. 'The weather was exceedingly hot and the gnats and other insects, particularly the small sand-flies, were very troublesome. The thermometer in the tent in which we sat exceeded, during the day, 120° F (50° C) and in the tombs, during the night, stood above 90° F (32° C). After having gone round the several works I was sent for about two o'clock to the Great Pyramid as the casing stones at the base had been discovered.'

Colonel Vyse averred that the casing stones were quite perfect, that they had been hewn into the required angle before they were built in and had then been polished down to one uniform surface; the joints were scarcely perceptible and not wider than the thickness of silver paper. The pavement beyond the line of the building was well laid and beautifully finished; but beneath the edifice it was worked with even greater exactness and to the most perfect level in order, probably, to obtain a lasting foundation for the magnificent structure to be built upon it. He considered that the workmanship displayed in the King's Chamber, in this pavement and in the casing stones was perfectly unrivalled; and there was no reason to doubt that the whole exterior of this vast structure was covered with the same excellent masonry.

Just how the ancient Egyptians placed these huge blocks of masonry in position is a matter for speculation. Most archaeologists agree that they probably constructed a main supply ramp of mud brick and packed earth up which they could haul the bulk of the stone. At the Great Pyramid this main ramp might have reached about a third of the way up the structure, to the level of the King's Chamber with its massive blocks of granite. Some archaeologists suggest the main ramp was successively raised to the final height of the pyramid; others conjecture that a system of subsidiary ramps gradually spiralled around the structure; while others, still, suspect that ramps were impracticable beyond a certain height and that the builders lifted the blocks from level to level as though up a staircase. The Egyptians had no cranes although some people have suggested that they could have counterweighted long levers with stones or sand to make a lifting device. A simpler idea is that they levered a stone and its rocker to and fro and by slipping planks beneath the runners gradually raised it up. Every theory accepts that they dressed the surface from the top down, gradually clearing away any foothold ramps, scaffolding or staircase blocks as they went.

Over and above the sheer ability to handle stone, the pyramid builders needed an effective organizational system. Bringing any one stone across the Nile and shaping and positioning it required effort but in itself was straightforward. The system, however, had to guarantee a smooth flow of thousands of blocks a year and keep track of the masons' work so as to deliver shaped blocks to the right place and in the right sequence. Most estimates suggest that the Great Pyramid took twenty to thirty years to build, that between four and ten thousand men worked on it continuously with hundreds more in the quarries, that during the three or four months when the Nile flooded, and no one could work on the land, levies of up to a hundred thousand men hauled the next year's supply of stone to the site and raised finished blocks to the construction level. At this time the total population of Upper and Lower Egypt was probably between one-and-a-half and two million people. Conscripting such a large proportion of the population, supervising their work and arranging for them to be fed and housed, and collecting the taxes that made it all possible, tied in with the making of the single state of Egypt out of a series of provinces.

Whatever the Egyptians themselves thought about pyramid building, later commentators tended to cynicism. During the first century AD, the Roman writer Pliny the Elder, in his *Natural History*, mentioned the pyramids as an idle and foolish exhibition of royal wealth. Many people, he claimed, believed that the kings constructed them to use up their treasures, rather than leave them to their successors or rivals, and to keep the people from idleness.

Virtually every description of the building of the pyramids has to start with the account left by Herodotus of what he learned when he visited Egypt. Intriguing though this is in telling what was known 2500 years ago, it must include some of the prejudices and misconceptions accumulated by the Egyptians themselves in the centuries since Cheops died. They told him that when Cheops became king he reduced the Egyptians to utter misery for he closed all the temples and kept them from offering sacrifices. He forced all the Egyptians to work for him. Some had to draw stones from the quarries in the Arabian mountains, on the east bank, to the Nile. Others received the stones after they had been carried over the river in boats and had to draw them up to the Libyan mountains on the west bank. They worked in bodies of a hundred thousand men at a time, for each three months continuously. This oppression continued for ten years during the construction of the causeway along which they drew the stones. This, in Herodotus's opinion, was a work not much inferior to the pyramid, for it was 915 metres (3000 ft.) long, 18 metres (60 ft.) wide and, at its loftiest, 15 metres (48 ft.) high. It was made of smoothed stone with figures carved on it. The ten years spent on this included the excavation of subterranean chambers in the hill on which the pyramid stands. There Cheops constructed his own sepulchral vaults on an island made by introducing a canal from the Nile. Twenty years went into the construction of the Great Pyramid itself.

Herodotus' informants went on to tell him that the pyramid was constructed in the manner of steps, called by some parapets and by some little altars. When they had constructed it so, they raised the remaining stones with machines made of short pieces of wood, raising them first from the ground to the first layer of steps. When the stone was let down on this it rested on a second machine standing on the first layer, from this it was drawn to the second layer where another machine lay to receive it. There were just as many machines as there were layers of steps, or perhaps they transferred the same single portable machine to each layer successively. Herodotus was not sure which as both accounts were related to him. The upper part of the pyramid was finished off first, then the next part, and last of all the parts near the ground.

This Cheops, the Egyptians said, reigned 50 years and was succeeded at his death by his brother Chephren, who pursued in all respects the same course as he had done. His pyramid, however, did not reach the same size: Herodotus claimed that he, himself, had measured it. Chephren's pyramid lacked any subterranean chambers; nor was there any canal flowing into it from the Nile. He built the lower courses of Ethiopian stone or granite of different colours. Chephren, the Egyptians said, reigned 56 years. This made up 106 years during which, according to their account, they were reduced to extreme misery and the temples were closed up.

Sir Flinders Petrie, at the start of his long career in Egyptology, spent many months carrying out a survey of the pyramids of Giza and spelt out how he believed Herodotus's hundred thousand men organized their work. According to him, the actual course of work during the building of the pyramid would have been somewhat along the following lines.

At the end of July, when the Nile had fairly risen, the levy of men would assemble to the work.

Not more than eight men, he thought, could work together on an average block of 1.1 cubic metres (40 cu. ft.) or 2.5 tonnes (tons) so the levies would probably be divided into working parties of about that number. If, then, he calculated, each of these parties brought over ten average blocks of stone in their three months' labour – taking a fortnight to bring them down the causeway at the quarries, a day or two of good wind to take them across the stream, six weeks to carry them up the pyramid causeway, and four weeks to raise them to the required place on the pyramid – they would easily accomplish their task in the three months of high Nile. They could then return to their own occupations at the beginning of November when the land was again accessible.

Besides these hosts of unskilled hands, he thought, there must have been a smaller body of masons permanently employed in quarrying the stone, and in trimming it at the pyramid. It was also likely that a year's supply of stone was kept on hand at the pyramid, on which the masons would work, and so the three months' supply of labourers would put up the stones which had been trimmed and ranged during the previous nine months as well as bringing over the supply for the next nine months. He estimated the number of skilled masons by looking at the accommodation provided for them in barracks behind Chephren's pyramid. These barracks were used by Chephren's workmen; but those of Cheops must have been equally numerous and have occupied a similar space, if not the identical dwellings. These barracks would hold about 3600 men or 4000 men easily. As about 120000 average blocks were required every year, this would be only one block of stone a month prepared by every group of four men, which would probably be the number of masons working together.

Sir Flinders Petrie's survey was accurate enough to allow him to speculate about the timing of the different parts of the construction, and even the career of a single supervisor, as well as commenting on some clumsy work: the Great Pyramid is not as perfect as it might be. During the course of building there was evidently a great change in the style of the work, a change belonging more to the builders than the masons. The pavement, lower casing, and entrance passage, he thought, were exquisitely wrought; the means employed for placing and cementing the blocks of soft limestone, weighing a dozen to 20 tonnes (tons) each, with such hair-like joints, are almost inconceivable; and the accuracy of levelling is marvellous.

But the higher parts are far from such excellence.

Petrie pointed out that the upper part of the Grand Gallery is very skew and irregular; the ramp surface being tilted more than 2.5 centimetres (1 in.) in a width of 51 centimetres (20 in.). In the antechamber the granite had never been dressed down flat, and defective stones were employed; where the limestone was very bad, it was plastered over and in many parts was strangely rough. In the King's Chamber the masonry is very fine, both in its accuracy of fitting and in the squareness and equal height of all the blocks; but the builders were altogether wrong in their levels and tilted the whole chamber over to one corner so that the courses are 6 centimetres (2.3 in.) higher at the north-east than at the south-west, a difference much greater than that in the whole base of the Great Pyramid.

An error like this in putting together such a magnificent piece of work Petrie found astonishing because the masons' work itself was close to perfection. The walls of the King's Chamber are composed of nearly 150 metres (490 ft.) length of granite blocks about 1.2 metres (4 ft.) high, and

probably as thick, all of which are gauged to the same height with an average variation of only 1 millimetre (0.04 in.). As it would be difficult to suppose any architect allowing such errors of building, after so closely restricting the masons' work, it strongly suggests, Petrie thought, that the granite had been prepared for the chamber long before it was built. The supervision was less strict as the work went on, because of more hurry and less care or the death of the man who had really directed the superfine accuracy of the earlier work.

Superfine or less than superfine, the Great Pyramid is still one of the Seven Wonders of the Ancient World, and the only one that exists today. Yet after they completed the three pyramids at Giza the Egyptians still looked forward to 2000 years or more of building pyramids, constructing tombs and temples, and collecting treasures.

The mysterious pyramids and Sphinx on the Giza plateau have always attracted investigators: this view was executed at the time of Napoleon's expedition to Egypt in 1798.

Tombs and Temples

AFTER GIZA, DYNASTIES of kings carried on their monumental ways. These living gods raised more pyramids, although smaller than the giants of Cheops and Chephren, and added tombs and temples, obelisks and colossi as they sought to ensure undisturbed enjoyment of the after-life and proper respect in the here and now.

Userkaf, first king of the Fifth Dynasty, constructed a pyramid at Saqqara, just to the north-east of Zoser's Step Pyramid, that was about 45 metres (147 ft.) high on a base somewhat over 70 metres (230 ft.) square. Like the Fourth Dynasty pyramids it had a core of large stones, faced off with better-quality limestone from Tura, but the interior was roughly put together out of unworked blocks bonded in place with coarse mortar. When the facing stones were quarried away by later generations the core began to collapse.

As well as the Saqqara pyramid, with its Mortuary Temple and subsidiary pyramid, Userkaf built a temple to the Sun-god at Abu Gurab, a little north of Abu Sir. Sahure, Neferirkare and Niuserre, the kings that followed him, did the same. Their pyramids are at Abu Sir and, like Userkaf's have disintegrated. Niuserre built a Sun-temple at Abu Gurab which had, as its main feature, a squat, obelisk-like structure, the symbol of the Sun-god, sitting on a truncated pyramid base. The others, too, built Sun-temples.

Unas, last of the dynasty, returned to Saqqara to build a pyramid maybe 43 metres (140 ft.) high on a base of 67 metres (220 ft.) square: today the remains stand less than 19 metres (62 ft.) high. It has a single inclined passage running from under

Ramesses II built the Ramesseum, an extensive funerary temple on the west bank at Thebes, in the thirteenth century BC. David Roberts sketched the remains in 1838.

The pyramid of Unas, built around 2350 BC but now a collapsing heap of rubble, was the first to have texts relating to the after-life incised in the chambers and passages.

the pavement on the northern side down into the bedrock: a level passage, blocked by three granite barriers, leads on to a square antechamber and the oblong burial chamber itself. So far it is similar to previous pyramids. However, for the first time the walls of the burial chamber and antechamber are covered with columns of hieroglyphs. These hieroglyphs, cut into the stone and picked out in a pale green-blue, record funerary rituals that guaranteed the dead king food and drink, prayers to the gods on his behalf and magical formulas to protect him on his journey to the other world. A typical section reads 'O Unas, you have not gone forth dead; you have gone to sit upon the throne of the god Osiris: you hold your sceptre in your hand to command those who dwell in hidden places.'

Over two hundred of these incantations appear on the walls of Unas's burial chamber and more than seven hundred are known in all. Some of the spells perpetuate much earlier rituals: 'Cast the sand from your face,' says one, referring to the time when the king was still buried in an open pit. Other spells have to do with the religious beliefs of later dynasties and even mention the pyramids themselves. These utterances are known as the *Pyramid Texts*. Later generations extended them

and took to painting them on their wooden coffins and, eventually, to writing them on papyrus. This *Book of Coming Forth by Day* or *Book of the Dead* was placed in a niche in the tomb or in the coffin with the dead person.

During the Sixth Dynasty kings continued to build at Saqqara. These pyramids were still substantial constructions but the core now consisted of small stones bonded with Nile mud. Once the limestone facing was stripped away the core fell apart. 'The present appearance of this Pyramid,' John Shae Perring reported of one in 1837, 'is that of a square heap of rubbish.' The emphasis was shifting to the Pyramid Complex which, at this stage, was developing into an ever more extensive range of subsidiary buildings and temples.

One of the kings of this Sixth Dynasty, Pepi II, whose pyramid once stood about 52 metres (171 ft.) high on a base 79 metres (258 ft.) square, apparently ruled for 94 years. At the beginning of his reign Egypt was still a united power capable of sending expeditions into the distant lands of Africa. Right

The dead depended on the living to provide for all their needs: this carving from around 2000 BC shows a son acting as a priest to make offerings to his father.

at the beginning of his reign the king, who was six years old, wrote to the leader of one caravan welcoming the news that they were bringing back a dwarf: 'Come northward at once to the Court and bring with you this dwarf, alive, sound and well. When he comes with you in the boat appoint trustworthy people to be beside him on each side of the boat; take care lest he fall in the water. When he sleeps at night appoint trustworthy people to sleep beside him in his tent. Inspect ten times a night.' But by the end of his reign Egypt was drifting towards separation into independent districts. The Sixth Dynasty, and with it the Old Kingdom, ended with Queen Nitocris on the throne of Egypt.

Herodotus collected a tale about a Queen Nitocris, the 'rosy-cheeked beauty', who came to the throne after her brother, who was perhaps her husband too, was killed in a riot. She built an immense subterranean hall and under the pretext of celebrating its completion, but in reality with a totally different aim, she then invited a con-

siderable number of those Egyptians she knew had taken part in the murder to a great feast in this hall. During the banquet she opened up a secret canal and let the waters of the Nile flow into the hall. This is what was related of her. Also, that after she had done this she threw herself into a great chamber full of embers in order to escape punishment.

During the First Intermediate Period that followed the end of the Old Kingdom, with Egypt split into provinces under a confusion of dynasties, vast monuments went out of favour. However, kings could still think about building tombs and could even confess, if only by implication, to stealing their predecessors' works. One of the Tenth Dynasty kings ruling at Heracleopolis, about 250 kilometres (150 miles) south of Memphis, passed on some practical advice to his son, Merikare, in a collection of *Precepts*: 'Do not destroy ancient buildings. The Southern Kingdom will supply you with granite, so do not break up other people's monuments. Fetch limestone from Tura and do not build your own tomb by tearing down others, taking what once was to make what will be.'

With the Eleventh Dynasty, kings from the

Religious texts and motifs came to figure on every item of funerary equipment: this owl was painted on the inside of a coffin dating from around 2000 BC.

southern capital of Thebes came to dominate Egypt. Neb-hepet-Re Mentuhotep, or Mentuhotep II, the king who actually conquered the northern provinces and re-unified the kingdom, developed an equally forceful attitude towards funereal architecture. Earlier kings shifted the emphasis from pyramid to temple: Mentuhotep's monument was nearly all temple. In addition, this temple was more a memorial of his life than a tribute to his death.

Mentuhotep II set his temple in a spectacular arena at the base of the cliffs at Deir el-Bahari on the west bank of the Nile slightly north of Thebes. An open causeway led to the temple through a formal grove of tamarisk trees. A ramp took the causeway up on to a colonnaded terrace which carried a square, colonnaded building. At the centre of this building was a solid platform which possibly supported a rubble-cored pyramid maybe 14 metres (46 ft.) high on a base 21 metres (70 ft.) square.

Mentuhotep II constructed and decorated his funerary chapel during his own lifetime, taking the opportunity to cover the walls with sculptures and reliefs that depicted the glorious events of his reign as they took place. Here were his wars, his triumphs and the hunting scenes which were his amusement. Through them all he moved as the living god of the temple. Some of these reliefs might have been the work of the sculptor Irtisen, who set out his claims on his own funerary tablet: 'I was an artist skilled in my art. I knew my art, how to represent the forms of going forth and returning so that each limb may be in its proper place. I knew how the figure of a man should walk and the carriage of a woman; the poising of the arm to bring the hippopotamus low, the movement of the runner. . . .'

One of the people who investigated this temple early in the twentieth century, Somers Clarke, co-author of the book *Ancient Egyptian Masonry*, tried to conjure up some picture of what it once looked like. He pointed out that we must not forget that an apartment, gloomy and squalid, such as we now see in many a temple, a ray of light struggling through a small opening in the roof slabs, did not by any means present this appearance in earlier times. The flat ceiling, instead of being stained and black with the filth of bats, was painted blue, thickly covered with light yellow stars; the walls were quite light in their general colour, adorned with many figures on a light ground; the floors were covered with a fine hard plaster, white or very light in general tint. A small ray of light from the glorious sky of Egypt was enough to illuminate such an apartment.

After the Eleventh Dynasty the capital shifted back to the north and the kings of the Twelfth Dynasty took to building pyramids once more, at Lisht, Dashur, Illahun and Hawara. By now they had fallen a long way from the standards of construction set by Cheops. Those pyramids built of stone often used limestone blocks taken from older tombs: in other pyramids the core was made of mud bricks. Herodotus noted that one pyramid carried an inscription saying: 'Do not despise me in comparison with pyramids of stone, because I excel them as much as Zeus excels the other gods; for those who built me thrust poles into the lakes and collecting the mud which stuck to them, made the bricks with which they constructed me.'

Ammenemes I, first king of the Twelfth Dynasty at about the beginning of the twentieth century BC, built at Lisht, south of Dashur, using blocks from Old Kingdom tombs to raise a pyramid maybe 56 metres (183 ft.) high on a base 90 metres (296 ft.) square. 'Many of the blocks have been taken away,' John Shae Perring reported, 'and their removal has disclosed its construction, which is very irregular and consists of differently sized stones, put together with Nile earth instead of mortar, and arranged in walls of unequal thickness.'

Sesostris I built at Lisht, too, raising a somewhat larger pyramid on a base about 107 metres (350 ft.) square. As well as the subsidiary pyramid about ten metres (33 ft.) high that was a standard part of the Pyramid Complex he dotted about a further nine small pyramids for queens and princesses, each with its own entrance shaft and offering chapel.

Ammenemes II built a pyramid at Dashur that was possibly around 50 metres (160 ft.) high on a base about 80 metres (260 ft.) square. He used fine

Tura limestone throughout but, in the event, this proved self-defeating as later builders found the pyramid a particularly attractive source of materials. The archaeologist Jacques de Morgan was prepared for disappointment when he excavated the pyramid at the end of the nineteenth century because it had been nearly all quarried away; its chambers had been opened up so many times by robbers that hardly a single object remained; the white walls were so bare of inscription that, for several weeks, he could not determine even in which dynasty it had been constructed. Only later did he learn it belonged to Ammenemes II. Because of the state of the ruins it was not possible

Statues could act as a substitute if a person's mummified body was destroyed: this granite statue from the nineteenth century BC commemorates a local official.

111

to estimate the height or other dimensions. Little remained except some of the lower courses of stone.

However, Jacques de Morgan did make his way into the royal burial chamber, although the sandstone sarcophagus had long been opened, and he gradually cleared the sand from the surrounding tombs. And here he found the Dashur treasure, jewellery once worn by the two princesses Khnumet and Ita. 'The real prize,' he wrote, 'is a delicate coronet formed from six ornamented Maltese crosses laced together with strands of gold threaded with beads of lapis lazuli and decorated with pretty little flowers made from emerald and cornaline. Any description hardly does justice to its airy grace and virginal appeal.'

When Sesostris II built his pyramid, at Illahun south of Meidum, his architects settled for an internal framework of stone walls and packed the spaces with mud bricks. His successors, Sesostris III and Ammenemes III, returned to Dashur where they, too, built with bricks. These three pyramids were much the same size, possibly as high as 75 metres (245 ft.) on a base 107 metres (350 ft.) square. All were faced off with Tura limestone and while this continued intact the brick core stayed solid enough. Once the facing stones disappeared, however, the pyramids crumbled away into little more than rounded hillocks.

Jacques de Morgan, in describing his discoveries, noted that the pyramid of Sesostris III was composed of sun-dried bricks placed in horizontal layers, the lowest resting directly on the desert gravel. The bricks in one course were all laid parallel but the courses were displaced so as to break up the rising joints. The bricks did not fit directly together but were bedded in a thin layer of fine, dry sand. They were about 42 centimetres (17 in.) long by 21 centimetres (8 in.) wide and 12 centimetres (5 in.) thick. Any differences were taken up by the sand that separated the courses and filled the rising joints. As it happened, Jacques de Morgan found collections of jewellery in the tombs around both pyramids at Dashur and the archaeologists who excavated at Illahun found even more.

Ammenemes III built a second pyramid of equal size at Hawara, between Illahun and Meidum. Sir Flinders Petrie, continuing as an Egyptologist after his survey of the pyramids of Giza, opened the pyramid and dug his way through the complicated and deceptive approaches to the burial chamber. The chamber, when he broke into it, was half-full of water and he had to work naked, sliding through the mud-blocked passages and feeling around for objects with his toes. This chamber, which contained two quartzite sarcophagi, was itself hollowed out of a single block of quartzite. Flinders Petrie could hardly believe this discovery: 'The sepulchre is an elaborate and massive construction. The chamber itself is a monolith 267.5 inches (6.8 metres) long, 94.2 inches (2.4 metres) wide and 73.9 inches (1.9 metres) high to the top of the enormous block with

Much Egyptian art was highly stylized; only particular poses were thought appropriate for depicting the great on the walls of their 'houses of eternity'. This wall-painting of waterfowl rising from a papyrus thicket, executed during the fourteenth-century BC reign of Amenophis IV or Akhenaten, shows close observation of nature and a mastery in presenting life-like detail.

a course of bricks 18.5 inches (0.5 metres) high upon that. The thickness of the chamber is about 25 inches (0.6 metres). It would accordingly weigh about 110 tonnes (tons). The workmanship is excellent; the sides are flat and regular, and the inner corners so sharply wrought that – though I looked at them – I never suspected that there was not a joint there until I failed to find any joints in the sides.'

South of the pyramid, Ammenemes III extended his Mortuary Temple into a vast, single-storey building that came to be called the Labyrinth. Herodotus visited it and felt amazed admiration as he circled through its pillars, wandering from courts to chambers to colonnades, and from colonnades into new rooms and courts not seen before. In the centuries since, the Labyrinth gradually disappeared as lime-burners quarried away the stone to turn it into mortar and plaster. George Sandys, an Englishman who travelled to Egypt early in the seventeenth century, recorded what was believed: 'That in the midst of this Labyrinth were 37 palaces, belonging to the 37 jurisdictions of Egypt. The passages thereunto were through caves of a miraculous length, full of dark and winding paths, and rooms within one another, having many doors to confound the memory and distract the intention, and leading into inextricable error, now mounting aloft, and then again redescending, not seldom turning about, walls infolded within each other, in the form of intricate mazes, not possible to thread or get out

of without a conductor.'

Sir Flinders Petrie identified the Labyrinth's site and speculated on its appearance: 'The gap in the desert hills, through which the Nile water flows into the oasis of the Fayum, is signalized by the ruins of two pyramids, one at either end of it. At the point where the stream of the canal turns away from the Nile valley the pyramid of Illahun rises on a rocky knoll; and at the edge of the basin of the Fayum stands the pyramid of Hawara, with various remains about it.' It seemed evident, he thought, that there was no other site but Hawara at which to look for the Labyrinth.

Ancient accounts told of the enormous extent of the buildings, and of their exceeding in vastness all the temples of the Greeks put together, and that they even surpassed the pyramids. Of the beauty and magnificence of the work, no one can now judge as almost every stone has long since been broken up and removed; but the extent of the area could be measured, marked out by the immense bed of chips of fine white limestone which lies on the south of the pyramid. On tracing these signs to their limits he found that they covered an area about 300 metres (1000 ft.) long and 240 metres (800 ft.) broad.

Within the Labyrinth, he noted, Herodotus had seen six great courts side by side, facing north, and

The mud-brick core of the pyramid of Ammenemes III at Hawara, sketched by John Shae Perring in 1837, crumbled once the facing stones had been taken for other buildings.

six others facing south, with one wall surrounding them all. Strabo, a Greek geographer who visited Egypt about 25 BC, gave further particulars of a row of courts all backing against one wall; long and intricate passages; and a hall of twenty-seven columns. The passages and chambers in front of the entrances to the courts would be quite enough to bewilder any stranger led through them by a guide, for a large temple appears confusing to anyone visiting it for the first time.

Petrie explained that people must get out of their minds the modern sense of a labyrinth. They must not compare it with the meanders of a mosaic pavement, or a maze made in a field, but should think of a building with many doors and galleries which confuse a visitor.

After Ammenemes III, Egypt once more drifted into confusion as the Middle Kingdom declined into the Second Intermediate Period. A few more kings may have raised pyramids and one that has been fully identified was built at Saqqara by a Thirteenth Dynasty king, Khendjer. This pyramid, with its core of mud bricks, stood maybe as high as 37 metres (120 ft.) on a base about 52 metres (170 ft.) square.

Pyramid builders, by this time, had developed increasingly sophisticated methods of trying to thwart robbers. The entrance to Khendjer's pyramid is to the west, rather than the north, concealed beneath the flagstones that supported the lowest course of casing blocks. Two quartzite slabs should have blocked the entrance passage but, apparently, could not be shifted when the builders came to close the pyramid: they still remain in the wall slots from which they should have slid portcullis-like. Once again the burial chamber consisted of a single block of quartzite, set in a pit beneath limestone slabs leaning against each other to make a pointed roof above. Two quartzite slabs 1.5 metres (5 ft.) thick formed a lid for the chamber. Until the funeral was over, twin props of granite, standing in vertical shafts filled with sand, held one part of the lid open. After the burial, stone plugs at the bottom of the two shafts were removed, the sand ran out and the quartzite slab sank slowly into place. Despite all the subtleties, thieves broke in, carved a hole in the quartzite chamber and took everything.

Kings of later dynasties came to one conclusion: pyramids were not worthwhile. Whatever mystical

Models from tombs reveal much about ways of life: in this nineteenth-century BC house, a farm steward sits upstairs while a woman kneads dough in a lower room.

function they served, the practical effect was to mark out the burial site for any tomb robber's attention. A king looking for peace in eternity could not count on the protection of a grave beneath a pyramid because robbers, given time and their sources of information, would eventually break in and destroy. So, when Egypt restabilized itself during the New Kingdom, under the Eighteenth to Twentieth Dynasties ruling from about 1550 BC to 1070 BC, the kings turned away from pyramids. They built individual temples, the equivalent of the Mortuary Temple that stood beside a pyramid. They built, rebuilt and added to the great temples at Karnak and Luxor on the east bank of the Nile near Thebes. They carved statues and raised monuments to themselves and their exploits. And they tunnelled secret tombs.

One of the finest funerary temples belonged to Queen Hatshepsut, fifth of the Eighteenth Dynasty rulers. She built alongside Mentuhotep II's temple at Deir el-Bahari, repeating on a larger scale the design of colonnaded terraces approached by ramps. The result again was a spectacular building in a spectacular setting. Every part of the temple had its statues of Hatshepsut, life-size and larger, and the walls were carved with scenes from her reign. Hatshepsut herself claimed that she was more beautiful than anything to look upon; her splendour and her form were divine; she was a maiden, beautiful and blooming. She also claimed divine conception: one series of carved reliefs told how the god Amun disguised himself as Tuthmosis I, third king of the dynasty and Hatshepsut's father, in order to visit Queen Ahmes, Hapshepsut's mother.

All Hatshepsut's works were carried through by one man, Senenmut, who rose from a lowly position as a priest of Amun to become Steward of the temple of Amun at Karnak, High Steward to the Queen herself, Overseer of the Overseers and Superintendent of virtually every administrative office. Senenmut's career hints at the kind of intrigues that beset these Egyptian courts. He put his own claims on record: 'I was under Hatshepsut's command from the moment of the death of her predecessor. I was one whose steps were known in the palace, secure in favour. I was one to whom the affairs of Egypt were reported. I was the greatest of the great in the whole land.' He even tunnelled his own tomb beneath the temple he built for the Queen. And yet he never lay in that tomb. It was never finished and those who wished him ill destroyed many of the statues and inscriptions. And yet again, suspicions about his power

re-emerged thousands of years later. The American archaeologist who excavated the temple in the 1920s, Herbert Winlock, slyly wondered whether some of the shoddier work resulted from Senenmut siphoning off the funds.

Whatever the queries about Senenmut's activities, he operated effectively in accomplishing the Queen's various projects. In one impressive feat he erected two granite obelisks, one of which still stands, in the great Karnak temple. Each of these obelisks was a single granite block weighing over 300 tonnes (tons) and standing 29.5 metres (97 ft.) high. The pyramid-shaped tip was itself 3 metres (10 ft.) tall. Each obelisk was 2.4 metres (8 ft.) square at the base, tapering to 1.8 metres (6 ft.) at the top of the shaft. These obelisks came from Aswan, 240 kilometres (150 miles) further up the Nile. An inscription still exists, carved in the Aswan rocks, saying: 'Senenmut came to conduct the work of two great obelisks. It took place according to that which was commanded because of the fame of her Majesty.'

An idea of the work involved can be pieced together from investigations of a half-finished obelisk still in the ground at Aswan, which was abandoned because fissures developed in the granite. If it ever had been raised it would have been the largest of them all, standing 42 metres (137 ft.) high and weighing over a thousand tonnes (tons).

Senenmut probably used fire and water to wear away the surface rock. Then he set to cutting out the obelisks themselves, putting shifts of maybe a hundred men at a time to work on each, bruising a trench about 0.8 metres (2.5 ft.) wide all round by pounding away with balls of the hard stone dolerite found in the desert. Next he freed them from the rock by pounding tunnels underneath. Then, probably using hundreds of soldiers for labour, he dragged them down to the river's edge, loaded them end to end on a barge and floated them down to Karnak. To raise them into position he may have hauled them up an earth embankment, perhaps lowering them into position down a cutaway pit filled with sand. Levers and counterweights were probably used to lift the obelisks, banking earth behind them as they rose. A later king, according to Pliny (who wrote his account more than a thousand years after the event), feared that the

A bureaucratic career in ancient Egypt could lead to power and riches. A 'block' statue from the time of Queen Hatshepsut commemorates a high official.

machinery raising one of his obelisks might not prove strong enough. To safeguard the monument he tied his own son to the summit of the obelisk as a guarantee of success. The king concerned, Ramesses II, had over a hundred children.

Senenmut carved the obelisks with Hatshepsut's prayers to the god Amun and as a final touch sheathed them in electrum, a mix of gold and silver. An inscription on the base reads: 'She made them as her monument to her father Amun, Lord of Thebes. Presider over Karnak, making for him two great obelisks of enduring granite from the south; their surfaces are of electrum, the best of every country; they are seen from both sides of the river. Their brightness floods the Two Lands when the sun rises between them as he dawns in

Queen Hatshepsut's temple at Deir el-Bahari near Thebes, built during the fifteenth century BC, reveals the glories of Egyptian architecture in a setting of splendour. The Valley of the Kings is in the hills behind.

the horizon of heaven.' All this, the inscription states, Senenmut accomplished in seven months.

Over the generations, these New Kingdom kings raised temple after temple and extended those that were already in being, particularly the great temple of Amun at Karnak. This became ever more impressive as king after king built and rebuilt. Here are Hatshepsut's obelisks, and here the obelisks quarried by Tuthmosis I; here are the pylons, or gate-towers, raised by Tuthmosis III and Amenophis III; here is the pillared Great Hypostyle Hall of Seti I, who also built a temple at Abydos dedicated to seven gods, including himself; here are some buildings added by Ramesses III; and here a carving in relief left by Merenptah.

Amelia Edwards thought Karnak was a marvel when she visited it in the nineteenth century. As she went in an immense perspective of pillars and pylons leading up to a very distant obelisk opened up before her. She entered the first court, where the great walls towered up like cliffs above her head. Here, in the midst of a large quadrangle open to the sky, she found a solitary column, the last of a central avenue of twelve, some of which, disjointed by the shock, lay just as they fell, 'like skeletons of vertebrate monsters left stranded by the Flood.' Crossing this court in the glowing sunlight, she came to a mighty doorway. The cornice of the doorway was gone. Only a jutting fragment of the lintel stone remained. That stone, when perfect, had measured 12.5 metres (41 ft.) across. The doorway must have been 30 metres (100 ft.) in height.

She went on and passed into the Great Hypostyle Hall of Seti I, a place, she decided, 'of which no writing and no art can convey more than a dwarfed and pallid impression; the scale is too vast; the effect too tremendous; the sense of one's own dumbness, and littleness, and incapacity, too complete and crushing. It is a place that strikes you into silence; that empties you, as it were, not only of words but of ideas. I could only look and be silent.'

In that silence, Amelia Edwards first contemplated the mightiest of the dozens of columns and tried to gauge their size. She stood at the foot of one, or of what seemed to be the foot, for the original pavement lay buried two metres (7 ft.) below, and reckoned six men standing with extended arms, finger-tip to finger-tip, could barely span it. It cast a shadow 3.5 metres (12 ft.) wide, such as might be cast by a tower. The capital that jutted out so high above her head looked to her as if it might have been placed there

to support the heavens: 'It is carved in the semblance of a full-blown lotus, and glows with undying colours – colours that are still fresh, though laid on by hands that have been dust these three thousand years and more. It would take not six men, but a dozen to measure round the curved lip of that stupendous lily.'

Such were the twelve central columns. The rest she found gigantic too; but smaller. Of the roof they once supported only the beams remained. These beams are huge, monolithic stones, 7.5 metres (25 ft.) long, carved and painted, bridging the gap from pillar to pillar. She obtained the measurements of the Great Hall, 52 metres (170 ft.) from doorway to doorway and 100 metres (329 ft.) across, and counted the columns. It contains 134 in all. The central twelve stand 19 metres (62 ft.) high in the shaft and measure 10.5 metres (34.5 ft.) in circumference. The smaller columns stand 13 metres (42.5 ft.) high and measure 8.5 metres (28 ft.) in circumference. And she described her feelings:

'Looking up and down the central avenue, we see at the one end a flame-like obelisk, at the other a solitary palm against a background of glowing mountain. To right, to left, showing transversely through long files of columns, we catch glimpses of colossal bas-reliefs lining the roofless walls in every direction. The king, as usual, figures in every group, and performs the customary acts of worship. The gods receive and approve him. Half in light, half in shadow, these slender, fantastic forms stand out sharp, and clear, and colourless; each figure some 6 metres (20 ft.) in height. There is, in truth, no building in the wide world to compare with it. The pyramids are more stupendous. The Colosseum covers more ground. The Parthenon is more beautiful. Yet in nobility of conception, in vastness of detail, in majesty of the highest order, the Hall of Pillars exceeds them every one. This doorway, these columns, are the wonder of the world. How was that lintel-stone raised? How were these capitals lifted? It has been calculated that every stone of these huge Pharaonic temples cost at least one human life. You are stupefied by the thought of the mighty men who made them.'

Most prolific of all the New Kingdom kings who built their temples and carved their statues was Ramesses II. Amenophis III left two impressive statues, a pair of seated figures over 20 metres (66

Queen Hatshepsut's High Steward, Senenmut, told how he raised a pair of magnificent obelisks in the temple at Karnak on her behalf. Only this one remains standing.

ft.) high called the Colossi of Memnon which dominate the empty plain near Thebes. Akhenaten left some of the finest carvings in the statues of himself at Karnak and in the ruins of the city he built at El-Amarna, half-way between Thebes and Memphis. But Ramesses II built as big as Amenophis and more extensively than Akhenaten. He finished the works his father, Seti I, had begun. He cut the vast temple in the rock at Abu Simbel, to the south in Nubia: the four huge statues, about 20 metres (66 ft.) high, set against the rock face are actually portraits of himself. Another temple at Abu Simbel belonged to Nefertari, one of his queens. He built a temple at Abydos; he carved and built in the temples at Luxor and Thebes and across the river, on the west bank, he raised his Mortuary Temple, the Ramesseum. A report of one of the statues of himself that Ramesses II erected led Shelley to write the poem *Ozymandias*, which was his name in Greek, setting out the ambivalent nature of the immortality he desired:

The impressive ruins of the temple of Amun at Karnak reveal its vast size: the distance from the western entry to the eastern gate totals about 500 metres (1650 ft.).

> I met a traveller from an antique land
> Who said: Two vast and trunkless legs of stone
> Stand in the desert . . . Near them, on the
>   sand,
> Half sunk, a shattered visage lies, whose frown,
> And wrinkled lip, and sneer of cold command,
> Tell that its sculptor well those passions read
> Which yet survive, stamped on these lifeless
>   things,
> The hand that mocked them, and the heart
>   that fed:
> And on the pedestal these words appear:
> 'My name is Ozymandias, king of kings:
> Look on my works, ye Mighty, and despair!'
> Nothing beside remains. Round the decay
> Of that colossal wreck, boundless and bare,
> The lone and level sands stretch far away.

For these Egyptian kings, personal immortality depended on keeping the body in being. As the pyramids had proved unsafe they tried another kind of security. They still equipped their tombs with riches and decorated them beautifully, but they hid them away, cutting them deeply into the rock and providing only an insignificant stone doorway to mark the entrance. From Tuthmosis I onwards they tunnelled their secret tombs in a bare and guarded valley in the hills north-west of Thebes, the Valley of the Kings.

Henry Rhind, a nineteenth-century British Egyptologist, described the scene: 'Deep in the mountains a break in the desert range opens up a narrow defile which, with many windings, leads to a desolate glen closed in by the arid hills. The

Valley of the Shadow of Death could offer no picture more sternly emblematic. No flower or shrub, intruding its message of vitality, fringes one single spot in the whole parched outline. Stray footprints in the sand of hyenas and jackals, although dim evidences of life, speak rather of the haunts of death. The cavernous entrances to the tombs, marked by deep dark shadows where they pierce the crags, look more than figuratively the gloomy portals of the grave.'

Inside, these tombs could be quite extensive. The entrance passage for Tuthmosis I's is only 15 metres (50 ft.) long but Queen Hatshepsut's stretches to over 200 metres (660 ft.) as though she tried to drive though the hill to position her tomb close to her temple at Deir el-Bahari. At the end of the passage, which usually sloped steeply down with a sharp turn or two, or even a concealed entrance into a second passage, a series of rooms contained the funeral goods and the sarcophagus itself. All the walls were painted with scenes from the funerary texts that would help the dead king on the journey to the other world. The most impressive tomb, which belonged to Seti I, was unearthed by Giovanni Belzoni early in the nineteenth century. The entrance into the tomb is at the foot of a high hill with a pretty steep

Ram-headed sphinxes forming an avenue in the temple at Karnak represent Amun, the local god who became one of the most significant in the Egyptian religious system.

ascent. The first thing the visitor comes to is a staircase, cut out of the rock, which runs down to the passage into the tomb. The walls of the passage are covered with carved and painted funeral processions, apparently escorting the sarcophagus down into the tomb.

All the figures and hieroglyphs everywhere in the tomb are sculpted and painted over. To do this the wall was previously made as smooth as possible. Where a figure or anything else was required, the sculptor seems to have made the first sketches of what was intended to be cut out in red lines. When the sketches were finished, another, more skilful artist, corrected any errors in black. Then the sculptor proceeded to cut out the stone all round, leaving the figures in relief, standing out over a centimetre (0.5 in.). Belzoni estimated that there was not a space on the walls more than 30 centimetres (1 ft.) square without some figure or hieroglyph. When the figures were completed and made smooth by the sculptor, they were white-washed all over. This white still appeared so beautiful and clear, Belzoni noted, that 'the best and whitest paper appeared yellowish when compared with it.' The painter came next and finished the figure.

After the passage comes the first hall, which has four pillars. On the right hand side wall are three tiers of figures, one above the other, and this is the general system all over the tomb. In this hall, facing the entrance, is one composition that Belzoni reckoned to be the finest ever made by the Egyptians: 'It consists of four figures as large as life: The god Osiris sitting on his throne receiving the homages of a hero who is introduced by a hawk-headed deity. Behind the throne is a female figure as if in attendance on the great god. The whole group is surrounded by hieroglyphs and enclosed in a frame richly adorned with symbolic figures. The winged globe is above, with the wings spread over all, and a line of serpents crowns the whole. The figures and paintings are in such perfect preservation that they give the most correct idea of their ornaments and decorations.'

Another hall leads straight ahead but the main tomb continues down a staircase and along a lower passage. On the wall to the left is a seated life-size figure. 'It is the hero himself on his throne,' wrote Belzoni, 'having the sceptre in his right hand while the left is stretched over an altar.' The upper part of each wall of the passage is divided into several small compartments, 60 centimetres (2 ft.) square, containing groups of figures 50 centimetres (18 in.) high. Further on a small stair-case drops down to a short passage leading to a section much wider than the rest. The charming sight of its many figures, all in such perfection, prompted Belzoni to name it the Room of Beauties. Next comes a great hall, with six pillars, which opens into a large, vaulted chamber 9.7 by 8.2 metres (32 by 27 ft.). The ceiling of the vault is painted blue, with a procession of figures and other groups relating to the zodiac.

It was here that the body of the king was deposited, as at its centre was placed a beautiful sarcophagus. This alabaster sarcophagus, which Belzoni later shipped to London, is 2.9 metres (9.5 ft.) long and 1.1 metres (3.5 ft.) wide. Its walls are only 5 centimetres (2 in.) thick. Belzoni was highly taken with his find: 'It is sculptured within and without with small figures incised in the surface and coloured with a dark blue, and when a light is put inside it is quite transparent.'

As well as painting the walls with religious scenes depicting their hopes for the after-life, all these kings stacked their tombs with treasure. And they had treasures and more to stack. Over two thousand years later, the Arab writer Murtada ibn al Khafif tried to imagine the riches these tombs had seen. According to him, when Masar, the first king after the Deluge, was near death, he

enjoined his children to make him a cave in the earth, to pave it with white emeralds, to dispose his body into it, and to bury with him whatever there was in his treasuries of gold, silver, and precious stones. They made a cave 150 cubits (maybe 75 metres or 250 ft.) in length, and built an assembly hall, lined with plates of gold and silver, which had four doors. Over every door they placed a statue of gold, wearing a crown set with precious stones and seated on a throne of gold.

Although this sounds like fantasy, the reality was exactly that amazing. When the archaeologist Howard Carter first peered into the newly discovered tomb of Tutankhamun, on November 26, 1922, he was struck dumb with amazement. Lord Carnarvon, his colleague and patron, asked in trembling tones, 'Well, what is it?' Howard Carter answered, 'There are some marvellous objects here.' The tomb was alive with the glint of gold.

Opposite: *The sheer size of the columns, some of which are 19 metres (62 ft.) high, amazes all who wander through the temple at Karnak.*

Below: *David Roberts sketched the sand-filled interior of the temple of Ramesses II at Abu Simbel in 1838.*

Tutankhamun was one of the least significant of Egypt's rulers, a boy-king who reigned for nine years and died aged only 18. His was one of the smallest tombs, just the burial chamber, an anteroom and two other rooms. And still the treasure brings gasps from all who see it. There are the two life-size figures of the king with gilded kilt and head-dress; there is the golden throne with an inlaid scene of the king and his wife; there is a little shrine encased in gold; there is a golden dagger, an exotic necklace with scarab beetles carved from lapis lazuli, jewellery that is a heady mix of beaten gold and semi-precious stones; there is the alabaster chest that contained his inner organs; there is the shrine containing his sarcophagus that is made of oak overlaid with gold and is 5 by 3.4 metres (17 by 11 ft.) and 2.7 metres (9 ft.) high; there is the inner coffin 1.9 metres (6 ft.) long made of solid gold and so heavy that it took eight men to lift it; and there is the golden mask on the mummy itself. This burnished golden face, with its eyes of lapis lazuli, obsidian and quartz, and its decorated head-dress and beard, symbolized the dead king as Osiris.

With treasure like this as the reward it is no wonder that thieves broke in to steal from all the

other 30 or so royal tombs in the Valley of the Kings. Tutankhamun's remained safe only because the entrance was buried in the rubble thrown down the cliff by the workmen cutting Ramesses VI's tomb. Ineni, the official who constructed a tomb for Tuthmosis I, the first in the valley, did record that he 'supervised the excavation of His Majesty's tomb all alone, no one saw, no one heard.' But of course they did. And the stone-cutters, sculptors and artists had their own problems. Theoretically their royal employers supplied them with rations; money played no part in the system. But what with holidays, feast days,

days when supervisors failed to organize any work and days when the rations just did not appear, the necropolis workers were often left hungry. From time to time they went on strike, claiming their due. From time to time they, and the guards and the officials and the priests, probably co-operated with the tomb robbers.

In the end, those responsible for preserving the royal mummies, and the royal hopes for the after-life, gathered together the despoiled bodies and hid them away once more, some in a rock-cut chamber near Deir el-Bahari, others in the tomb of Amenophis II in the Valley of the Kings. These caches eventually came to light late in the nineteenth century and Gaston Maspero, Director of the Egyptian Antiquities Service, reconstructed the pressures that led the Ancient Egyptians to treat their deceased kings like so many sacks of coal. People in modern times, he thought, could

Opposite: Kings in Nubia built pyramids long after the Egyptians themselves had stopped. These are at Meroe.

Below: Tutankhamun's tomb contained sumptuous vessels in alabaster, such as this lotus-flower drinking cup.

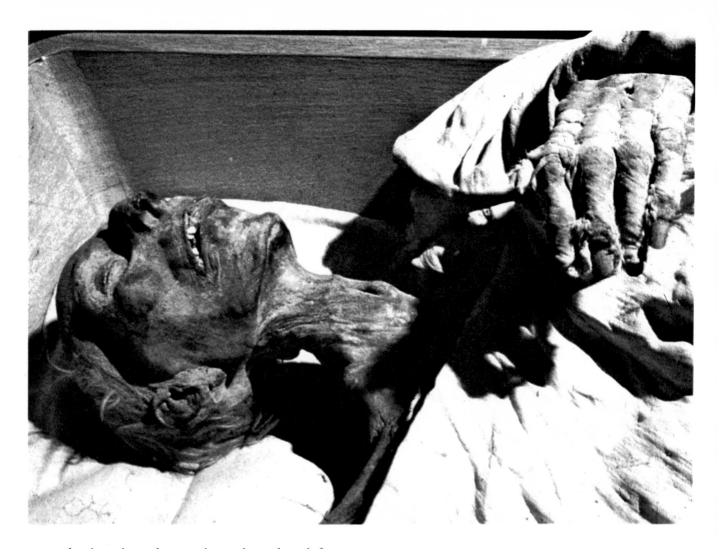

scarcely imagine the anxiety that the defunct Pharaohs caused their successor the day after the burial. As the splendour of their funeral equipment should equal or at least approach that of their terrestrial life, they were allotted not only quantities of furniture and painted and decorated plates and dishes, but masses of jewels and royal orders, necklaces, bracelets, rings, amulets, weapons of war and of the chase, mostly in gold or silver, inlaid with enamel and precious stones. And these valuables were not delivered to them at night or furtively: the pieces of jewellery that were not applied to the corpse during the wrapping of the mummy cloths round it were displayed in full daylight to the sight of the crowd who assisted at the funeral ceremony, so that everyone in the land knew their value and number. So much wealth would certainly attract the robbers who exploited the Theban burying places, and they would soon have carried them off had not efficient measures been taken to guard against their enterprises. Each tomb had its guards, who were relieved night and day and never lost sight of the entrance. Sentry-posts were placed all along the valley and enclosed it with an

impenetrable barrier for all who did not know the password, while police made continuous rounds in the outskirts and relentlessly challenged anyone who ventured too near.

At irregular intervals distinguished persons, appointed by the High Priest of Amun or by the King, descended on the places unexpectedly. They visited the hall, opened the sarcophagus, examined the mummy, clothed it with a new shroud or wrapping if they found the old ones in bad condition, and before leaving wrote an account of their proceedings on the wooden cover of the coffin or on the shroud itself. Even if these precautions checked the violation of the tombs, they did not succeed in entirely preventing it, and the sacrilege that professional robbers did not dare to risk was often accomplished by the guards themselves. They were underpaid, ill-fed, and ill-lodged, and only performed their duty from fear of punishment, and so, as soon as they saw an opportunity of plundering the Pharaohs entrusted to their care, they profited by it either alone or in partnership with persons outside.

It was not unusual, Maspero revealed, for a professional excavator of his own time, making an incursion into forbidden ground, to furnish himself with food, water, and means of artificial light for several days, then to shut himself up in a tomb and not to stir until he had finished despoiling it. The predatory spirits of former days did the same. Once shut up with the dead, they stayed as long as was necessary to rob him. They unwrapped the mummy at leisure, tore off its necklaces, bracelets, rings, jewels, and bared the breast in the hope of finding some valuable amulet. Sometimes they left it half-naked and bruised on the ground; sometimes, to save the guards (their accomplices) from punishment, they put everything tidy again, and left it, outwardly at least, as if it had not been touched. Indeed, so skilful were they in that sort of fraud, that unless a very detailed inspection was made, no one would believe that under the eminently correct wrappings there was merely a parcel of broken bones, supplemented with palm branches or pieces of wood.

In fact, the royal mummies so unceremoniously bundled into a single tomb at Deir el-Bahari themselves came to light as the result of nineteenth-century tomb robberies. During the 1870s quantities of fine antiquities, identifiable as coming from royal burials in Thebes, steadily appeared in museums and private collections, supplied by surreptitious and illegal trading. In 1881, an English tourist passing through Paris showed some photographs of a Twenty-first Dynasty papyrus to Gaston Maspero and revealed that he had bought it from a dealer at Thebes named Ahmed Abd el Rasul. This confirmed Maspero's suspicions about tomb pillage and when, later in the year, he travelled to Thebes, he had Ahmed Abd el Rasul arrested. All concerned kept silent however, and after two months Maspero had to return to Paris, announcing, as he left, a reward of £500 for information.

At this point, Mohammed Abd el Rasul, Ahmed's elder brother, betrayed the secret. Emil Brugsch, a colleague of Maspero's and Keeper of the museum in Cairo, dashed to Thebes and was taken to a lonely spot in the most desolate and unfrequented part of the necropolis which stretched for three or four miles along the western bank of the Nile. Here, hidden behind a huge fragment of fallen rock, he found the entrance to a shaft 12 metres (39 ft.) deep. From the bottom of the shaft a gallery 74 metres (243 ft.) long led to a sepulchral vault seven by four metres (30 by 13 ft.). The mummies of more than twenty kings and queens were packed into the gallery and vault, including those of Amenophis I, Tuthmosis II and Tuthmosis III from the Eighteenth Dynasty and Seti I and Ramesses II from the Nineteenth. With the aid of 500 labourers, Emil Brugsch carried them all off to the safety of Cairo just as fast as he could.

Even though the kings of Egypt gave up building pyramids, the impulse lingered. If kings could find new ways of approaching the other world, so could their subjects. In one cemetery at Deir el Medina, close by the Mortuary Temples raised near Thebes by the New Kingdom rulers, people who had worked on the royal projects developed their own kind of two-part tomb. Below ground, a vertical well about 4 metres (13 ft.) deep led down to two or three chambers where the bodies of several generations of the family might lie. The chamber walls were painted with scenes intended to help the dead enjoy the after-life. Above ground, the tomb consisted of a courtyard and chapel quite similar to the owner's home in life. This chapel was topped off with a stone or brick-built pyramid maybe 4 metres (13 ft.) high on a base about the same square. On the east side of the pyramid, the entrance side of the chapel below, might be a statue of the owner. The four sides of the solid capstone, or pyramidion, showed him worshipping the sun at four stages in its daily cycle.

And far to the south, and centuries later, kings from Nubia or Northern Sudan, who at one point conquered Egypt itself, continued to build pyramid tombs. These southern kings, who set themselves to preserve the old traditions, raised literally dozens of pyramids in the cemeteries of Napata, Kuru, Nuri and Meroe, about 800 kilometres (500 miles) south of Aswan. All were steep-sided, sloping at around 70 degrees, and most were small, maybe 20 metres (66 ft.) high on a base about 12 metres (40 ft.) square. Some, however, may have been as high as 80 metres (262 ft.) on a base about 49 metres (160 ft.) square. They came in every type, stepped or smooth-faced, built with stone or brick or even rubble. These were the burials that reverberated through fantasy and fiction because the southern kings expected their servants to accompany them into death: they may even have buried them alive. And as a final luxury for that life that follows death, they had their horses killed and buried with them too.

Chapter 6

The Story of Mummies

LIFE AFTER DEATH, for the ancient Egyptians, required the preservation of the earthly body. Although they developed a confused multiplicity of beliefs about a variety of intangible here-afters they also kept in mind the simpler hope that death would be a lot like life. They realized they could not know for certain. One of their own poems said: 'No one has come back from there who can tell their state, who can tell their needs, who can set our hearts at rest. No one ever comes back.' But they could plan ahead.

When a person dies, they thought, a kind of spiritual double called the *ka* continued to exist. A person and the *ka* went through life together and after death the *ka* went on. A person also had a sort of external soul, called the *ba*, imagined as a human-headed bird. After death the *ka* needed a home and the *ba* a link with the person whose soul it was, so an Egyptian built and even furnished a tomb that was like a house, relatives and priests gave offerings of food and drink and they preserved the body.

At first this had been almost accidental. In the earliest burials, when they laid the body in a shallow pit with a few pots and tools as furnishings, the hot desert sand dried the flesh. Later, when they built more elaborate tombs with a chamber for the body, they could no longer count on this natural dessication. So they took to wrapping the body in linen in the hope that this would ensure its survival. Among the human remains found in a Second Dynasty cemetery at Saqqara was the skeleton of a woman about thirty-five years of age, lying on the left side and sharply bent up as in pre-dynastic burials. The body had been completely wrapped in a complex series

Professional mourners ensured that the passage to the other world was marked with lamentation: this group from a fourteenth-century BC tomb painting includes an apprentice.

of broad bandages. More than sixteen layers remained intact.

During the old Kingdom, the great age of pyramid building, they took the process further. The embalmers first did what they could, although they probably realized that their efforts would not produce a life-like corpse, and then concentrated on the wrapping. They moulded the linen bandages into shape, using linen pads to produce realistic-looking bulges for muscles, and even modelled the face, marking the eyes with green paint and the moustache with brown.

By the time of the New Kingdom, which began around 1550 BC, and continuing on into the Twenty-first Dynasty and later, the embalmers were more confident. They now worked extensively on the body itself, packing linen, mud or butter beneath the skin to plump it out, setting artificial eyes in the sockets and providing a wig. The body became its own statue before it was wrapped. Later still, as the art deteriorated, the corpse was hardly treated at all but the wrappings were soaked with resins that hardened into an airtight case concealing a putrefying body. As these resins aged they darkened to look like pitch, which is called by the Arabs *mumiya*. This is why these ancient Egyptian corpses are known as mummies.

Masks of the face, made for mummies from the Old Kingdom onwards, followed much the same pattern of development. At first they consisted of

cartonnage, layers of linen moulded together and covered with plaster, and might be gilded as well as painted. Gradually these extended into full-length cases and then into a wooden, form-following coffin. Tutankhamun's mummy, a dried and emaciated body within its ointment-soaked wrappings, had a gold portrait mask and lay within a nest of three coffins, the inner one solid gold, which themselves were shaped into three-dimensional portraits. Eventually, too, these masks gave way to a simple portrait painted on board and bound over the mummy's face.

Mummification involved religious ceremonies as well as the practicalities of embalming and the standard ritual lasted seventy days or longer. A memorial inscription for a priest of Amun-Re reads: 'The length of his life on earth was seventy-two years, five months and fourteen days, when he was placed in the mortuary workshop in the hands of Anubis. There was done for him all that is to be done for every great and excellent blessed dead person. He completed seventy-two days in the House of Embalmment. Becoming content with the venerated state, he was drawn to his house of eternity, resting therein for ever.' Priestly supervisors marked each phase by reciting the prayers laid down 'according to that which comes in writing' and superintended the purification of the body before its anointing and wrapping.

Soon after a person's death, the relatives delivered the body to the embalmers' workshop, usually called 'the pure place', which might be a temporary studio close to the tomb itself. The embalmers stripped the body and laid it on a table-top about 2.1 metres (7 ft.) long by 1.2 metres (4 ft.) wide set on two trestles. In the later, cleaner, stages of embalmment the body might lie on a more impressive animal-headed couch.

Now came the first operation, removing the brain. Usually the embalmers forced a chisel up through the left nostril into the skull, sometimes at the expense of a fair amount of facial damage, chopped the brain apart with a metal hook and picked out the pieces. In many cases they then washed out the last fragments. They also washed out the mouth.

Next the embalmers made an incision about 15 centimetres (6 in.) long in the left side, through which to remove the entrails. According to one account, the man who made this cut, the ripper-up, immediately fled away, with the other embalmers shouting ritual curses after him, because wounding a body was sacrilegious. Now the embalmers reached in, cut the internal organs free and pulled them out to preserve separately, all except the heart which was usually left in the the body. Then came dehydration. For this they probably laid the corpse out on a mat and covered it over with the drying agent natron. Natron, a mixture of sodium carbonate and bicarbonate collected from places in the desert, acted by drawing moisture from the body in the same way that ordinary salt draws moisture from damp air. The body was probably left to dry in this way for about 40 days. After this drying, the embalmers washed

In this twentieth-century BC carving a dead man accepts offerings: mummification was part of a series of rituals intended to guarantee a pleasant life after death.

131

the body inside and out before the priests carried out a ceremony of purification in which they stood or sat the body upright to pour over it what was probably a weak solution of natron. They then anointed the body with oil.

Before starting to wrap the corpse, they packed the body cavity with pads of linen, gums and spices and covered the slit in the side with a gold plate or piece of leather. They might pack the skull and they plugged the mouth, nose and ears. They put rings on the fingers, bracelets on the wrists and ankles and they often placed a large, stone-carved scarab beetle over the heart. This carried an inscription beseeching the dead person's heart to act true when questioned by the gods. Then they poured heated resin over all and began the wrapping.

Each stage of wrapping had its own ceremonies, and bandages for different parts of the body had their own names. In the first stage, the embalmers bandaged the body, the hands and feet, and the arms and legs separately. Part of the ritual of wrapping read: 'Wrap the toes in a piece of cloth, draw two jackals upon two pieces of linen with colours mixed with perfumed water. Each jackal shall have his face turned towards the other; the jackal on the one bandage is the god Anubis, the jackal on the other is the god Horus. Put Anubis on the right leg and Horus on the left leg, and wrap them up in fine linen.' Then, after crossing the arms over the breast, the embalmers continued by wrapping the whole, body and limbs together, laying folds of linen vertically, placing amulets and images within the folds and wrapping bandages around horizontally. As much as 2000 metres (6600 ft.) of material of various widths went into a mummy wrapping, some of it large pieces of linen perhaps torn from sheets, some of it finely-made bandages up to 4 metres (13 ft.) long by 10 centimetres (4 in.) wide. Skilled wrappers could produce an impressively tidy pattern of bandaging in the outer layers to complete the mummy. Finally it might be placed in a form-fitting wooden coffin painted with scenes from the journey to the next world and, together with the four canopic jars containing the preserved entrails, delivered up for the funeral ceremonies.

Herodotus, travelling through Egypt when mummification was commonplace, noted down what he learned about the arrangements for embalming:

The ka, *or double, was often shown with upraised hands set on its head: this wooden, near-life-size* ka *statue commemorates the Thirteenth Dynasty king Hor.*

'Embalmers, when a corpse is brought to them, show to those who brought it wooden models of corpses painted to look like the reality. The best method of embalming they show is that of him whose name I think it impiety to mention when speaking of a matter of this kind. The second method they show is inferior but less expensive, and the third is cheapest of all. Having explained this, they ask in which way they should prepare the body. After the price is agreed the relatives depart.' The name he left out was probably the god Osiris.

Herodotus went on to describe the three methods of embalming, adding the information that a person killed by crocodiles or by drowning in the Nile was treated as sacred. He started with the most expensive method, in which the embalmers first drew out the brain through the nostrils with a crooked iron tool, extracting it partly in this way and partly by pouring in drugs; after this they made a cut along the side with a sharp stone and took out the whole contents of the abdomen. When they had cleared out the cavity and rinsed it with palm-wine they cleansed it again with pounded-up spices: then they filled the abdomen with pure myrrh pounded up, and with cassia and other spices except frankincense, and sewed it together again. Having done so, he noted, they kept it covered up in natron for seventy days, but it was not permitted to embalm it for a longer time than this.

Herodotus possibly confused the time the body spent drying out with the time taken for the entire process. He carried on to explain that, when the seventy days were past, they washed the corpse and rolled its whole body up in fine linen cut into bands smearing these beneath with gum. Then the relatives took the body back again and enclosed the corpse within a wooden figure made in the shape of a man. Having shut it up, they stored it in a sepulchral chamber, standing it upright against the wall. This was how they dealt with the corpses which were prepared by the most costly method.

Herodotus went on to describe the middle way, for those who wished to avoid great cost. The embalmers filled syringes with oil of cedar-wood which they injected into the belly of the corpse. They did this, without having either cut it open or taken out the bowels, by injecting the oil through the anus. Having stopped the drench from escaping, they kept the body the appointed number of days for embalming. On the last day they let the cedar oil out from the belly; it had

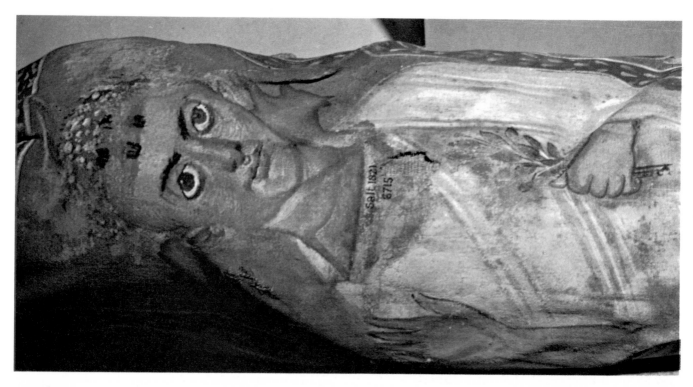

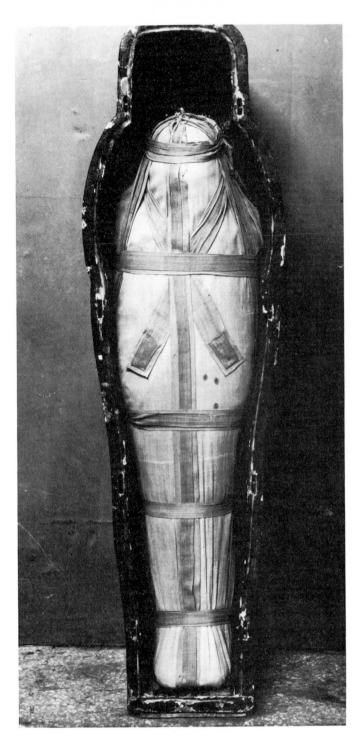

Above left: *Mummification persisted long after Egypt fell to Rome in 30 BC. This mummy of a boy, with a full-length portrait on the shroud, is from the third century AD.*

Above: *Embalmers gradually changed their methods of mummification: this tidily-wrapped specimen dates from the Twenty-second Dynasty around the ninth century BC.*

Left: *Ceremonies of purification completed the process of mummification: this fourteenth-century BC scene depicts streams of water being poured over the mummy.*

such great dissolving power that it brought with it the bowels and interior organs of the body. The natron dissolved the flesh so that the corpse was left only skin and bones. When they had done this they gave the body back at once without working on it any more.

In the third kind of embalming, used for the bodies of those who had even less means, they cleansed out the belly with a purge and then kept the body for embalming during the seventy days. Immediately after that they gave it back to the bringers to take away.

Herodotus discovered that when the wives of men of rank died they were not given to the embalmers at once, nor were women who were very beautiful or of greater importance than others. Only on the third or fourth day after their death, and not before were they delivered to the embalmers. He also found out the reason why: 'They do this in order that the embalmers may not abuse their women. They say that an embalmer was once taken abusing the corpse of a woman lately dead and his fellow craftsmen gave information.'

Death called forth mourning. However pleasant the other world might turn out to be, life was enjoyable and leaving it gave cause for sorrow. According to Herodotus, their fashion of mourning involved agitated lamentation following immediately upon a death. Whenever any household lost a man who was of any regard amongst them, all the women of that household plastered mud over their heads and even their faces. Then, leaving the corpse within the house, they went to and fro about the city, beating themselves, with their garments bound up by a girdle and their breasts exposed. With them went all the women who were related to the dead man. The men, too, bound up their garments and beat themselves. When they had done this they then conveyed the body to the embalmers.

Thomas Greenhill, an eighteenth-century English surgeon who made a study of embalming, felt their grieving might appear even more distressful when any of their kings died: 'They lamented his death with a general mourning, making sad lamentations, putting dirt upon their heads, rending their clothes and beating their breasts. They shut up their temples and markets and prohibited all festivals and rejoicings; they abstained from all delicate meats and costly apparel, from baths, perfumes and ointments, and neither made their beds nor accompanied with their wives, but expressed all the signs of an extraordinary afflic-

tion that they would have done for their own child. This, their mourning, continued till the body was buried, which was no less than seventy-two days. During this period, both men and women, about two or three hundred in number, went about the city twice a day without anything on but a linen cloth girt about their bodies, from beneath their breasts downwards, renewing their grief, and intermixing the virtues and praises of the deceased prince with their sighs and outcries. Much the same ceremonies were observed in their private funerals.'

For people of wealth and position, the private funeral, when they carried the mummy to the eternal habitation of its tomb, meant a grand procession. First might come several servants, carrying tables laden with fruit, cakes, flowers, vases of ointment and wine, with a calf for sacrifice and other things. Then came others bringing the small closets in which the mummy of the deceased and of his ancestors had been kept. Next came a table of offerings, couches and boxes; then a charioteer with a pair of horses yoked to a chariot which he drove as he followed on foot, in token of respect to his late master. After these were men carrying gold vases on a table, with other offerings, boxes, and a large case upon a sledge borne on poles by four men, then others bearing small images of his ancestors and things to do with the king in whose service he had held an important office. After these came the bearers of a sacred boat, and the mysterious eye of Horus as god of stability. Others carried small images of blue pottery representing the deceased under the form of Osiris, and the bird emblematic of the soul. Following these were more men bearing cases filled with flowers and bottles for libation; and then seven or eight women, with their heads bound with fillets, beating their breasts, throwing dust upon their heads, and uttering doleful lamentations for the deceased, intermixed with praises of his virtues.

Next came a sacred case containing the emblem of the god of letters, Thoth, placed on a sledge drawn by four men; the officiating high priest or pontiff, clad in a leopard skin, followed, accompanied by his attendants. Then came the hearse, placed in the consecrated boat, which was on a sledge drawn by four oxen and seven men. A high functionary of the priestly order walked close to the boat, in which the chief mourners, the nearest female relatives of the deceased, stood or sat at either end of the sarcophagus; sometimes his widow, holding a child in her arms, united with her lamentations prayers for her tender offspring. The sarcophagus was decked with flowers, and on the sides the emblems of stability and security were painted alternately on separate panels, one of which was sometimes taken out to expose to view the head of the mummy within.

Behind the hearse followed the male relations and friends of the deceased; some beating their breasts; others, if not giving the same tokens of grief, at least showing their sorrow by their silence and solemn step as they walked, leaning on their long sticks. These closed the procession.

Once in the tomb, the mummy provided a connection between the dead person's *ka*, the *ba* and the worlds of the living and the dead. For the ancient Egyptians this link was very close. The soul, or double, they believed, required the family to provide offerings of food and drink. Part of the funeral ritual involved the ceremony of symbolically opening the mouth of the mummy to allow the double to eat and drink. Even so, the double was likely to regret the bright world it had left.

In one poem, the double advised those who still lived in the world to enjoy themselves while they could: 'My brother, withhold not from drinking and from eating, from drunkenness, from love, from all enjoyment, from following your desire by night and day; put not sorrow within your heart for what are the years of a man on earth? The place of the dead is a land of sleep and of heavy shadows, a place wherein the inhabitants, when once installed, slumber on in their mummy-forms, never more waking to see their brethren; never more recognizing their fathers and their mothers; with hearts forgetful of their wives and children. The living water, which earth gives to all who dwell on it, is for me but stagnant and dead; that water flows to all who are on earth, while for me it is but liquid putrefaction, this water that is mine. Since I came into this funeral valley I know not where

137

nor what I am. Give me to drink of running water! Let me be placed by the edge of the water with my face to the north, so that the breeze may caress me and my heart be refreshed from its sorrow.'

For their part, the living ate and drank and remembered that they, too, would someday die. During the entertainments of the rich, apparently, when they had finished eating, a man bore round a wooden figure of a dead body in a coffin, painted and carved to look as real as possible. This he showed to each of those drinking together, saying: 'When you look on this, drink and be merry, for you shall be such as this when you are dead.'

Some of the poorer Egyptians found themselves in even closer contact with those who had gone before. Tombs built as abodes for the dead turned out to make acceptable dwellings for the living. Henry Westcar, an Englishman who toured Egypt early in the nineteenth century, visited the village of Qurna, once one of the cemeteries near Thebes, and recorded what he saw: 'They dwell in those mummy pits that are not too high to be a convenience to get water from the Nile. They sometimes take the trouble to throw out the bodies, sometimes not. We saw one man, who they told us would die in three days, lying with the dead. The sight of these mummies is disgusting. I went into two or three. They had two or three rooms and invariably one was crammed with mummies.'

Mummies fascinated later ages and travellers always mentioned them. Abd al Latif made some observations when he was in Egypt around AD 1200. He told how the Egyptians occasionally discovered vast underground caverns, of very solid construction, containing an immense number of corpses. The corpses were enveloped in winding sheets of hempen cloth. In the first place,

all the separate members, the hands, the feet, the fingers and toes, had been wrapped individually with extremely fine bandages. The whole body was afterwards swathed in a single piece, so as to resemble a great bale. The Bedouins, apparently, carried away the winding sheets, which they made into dresses or sold to the paper-manufacturers who used them for making paper for the grocers. On the forehead, eyes and nose of these corpses, when unwrapped, leaves of gold were often seen, resembling a thin skin. This was noticed on the sexual parts of women; and some bodies were wholly covered with similar leaves of the metal.

Abd al Latif recorded one particularly shuddery little tale: 'A person of credit informed me that, being once occupied with others in search of treasures in the neighbourhood of the pyramids, they found a pitcher closely sealed; on opening this, and finding honey, they ate of it. One of them remarked a hair that stuck to his finger; he drew it towards him, and a small infant appeared, the body of which still seemed to preserve its original freshness. . . .'

Pietro della Valle, a seventeenth-century Italian who travelled as an alternative to suicide after a disappointment in love, although he later married twice and had fourteen sons, was much impressed by two decorated mummy-cases he was shown: 'Upon one was the figure of a young man, dressed in a long gown, gilded and sprinkled over with hieroglyphic emblems from head to foot, set off with precious stones, with the hair of his head black and curled, and his beard of the same colour, but short. A chain of gold hung about his

A fourteenth-century papyrus depicts mourners following the boat-shaped hearse on which the mummified body lies. The widow kneels beside it.

138

Above and left: *The Egyptians mummified such animals as cats, crocodiles, ibises and snakes as eagerly as they attempted to preserve human bodies. Mummies of cats, as here, were buried near the sanctuary of the cat-headed goddess Bast.*

The most ambitious animal mummification was that of the Apis bulls. Each bull was interred in an enormous granite sarcophagus in the vast underground galleries of the Serapeum at Saqqara. This statue of an Apis bull is in bronze.

neck, having a medal with the image of the ibis bird on it, with many other marks and characters, which gives us to understand this young man was possessed of great dignities. In his right hand he held a golden basin full of red liquor, and in his left a fruit somewhat resembling an apple. He had a gold ring on his thumb and another on his little finger, likewise sandals which covered only the soles of his feet. By his side was a woman yet more richly and mysteriously adorned, with an ox, the image of Apis, at her feet. In a word, both these figures were painted like saints of the ancients.'

A Monsieur Villoteau, one of the members of the commission of sciences and arts that accompanied Napoleon's expedition to Egypt in 1798, investigated briefly. His party encamped opposite the village of Qurna and scarcely had they pitched their tents than they saw men advancing towards them with dead bodies on their shoulders, mummies which they offered to sell.

One was the corpse of a woman in excellent preservation. After taking off the covering, they carefully unwound a great number of folds, some of which went round the legs and feet, others round the thighs, the body, the arms and the head. They raised in one single piece the part covering the face and found that it minutely preserved the underlying forms. The other parts were more thickly covered and revealed black and withered limbs. Nevertheless, all the parts of the body, although withered, preserved their natural form. The hair, the eyes, the nose and mouth were so well preserved that the investigators thought they could tell the character the features would give the face. The head was a regular oval. The body had been opened on the left side of the belly, to allow the entrails to be withdrawn, and for aromatic resins to be packed in.

Monsieur Villoteau wanted more adventure: 'At four in the evening of the next day we visited several grottoes and entered the caverns of the mummies. They can only be penetrated, in most parts, by crawling on hands and feet. After dragging ourselves over arms, legs, heads and carcases of mummies, all more or less damaged, we reached at length the cave where they are deposited. I reflected on the danger with which we should have been menaced if the least spark should have fallen from our lighted torches on to these heaps of mummies full of very combustible resinous substances. We caused several mummies to be dragged out upon opening one of the caves and a sailor among our company had the imprudence to light his pipe near the spot. A spark carried by the wind fell on one of these mummies. In an instant, a fire was kindled that lasted several days.'

With such excitements on offer Henry Westcar was eager to see more: 'I had a great desire to see a mummy-pit with the bodies in it, but there was none to be seen except where the mummies were broken to pieces, lying one on the other. So being determined to see what I could, I went into one of them. They were the lower class of people and therefore placed merely in a cave without ornament or anything extra. I entered, and what a horrid spectacle met my sight! Arms, legs, heads, etc. were scattered about on all sides; as I walked along a head or leg cracked in a thousand pieces under my foot. I was obliged to trample on hundreds of bodies, cracking like sticks.'

Such a robust attitude was, in its way, part of the tradition of mummy fancying. Even the ancient Egyptians themselves could be less than respectful of their corpses. When the embalmers had to cope with an incomplete corpse they just substituted a palm branch for the missing limb and continued wrapping: it really was the appearance that counted. The defects they were compensating for might be the result of death from a crocodile bite or, that other hazard of Egyptian life, falling masonry. A description of the mummy of Tuthmosis I in the Cairo Museum mentioned that during the Eighteenth Dynasty the art of mummification had reached near perfection, for the corpse was well preserved without being encrusted with a thick layer of resinous material. It went on to reveal that the hands had unfortunately been broken off and were placed not at the sides or on the thighs but over the genitals.

When the embalmers had finished, the mummy may have had more than purely sentimental or religious value: Herodotus noted that a man who needed a loan might offer the dead body of his father as security. In medieval times quacks and apothecaries decided that ground-down mummy was a valuable medicine. Arab physicians, who believed that the mineral pitch which oozed from the ground was a useful remedy for many ills, thought the blackened mummy-resin appeared very similar and was much easier to collect. When the trade was at its height, during the sixteenth and seventeenth centuries, speculators were in their element. John Sanderson, a commercial agent who visited Egypt at the end of the sixteenth century, shipped out more than 270 kilograms (600 lb.) of mummy, bringing 'heads, hands, arms and feet' back to England.

Most surprising of all, to those who discovered them, were the vast collections of mummified animals. Giovanni Belzoni, in his explorations of the tombs around Thebes at the beginning of the nineteenth century, came across examples of nearly every creature the Egyptians knew. Among the tombs he saw some which contained the mummies of animals intermixed with human bodies. There were bulls, cows, sheep, monkeys, foxes, bats, crocodiles, fishes, and birds; he often found idols, and one tomb was filled with nothing but cats, carefully wrapped in red and white linen. The head was covered by a mask representing the cat, and made of the same linen.

'I have opened all these sorts of animals,' Belzoni revealed. 'Of the bull, the calf, and the sheep, there is no part but the head, which is covered with linen, and the horns projecting out of the cloth; the rest of the body being represented by two pieces of wood, 45 centimetres (18 in.) wide and 1 metre (3 ft.) long, in a horizontal direction, at the end of which was another, placed perpendicularly, 60 centimetres (2 ft.) high, to form the breast of the animal. The calves and sheep are of the same structure, and large in proportion to the bulls. The monkey is in its full form, in a sitting posture. The fox is squeezed up by the bandages, but in some measure the shape of the head is kept perfect. The crocodile is left in its own shape, and after being well bound round with linen, the eyes and mouth are painted on this covering. The birds are squeezed together, and lose their shape except the ibis, which is found like a fowl ready to be cooked, and bound round with linen, like all the rest.'

In 1851, Auguste Mariette, who later became the first director of the Egyptian Antiquities Service, cleared the sand from an avenue of sphinxes at Saqqara and revealed, as he suspected he would, the entrance to the Serapeum, an astonishing find. In the Serapeum the Egyptians interred the mummified bodies of the sacred Apis bulls. Each bull, which was recognized by its special markings, had been the incarnation of the supreme god. It was worshipped in life and, in death, received a ceremonial funeral.

Auguste Mariette could hardly credit what he found. The underground galleries stretched for more than 250 metres (820 ft.). 'There were numerous vaults,' he wrote. 'Some were empty, some contained enormous sarcophagi. I counted twenty-four.' Each sarcophagus was about 4 metres (13 ft.) long and 2.3 metres (7.5 ft.) wide and high. The lid was 1 metre (3 ft.) deep. The whole weighed over 6 tonnes (tons). The underground tomb was in chaos, the lids to the granite coffins pushed aside, but in a further series of chambers he found an intact sarcophagus. It appeared to contain a mummified Apis from the time of Ramesses II with a golden mask still covering the face: the body turned out to be that of a man, a High Priest of Ptah, who had wanted to be buried among the Apis bulls.

Mummies, whether animal or human, worm their way into the imagination. The ancient Egyptians hoped that in some future world all the aspects of soul and body split apart by death might be reunited in new life. But in the meantime, they half-suspected the double could re-enter the corpse so that the dead person might, perhaps, walk to the door of the tomb to see the sun rise. When the Egyptians turned to Christianity, in the second and third centuries AD, some remembrance of this mummified semi-life persisted: the early Coptic Christians were well aware of mummies as they had taken to living in tombs. As a result, the Coptic tradition contains such tales as *St Pisentius and the Mummy*, in which John, a lowly monk, told how he helped Pisentius, his father in God, seek a life of seclusion in the desert. The two of them found a tomb, a place in the rock like a wide-open door, which inside was like carved stone, with six pillars supporting the roof and mummified bodies lying about. These they piled up. John noticed that the one nearest the door was wrapped in the pure silk of kings with its fingers and toes bandaged separately.

Pisentius then said to him 'Go away, my son. Live in your monastery and come to me only on Saturdays.' So, on the next Saturday, John filled a pitcher of water, took a little moistened wheat and went to the place where Pisentius was dwelling in solitude. But when he came near, he heard someone weeping and pleading with Pisentius. It was the mummy, the one nearest the door.

Pisentius asked 'Did you not hear before you died that Christ had come into the world?' He said 'No, my Father. My parents were pagans and I myself followed their way of life. And it befell me, when I was come to the straits of death, that spirits surrounded me who told me all the evils I had done. They had iron hooks in their hands, and also pointed iron spikes like spears, and they were stabbing my sides with them, and gnashing their teeth at me. And forthwith, my Father, the spirits drew my miserable soul out of my body and delivered it into the hands of many pitiless torturers, each one different in form. My Father, pray for me that I may be given a little rest and not carried off to that place again.'

Pisentius said to him 'The Lord is compassionate and merciful. He will have mercy on you. Return then and sleep until the day of general resurrection.' And the mummy lay down in his place as before.

John went into the tomb at this point and Pisentius asked if he had seen anyone, or heard anyone talking. 'No, my Father,' said John. But Pisentius knew. 'You have told a lie,' he said. 'If you reveal this matter in my lifetime you are excommunicated.' So John concealed his knowledge until he dared to tell of it.

Magicians, treasure-hunters and others have always speculated about raising the dead and whenever people talk about reanimation they sooner or later speak of mummies. In 1827, ten years after Mary Wollstonecraft Shelley wrote *Frankenstein*, Jane Webb published *The Mummy*. The main plot of this three-volume novel, set in the year 2126, revolved around the question of who was to be Queen of England, but some of the characters had other concerns. Edric Montagu, younger brother of Queen Claudia's commander-in-chief, told his tutor, Dr Entwerfen, 'I wish to resuscitate a mummy.' The pair set off for Egypt by fast balloon, taking with them a galvanic battery of fifty surgeon power. They landed beside the Great Pyramid and climbed through its passages to the inner chamber.

Our travellers shuddered, and opening with trembling hand the ponderous gates, they entered the tomb of Cheops. In the centre of the chamber stood a superb, highly-ornamented sarcophagus of alabaster, beautifully wrought; over this hung a lamp of wondrous workmanship, supplied by a potent mixture, so as to burn for ages unconsumed. A secret voice seemed to whisper in their bosoms: 'Retire whilst it is yet time: soon it will be too late.' Edric turned but saw that the doctor had already seized the lid of the sarcophagus and removed it from its place, displaying in the fearful light the royal form that lay beneath. Awful indeed was the gloom that sat upon that brow, and bitter the sardonic smile that curled those haughty lips. All was perfect.

'Let us go,' whispered the doctor. The die, however, was cast. Edric seized the machine and resolutely advanced towards the sarcophagus. As the flickering light of the lamp fell upon the face of the mummy, he fancied that its stern features relaxed into a ghastly laugh of scornful mockery. Worked up to desperation, he applied the wires of the battery, whilst a demoniac laugh of derision appeared to ring in his ears.

Edric stood aghast, gazing intently upon the mummy, whose eyes had opened with the shock. A fearful peal of thunder rolled in lengthened vibrations above his head as the mummy rose slowly from its tomb. Edric saw the mummy stretch out its withered hand as though to seize him. He felt its tremendous grip. Then all was darkness. . . .

But this is fantasy. In reality, people confronted with an actual wrapped-up corpse four thousand years old or more might more likely feel the urge to unwrap it, to see how it was prepared, to see what could be learned. Nowadays archaeologists tend to keep mummies intact, investigating them with such non-destructive tests as X-ray photography, though mummies are still dissected from time to time. From time to time, too, scientists have experimented with chickens, pigeons and rats to see what does happen to a body treated with natron.

One of the first scientific investigations of mummification took place in 1763 when Dr John Hadley of London dissected a mummy in front of a number of other medical men: 'This Mummy had been greatly injured, before it came into our hands; the head had been taken off from the body; and the wrappers, with which they had been united, having been destroyed, the cavity of the thorax was found open towards the neck. There were not the least remains of hair or integuments, on any part of the head; some parts of the skull were quite bare, particularly about the temporal bones. To other parts of the skull adhered several folds of pitched linen. The fillets in general externally did not adhere to each other; but though pieces of a considerable length could be taken off entire, yet, from the great age, so tender was the texture of the cloth, that it was impossible regularly to unroll them. The filleting, which went round the upper part of the body included the arms also; but they had evidently been first wrapped separately, then laid up in the position in which we found them, with the hands across upon the breast, and the hollows which they formed filled up with pieces of pitched cloth.'

In the nineteenth century, another surgeon, Thomas Joseph Pettigrew, organized a series of public unwrappings before audiences of 500 and more. An account of one of his lectures at the Royal College of Surgeons, London, in 1834, stated: 'Visitors in considerable numbers arrived very early and filled all the seats; many were obliged to stand; and many others retired from all the doors who could not find admission.' Among those turned away was the Archbishop of Canterbury.

Pettigrew first described the various methods of mummification, then set to work: 'The bandages were now removed as carefully as circumstances and time permitted. The outer smooth cloth being removed, exposed the circular hand-breadth rollers, which extended from head to foot several times in succession: others were placed oblique and diagonal very neatly but without much regularity or uniformity till we reached the very innermost layer or two which firmly adhered to the surface by a coat of asphaltum.. On the breast was a small protuberance, which when divested of the bandage, exposed a small carved Scarabous of a pale semi-transparent white colour – and on the upper part of the sternum a cluster of four or five small tally-shaped bodies enveloped in, and sticking to the body, by asphaltum. Part of the face was exposed and showed that a pair of artificial eyes, apparently of enamel, had been placed on or substitued for the natural ones. Here the examination of this part ceased for the present.'

A twentieth-century unwrapping, carried out in less public circumstances by Herbert Winlock at the Metropolitan Museum of Art, New York, exposed the embalmers' casual approach. They used old linen sheets which they tore into strips as they needed them. When they poured molten resin over the body it splashed about on to the heaps of linen waiting to be used. To add to that, they wiped their sticky fingers on the inner bandages. At some point they killed a mouse and stuck it out of the way under the last few layers of bandaging. They were careful, however, to keep their fingerprints off the wrappings that showed.

Even before a mummy is unwrapped, scientists can learn a lot from X-ray photographs. Any amulets and other decorations show up. The bone structures of the skull may reveal family resemblances and other bones may indicate conditions such as arthritis. In one case X-rays showed that a small mummy thought to be the baby princess Moutemhet was actually a baboon.

Once the wrappings have been taken off, the scientists can go even further, conducting a kind of long-delayed post-mortem. From the worn away teeth of most mummies they can tell that the flour from which the ancient Egyptians made their bread was probably very sandy. By diagnosing the diseases from which the ancient Egyptians suf-fered they can tentatively reconstruct their living conditions. Finding infectious diseases such as tuberculosis suggests that many members of different generations of a family lived close together in a single household; other conditions reveal that the ancient Egyptians were advanced

Rituals prepared the mummy for a kind of shadowy continuation of real life in which the tomb became its home where it lived on offerings left by relatives.

enough to cope with the problems of nursing a life-long cripple.

Most intriguingly, for those more interested in kings than common people, blood and tissue samples can help sort out just who was related to whom. The parenthood of Tutankhamun is one case. Most probably his father was Amenophis III, rather than his more immediate predecessor Akhenaten or Amenophis IV, but this still leaves the problem of his mother. Amenophis III, whose mummy is in Cairo Museum, had as his chief wife Queen Tiye, and the mummies of her parents have been found. Analysis of tissue samples from Tutankhamun himself and the other three mummies available suggests that Amenophis III and Queen Tiye quite probably were his parents. He could, however, just possibly be the son of Amenophis III and Sitamun, herself the daughter of Amenophis III and Queen Tiye.

All this digging up and dissecting of the bodies of people who hoped to lie in peace for eternity has had its critics. Sir Wallis Budge, who collected mummies by the dozen and more during the late nineteenth century, defended his activities on the grounds that they were better off in museums anyway. But Ambrose Bierce, the American satirist, characterized *mummy* as 'An ancient Egyptian, formerly in universal use among modern civilized nations as medicine, and now engaged in supplying art with an excellent pigment. He is handy, too, in museums in gratifying the vulgar curiosity that serves to distinguish man from lower animals.' He went on to note that tombs have a certain sanctity but 'when they have been long tenanted it is considered no sin to break them open and rifle them, the famous Egyptologist, Dr Huggyns, explaining that a tomb may be innocently "glened" as soon as its occupant is done "smellynge", the soul being then all exhaled.'

It is a dilemma for archaeologists. The mummy of Tutankhamun, after the unwrappings and investigations, was laid once more in one of its gilded coffins and returned to its original, and guarded, tomb in the Valley of the Kings: and the travelling exhibitions of the funeral goods do serve to keep the name of Tutankhamun in being. Gaston Maspero, who himself moved some of the royal mummies to Cairo in the late nineteenth century, revealed his thoughts about them:

'The sight of the royal mummies rouses a curious feeling. The heroes of classic times, those of Greece and of Rome, have cast off for ever their mortal coil, but the actors in the old Egyptian drama, their elders by so many centuries, are shown to us with all the substance of the body they inhabited, flesh and bone, figure, hair, the shape of the head, the features of the face. That slender, short personage is Thutmosis III, the conqueror of Syria, and the most formidable of the Theban Pharaohs, almost a dwarf in stature. The slim hands that Ramesses II peacefully crosses on his breast strung the bow and manipulated the lance for a whole spring day under the walls of Qodshou, until his determined effort brought back victory to the Egyptian banners. Seti I possesses the serene countenance of a priest, a fact that did not prevent him from fighting boldly when the call came. Ramesses III, on the other hand, appears like a stout, heavy rustic. History, certainly, gains a singular reality when written in the very presence of those who made it, and yet the advantages for many are more than outweighed by the horror with which this funeral parade fills them. It is, they say, a want of respect, not to a royalty so long departed, but to humanity itself, to exhibit these emaciated bodies, wrinkled and blackened skins, grimacing faces, torn shrouds, and mummy cloths reduced to parcels of rags.

And yet, in museums around the world anybody can confront a mummy. At the British Museum in London, school-children gasp as a lecturer tells them how the embalmers worked.

'They took out the brain,' he says, 'by pushing chisels up through the nose and using hooks and spoons to scoop it out.'

'Ugh,' say the audience.

'What else do you think they took out?' he asks.

'The guts and innards,' say the audience. 'The insides and that.'

'Yes,' he says. 'Except for the heart. They left the heart in.'

He tells them about natron and wrapping the body in bandages, about packing out the flesh to keep the life-like contours and about pushing artificial stone eyes into the eye sockets. 'It looks as though the person is still staring at you,' he says.

In the Mummy Room the children cluster in silence around the model grave that contains the body the staff call Ginger. He lies crouched up just as he was buried in the desert more than 5000 years ago, his blackened skin and orange hair preserved by the hot sand.

'It's a bit eerie,' they say. Then they go on to look at the wrapped-up mummies and the golden coffins. 'It's funny to think they're so old,' says one eleven-year-old. 'You look at them and you think they're still alive and not really dead.'

145

Chapter 7

The Fascination of the Pyramids

EGYPT IS AN alluring concept. One moment it is a far-off country with an impressive array of antiquities, a tantalizingly-lucid style of art and a vaguely-sensed sweep of history; the next it is an obsession. Travellers swear that nowhere else is like it; emperors and strategists see in it the key to Europe and the East; scholars pin down the minutiae of aeons; collectors dream of rich discoveries; initiates believe that esoteric knowledge from the past foretells the future and releases secret powers; anyone can succumb.

Pyramids are a centre and symbol of Egypt's hypnotic powers, looming giants that force themselves on the world's attention yet reveal so little that almost any fantasy can be spun around them. Even as they were being built they became a source of wonder to the ancient Egyptians themselves, who virtually worshipped them as sacred objects, who visited them as though on a pilgrimage and who scratched their awe-struck comments in the gleaming stone itself. Amenophis II, one of the Eighteenth Dynasty kings, built a sanctuary close to the pyramids at Giza and set in it a slab of limestone inscribed with the record of a visit he made to the two greatest pyramids before becoming king: 'He yoked the horses in Memphis, when he was still young, and stopped at the Sanctuary of the Sphinx. He spent a time there in going round it, looking at the beauty of the Sanctuary of Khufu (Cheops) and Khafre (Chephren) the revered. His heart longed to keep alive their names and he put it in his heart.' Humbler pilgrims to the pyramids and other great religious monuments left marks in their own way: a slab from the pavement of the Eleventh Dynasty temple of Mentuhotep II at Deir el-Bahari near

By the time this drawing was published, in 1908, a jaunt to the top of the Great Pyramid, hauled up by Arab guides, had become part of the itinerary of every tourist in Egypt.

Thebes bears the outlines of two feet, roughly cut into the stone, with an inscription in one to say 'The builder Ptahemheb was here.'

Foreign visitors, too, venerated antiquity. The Greek historian Herodotus, who travelled through Egypt around 450 BC, wrote a lengthy account of what he saw and learned, the earliest record from outside Egypt. He confessed his enthusiasm for things Egyptian: 'No other land possesses so many wonders, nor has such a number of works that defy description.' Herodotus saw the country when pharaohs still occupied the throne and when the temples still had priests who claimed to know their history, although he warned against believing everything they said: 'Now as to the tales told by the Egyptians, anyone may accept them who finds such things credible; but understand that I write the hearsay reported by the people of each place.' He enjoyed a good story, however, and happily wrote down anything they told him. One tale he noted concerned *The Treasures of King Rhampsinitus*, who was probably Ramesses II.

King Rhampsinitus built a great treasure chamber for his riches. But the builder left one stone in the wall so that it could be removed from outside. On his death-bed, he told his two sons the secret and they went and took what treasure they pleased. The king was greatly enraged by his losses and set traps about the silver. Next time the thieves entered the chamber one found himself caught fast.

'I am lost,' he said to his brother. 'Cut off my head so that the king cannot recognize who has robbed him. In this way our family shall be safe.' When the king entered the treasure chamber he found the body of the dead man. Astonished, but unable to do anything further, he hung the body up in public with guards around it. The other brother, giving way to his mother's pleas, tricked the guards into a drinking-bout and, when they fell into a stupor, stole the body back.

By now the king was thoroughly vexed. As a last resort he set his own daughter in a brothel with orders to find the man who had done these things. The brother, hearing of this, cut off an arm from the body of a man who had just died, concealed it under his cloak and went in to visit the king's daughter. He told her everything he had done but when, in the darkness, she tried to catch hold of him, he slipped away, leaving her to clutch tight to the hand of the corpse.

After the king heard of this latest ingenuity he announced that he would pardon the robber if only he would make himself known. The thieving

brother came to see the king and Rhampsinitus rewarded his boldness by giving him his daughter in marriage.

After Herodotus and the Greeks came Julius Caesar and the Romans. Caesar conquered Egypt, established the heiress-queen Cleopatra (actually the seventh Cleopatra) firmly on the throne and may have fathered her son, Ptolemy Caesar. After Caesar's death, Mark Antony married Cleopatra, although he already had a Roman wife, so that he could draw on the resources of Egypt in a bid for power within the Roman empire. In both cases Cleopatra probably hoped to safeguard Egypt through her personal alliance with the most powerful Roman of the time. However, Antony, with the Egyptian forces, suffered a ruinous defeat at the naval battle of Actium. In 30 BC, faced with ruin, Antony chose suicide. Cleopatra followed him, rather than allow the victor, Octavius, to make her his chattel. Even in the manner of her dying, by the bite of an asp, she emphasized that she was Queen of Egypt: the asp was quite probably a kind of cobra, the royal emblem. Octavius went on to proclaim himself Augustus, Emperor of Rome, and casually dealt with the question of succession to the throne of Egypt by murdering the male heirs and marrying off Cleopatra's daughter by Antony to an unimportant prince in a distant country. Egypt became the personal estate of the Emperor, a prosperous garden province that, later, could be taxed to distraction to supply luxuries for Rome.

While the Roman empire lasted, tourists could travel safely and reasonably quickly to its furthest frontiers. Thousands went to inspect Egypt and this civilization that was so much older than Rome itself. One of the most popular attractions was a visit to the great statues of the Eighteenth Dynasty king, Amenophis III set on a plain on the west bank of the Nile near Thebes. The Romans thought the two colossi represented Memnon, King of Ethiopia, who according to legend had been slain by Achilles as he fought with Troy against the Greeks. At some point the upper half of one of the figures had broken off, perhaps as the result of an earthquake in 27 BC. Early in the morning this damaged statue made strange sounds, probably because the stones expanded in the first heat of the sun. The Emperor Hadrian, in AD 130, came two days running to listen for them because the first passed in silence. One of his party, Julia

This model pyramid, found at Memphis, bears the figure of a man worshipping the all-powerful sun.

Balbilla, inscribed some lines of poetry on the base of the statue entreating the god to greet the Emperor, and rejoicing when he did so on the second day: 'I heard the stone begin to sing. I, Balbilla, I heard the divine voice of Memnon.' Another Emperor, Septimius Severus, felt that the statue's silence during his own visit in AD 202 reproached him for its ill treatment. He restored the head and body with great blocks of stone but the god stayed silent.

Christianity came to Egypt as early as the first century but, for a hundred years and more, Christians were harshly persecuted. Eventually, in AD 313, Constantine the Great made Christianity one of the recognized religions of Rome. The Bible was soon translated into Coptic, the language spoken by Egyptians, and the newly-official belief quickly spread from the educated city folk, who first took it up, to the country villagers. The Coptic converts turned against the old religion, their one true God countenanced no others. They defaced temple decorations; they probably demolished the Serapeum at Memphis, the centre where once their ancestors had worshiped the Apis bulls; they almost certainly destroyed the books in the great library at Alexandria. Ironically, monks and hermits withdrawing into a life of contemplation, as well as a growing number of Egyptians seeking to avoid the tax gatherers, took to living in the ancient tombs scattered in the hills and desert. With the mummies piled to one side these houses of eternity made excellent monastic cells.

After Christianity came Islam. In the seventh century an army of sixteen thousand sweeping in from Syria wrenched Egypt from the grasp of the Roman empire: Alexandria fell to the Arabs in AD 641. At first the country was ruled by governors appointed by the caliph of eastern Arabia but, in time, independent sovereign dynasties of caliphs and sultans gained power. In the early years of Islamic rule the Copts frequently revolted, mainly protesting against extortionate taxes, but they were finally crushed by the caliph Mamun in a decisive battle in AD 832: the men were massacred, the women and children sold into slavery.

According to legend, Mamun's father, the Caliph Harun al Raschid who listened so eagerly to the *Tales of the Arabian Nights* spun out by his bride Scheherazade, was the first to try to penetrate the Great Pyramid of Cheops at Giza. He drove a pit about 10 metres (33 ft.) into the side of the pyramid but his expenses mounted so quickly he decided to stop. Luckily, at the very point he ceased digging, he found a vessel filled with 1000 gold coins, which equalled what he had spent. He was, apparently, at a loss to imagine how the cost of his operations could have been accurately foretold, and how the money could have been placed exactly at the farthest point of his excavation.

Mamun succeeded where his father had given up, and broke into the passages within the pyramid. After that people went in and out as they wished. One party, it was said, discovered several golden statues covered with jewels which they carried away, another discovered a mysterious goblet of fine glass which weighed the same whether empty or full of water. Unfortunately, in both cases a member of the party was left behind and fell victim to the enchantment of the place. Each one came out naked and laughing wildly, shrieked out 'Do not follow me or look for me,' and rushed back into the pyramid.

Some visitors, however, gave a soberly factual description of what they saw. Abd al Latif, a doctor from Baghdad who travelled to Cairo about 1200, left a particularly impressive account of his observations. He admired the Sphinx and thought the statues found among the ruins of Memphis surpassed description, both because of their number and their extraordinary size: 'Most worthy of admiration is the nicety observed in their forms, their exact proportions, and their resemblance to nature. Some of these figures are represented holding in their hand a sort of cylinder that appears to be a volume of writing; the artist has not forgotten to express the lines and wrinkles formed on the skin of the hand, when closed, at the part adjoining the little finger.'

Abd al Latif went into the Great Pyramid, but had to retreat, half-dead with fear. He described the other two pyramids and was scathing about an attempt he saw to demolish one of them. Malik al Aziz Othman, son of the great Saladin who tormented the Crusaders, was persuaded by members of his court, 'people totally devoid of sense and judgement', that he should destroy the pyramids. He hired miners and quarrymen, setting them to work on the red pyramid of Mycerinus, the smallest of the three. After eight months of assiduous effort, and at vast expense, they tumbled down *one* or *two* stones. The noise was heard at an immense distance and the concussion shook the ground. Even then, the stone had still to be

Ancient Egyptian tombs, 'houses of eternity', sometimes became in later ages dwellings for those without homes: this one was drawn by Luigi Mayer around 1800.

broken up before it could be carried away. In the end they gave up the project as hopeless. When Abd al Latif asked an overseer if he could replace the stone in its original position, the man answered that even if he were given thousands of pieces of gold he could not do so.

Arabian writers collected together legends connected with the building of the pyramids. Some said that wise men foresaw the Flood, the judgement from Heaven by submersion, and erected many stone pyramids as a refuge against the rising waters. Some said they were granaries built to store the produce of the seven years of great plenty promised by Joseph when he interpreted the pharaoh's dream of seven fat cattle eaten up by seven lean cattle. Some said they were tombs for the kings of ancient Egypt. One Coptic tradition, that the pyramids of Giza had been built by Surid, king over Egypt before the flood, was written down by Masudi, a tenth-century historian and traveller who gave to one book summing up his observations the intriguing title *Meadows of Gold and Mines of Precious Stones*.

Surid dreamed that the earth was overthrown and its inhabitants laid prostrate upon the ground; that the stars came down to earth in the form of white birds, seized the people and shut them in a cleft between two great mountains. Early in the morning he called the chief priests together, all 130 of them, and asked for their interpretations.

'Grand and mysterious are your dreams,' they told him. 'And some disaster must surely come to pass, for your majesty is sacred.' The priests and astrologers determined that a deluge would drown the land but eventually the waters would retreat and the earth become fruitful again. So the king ordered pyramids to be built and the predictions of the priests to be inscribed upon large stones; and within the pyramids he placed all his treasures, together with the bodies of his ancestors. He told the priests to set down their knowledge of the different arts and sciences and placed these accounts within the pyramids, too. He filled the passages with talismans, with wonderful things, with idols and with the priestly descriptions of medicine, arithmetic and geometry; and he did this for the benefit of those who would come after and comprehend them.

In building the pyramids, he ordered pillars to be cut and an extensive pavement laid out. He brought stone from the neighbourhood of Aswan by placing sheets of papyrus inscribed with certain characters under the stones prepared in the quarries. When these blocks were then struck they moved about the distance of a bowshot each time and in this way were brought to the pyramids. When the buildings were finished the king covered the pyramids from top to bottom with coloured brocade, assembled all the people in the country and gave a great feast.

In the eastern pyramid (Cheops'), the king depicted the heavenly spheres and figures representing the stars and planets in the form in which they were worshipped; he also placed there the instruments with which his forefathers had sacrificed to the stars. He also deposited written accounts of the history and chronicles of time past, of that which is to come, and of every future event which would take place in Egypt.

In the western pyramid (Chephren's), he placed thirty caskets, hollowed from coloured granite, into which he piled sacred symbols, talismans of sapphire, weapons fashioned out of iron that could not rust, glass which could be bent without breaking and many sorts of medicine. The coloured pyramid (Mycerinus') contained the bodies of deceased priests laid in sarcophagi of black granite. Beside each priest lay a book made of leaves of gold which related his acts during life, the mysteries of his profession, the history of the past and prophecies for the future.

After describing the building of the pyramids, Masudi told how King Surid assigned a guardian to each one. The guardian of the eastern pyramid was an idol of speckled granite, who stood upright with a spear in his hand and a serpent wreathed about his brow. This serpent seized upon and strangled anyone who approached. The guardian of the western pyramid was an image of black and white onyx with fiercely-sparkling eyes, seated on a throne and holding a spear. Strangers who came near heard a dreadful noise, which made their hearts faint, and then the image destroyed them. The guardian of the coloured pyramid was a statue, placed on a pedestal, which had the power of entrancing any who looked on it, holding them motionless until they perished.

After appointing the guardians, Surid offered up sacrifices to prevent the entry of all people, except those who were worthy, and caused the pyramids to be haunted by living spirits. The spirit of the eastern pyramid passes round it in the shape of a beardless boy with large teeth and a sallow countenance; the spirit of the western

The Grand Gallery within the Great Pyramid, drawn by Luigi Mayer around 1800, has been a source of inspiration to the Egyptological fringe.

pyramid is seen only as a naked woman who draws anyone to her and besots him with love so that he grows mad; the spirit of the coloured pyramid is an old man who scatters incense around the edifice.

When all this was finished, the king inscribed this challenge to the future: 'I, Surid, built these pyramids and finished them in 61 years. Let him who comes after me, and imagines himself a king like me, attempt to destroy them in 600 years. To destroy is easier than to build.'

As Arab writers speculated about the riches disposed of by the ancient kings, their descriptions came to seem almost prescriptions for treasure-hunting. Murtada ibn al Khafif, in *A History of the Marvellous Things in Egypt*, told of the revelations made by a nymph: 'There is in this ruined city an empty round place, and about that place there are seven pillars with a brazen statue standing on the top of each of them. Measure from every pillar, on that side that the statue upon it faces, the space of 100 cubits [about 53 metres or 175 ft.] and then cause people to dig there. After you have dug 50 cubits [about 27 metres or 88 ft.] you will find a great floor; cause it to be taken away. Now you will descend into a cave 50 cubits [about 27 metres or 88 ft.] in length, at the end of which you will find a store-house made of stone. Enter: you will meet with an idol made of brass, with about its neck a plate of the same metal on which you will find written whatever is in the store-house, of silver, precious stones, statues and other wonders. Take what you please, but do not stay before a dead person you shall find there, nor touch his jewels and precious stones. Do afterwards as much to every pillar and its statue for they are the tombs of seven kings buried with their treasures.' Treasure-hunting became a serious, and taxable, industry that merged with the search for antiquities to ship to Europe and America: manuals such as *The Book of Hidden Pearls* gave the incantations and recipes for magic potions that were necessary for success.

Even when Abd al Latif visited Egypt around 1200 some of the smaller pyramids had already been taken off, by Saladin and his successors, to provide stone for building a series of arches near Giza, a wall round Cairo and the high-set Citadel that still dominates the city. Abd al Latif saw the Sphinx in its perfection and some pyramids, at

least, still complete with smoothed-off facing stones: he noted that the stones of the two main pyramids carried numerous inscriptions in ancient characters. The Cairo building programme, however, eventually made off with all the fine Tura limestone facing from Cheops' Great Pyramid and with all but the topmost cap from Chephren's. In 1300 the Sphinx, too, lost its looks when the Sultan Mohammed en-Nasir, the 'ever-fasting', mutilated it, and possibly many of the other statues around the site of Memphis.

Determined European traders and travellers did continue venturing into Egypt: around 1440 one Cyriacus was greatly astonished at the size of the pyramids but still climbed to the top of the Great Pyramid. After the Turkish conquest of Egypt, in 1517, the stream of merchants and visitors grew steadily greater, perhaps because the Turkish-appointed governors, the pashas, were ready to give greater protection to non-Muslims. These pashas, however, like some of the sultans and caliphs before them, regarded the existence of the pyramids almost as a personal affront. In 1584 Ibrahim Pasha first enlarged the entrance to the Great Pyramid, so that a person could walk in upright, and then proposed to blow up the entire edifice by filling the passages with gunpowder. He was dissuaded by the thought of huge blocks of up-flung stone crashing down on Cairo.

Most of the early visitors to Egypt were mainly intent on making a pilgrimage to the holy places of the Bible or on finagling a fortune out of the trade in medicinal mummy. The seventeenth-century philosopher Sir Thomas Browne noted sharply: 'Mummy is become merchandise, Mizraim (Egypt) cures wounds, and Pharaoh is sold for balsams.' Some travellers, however, began taking a more serious interest in the history of ancient Egypt and the antiquities that still remained, although even the investigatively-minded could be less than subtle in their methods. The Frenchman Jean Palerme, secretary to the Duke of Anjou, who climbed as far as the King's Chamber on an excursion to the Great Pyramid in 1581, broke off a piece of the sarcophagus to bring away out of curiosity. Thirty-five years later, the love-lorn Italian traveller Pietro della Valle hit that same sarcophagus as hard as he could with a hatchet: it rang like a bell but did not break.

Another of this new breed, the English poet George Sandys, described his experiences at Giza in a book *Relation of a Journey begun in 1610*. He climbed the Great Pyramid, counting the number of courses and observing that 'the stones were too

Some of the rock-cut tombs near Thebes are palatial in scale: just how the excavators and artists managed to work so deep in the hill-sides is one of the mysteries of Egypt.

large to have been borne by our own carriages,' and went inside after the guards with his party had fired their guns into the entrance 'lest some should have skulked within.' He commented on the dreadful heat of the interior, which forced him to take off most of his clothes, and on the foul, grave-like smell, but he managed to describe the passages, the chambers, the sarcophagus, and the shafts opening into the walls of the upper chamber. These were 'not big enough to be crept into – sooty within, and made, as they say, by a flame of fire which darted through it.'

Around 1638, an English professor of geometry, John Greaves, visited Giza and systematically measured the Great Pyramid. His observations, reported in his book *Pyramidographia or a Description of the Pyramids in Aegypt*, remained the most accurate available until nineteenth-century investigators re-surveyed the structure. He estimated the height as 152 metres (499 ft.) and the base as 211 metres (693 ft.) square. He mentioned the ancient tradition that the pyramids cast no shadows but pointed out that this was true only around midday when the sun rose high enough to shine on all four sides. He climbed to the top and went inside, measuring the passages and chambers. He made the interior of the sarcophagus in the King's Chamber 1.9 metres (6.5 ft.) in length and commented that this showed human beings had always been about the same height.

During the seventeenth and eighteenth centuries, as more people journeyed to Egypt and as increasing amounts of titillating information trickled back to Europe, Egyptiana was taken up by the fashionable as part of the general enchantment with classicism. Artists added pyramids, obelisks and sphinxes to their fantastic landscapes, drawn as much from hearsay and extravagant invention as from real knowledge. Giovanni Piranesi took his Egyptian motifs from wall paintings in Pompeii, developed them into imaginative designs and praised their heraldic strength: 'How artfully are those parts set off which are agreeable to architecture, while those are suppressed which are not advantageous to it.' Some people began collecting Egyptian antiquities: when the British Museum opened in 1759 it already possessed statuettes and papyri given by some of its founders. Others turned their attention to clarifying the history of ancient Egypt.

One amongst them was the scientist Sir Isaac Newton. In *The Chronology of Ancient Kingdoms Amended*, published in 1728, Sir Isaac disclosed the results of his cogitations while trying to synch-ronize the list of Egyptian kings provided by Manetho with his knowledge of Greek, Roman and Biblical history. From Newton's viewpoint, Manetho's gods and demi-gods stretched back well beyond the beginning of creation itself. He solved the problem, so rectifying the chronology of Egypt, by leaving most of them out, proving that kings with different names were, in fact, one and the same, and generally shrinking about 12000 years of legend into a few hundred.

'Historians agree,' he wrote, 'that Menes reigned in Egypt next after the gods, and turned the river into a new channel, and built a bridge over it, and built Memphis and the magnificent Temple of Vulcan. He built only the body of the Temple of Vulcan, and his successors Ramesses or Rhampsinitus, Moeris, Asychis, and Psammiticus built the western, northern, eastern and southern porticos thereof. The Egyptians originally lived on the fruits of the earth, and fared hardly and abstained from animals: Menes taught them to adorn their beds and tables with rich furniture and carpets, and brought in amongst them a sumptuous, delicious and voluptuous way of life. Now Menes built the body of the Temple of Vulcan, Ramesses the first portico, and Moeris the second portico thereof; but the Egyptians, for making their gods and kingdom look ancient, have inserted between the builders of the first and second portico of this Temple three hundred and thirty kings of Thebes, and supposed that these kings reigned eleven thousand years; as if any Temple could stand so long. This being a manifest fiction, we have corrected it by omitting those interposed kings, who did nothing, and placing Moeris next after Ramesses.'

At around the same time as Sir Isaac Newton was recasting Egyptian history, a French writer, Jean Terrasson, collected together all the Greek and Roman descriptions of Egypt and turned them into a vast novel, the *Life of Sethos*. Sethos was supposed to be a Prince of Memphis living about 200 years after the time of Ramesses II and Jean Terrasson presented the tale as though translating a Greek author of ancient times, setting down just about every possible speculation about ancient Egypt. He mentioned that some people believed the ancient Egyptians must have been accomplished alchemists who knew the secret of turning all metals into gold: what else could explain the extent of their riches? He recorded the notion that the poets of ancient Egypt devoted themselves to examining questions of virtue and vice: 'But poetry was absolutely forbid to persons of dissolute and irregular morals, by this they secured themselves from a public evil. . . .' And he revelled in the thought of secret places beneath the pyramids where every sort of religious ceremony could take place.

According to Terrasson's story, when Sethos was sixteen years old, his tutor Amedes, took him into the Great Pyramid by night. Their winding descent led to two folding doors of brass which opened with the least push, and without any noise; but in shutting again they made a very great sound, which echoed till it lost itself a good way off in the vast edifice. They were then at the bottom of the well, which is in all 45 metres (150 ft.) deep. Opposite this gate, which was on the north side, there was another, shut with iron grates, each bar of which

The Papyrus of Ani, a fourteenth-century BC royal scribe, is a richly illustrated and important source for our knowledge of Egyptian ethics.

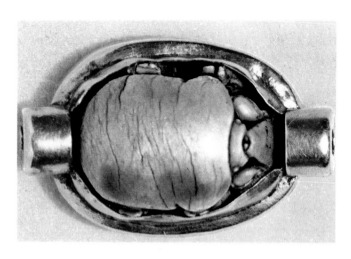

With pieces such as this gold and turquoise ring to uncover – it dates from the Hyksos period around the seventeenth century BC – the search for knowledge of Egyptian antiquity often took on a hint of treasure hunting.

in twenty-four large and lavishly illustrated volumes, the *Description de l'Egypte.*

Edmé Jomard, leader of the Commission, went into the Great Pyramid and reported that his party, on coming out of the King's Chamber, discharged their firearms so as to listen to the resounding echoes of the Grand Gallery: 'I have never heard anything quite so impressive. As the noise dies away the observer becomes ever more aware of the profound silence that rules these places. It is an experience I would like to repeat.' He climbed to the top, mentioned that a stone thrown with the greatest force would not clear the base and added a warning against jumping from step to step on the way down.

One of the artists who ranged so effectively through Egypt, Dominique Vivant Denon, hurried out his own account, *Travels in Lower and Upper Egypt*, in 1801, mentioning the difficulties under which the Commission laboured. When he visited the Great Pyramid a detachment of two hundred soldiers went along as a guarantee of safety, 'an advantage that could not be frequently expected'.

Most important of all, the expedition happened to discover the key to the deepest mystery of ancient Egypt, the meaning of the hieroglyphs. Everyone concerned with Egypt accepted that the hieroglyphs would prove significant, although, as yet, they had no way of translating them. Napoleon adopted as his emblem the bee, spangling it over the robes he and Josephine wore when he crowned himself Emperor in 1804; by then, he knew the hieroglyphic bee appeared among the titles of the god-kings of Egypt.

In previous decades anyone with an urge to speculate might come up with an interpretation of the hieroglyphic symbols. In 1705, Thomas Greenhill, a London surgeon, confidently proclaimed in a book sub-titled *The Art of Embalming*, that the crocodile was the emblem of malice, the eye the preserver of justice and the guard of the body, the right hand with its fingers open signified plenty and the left, with its fingers closed, preservation and the custody of men's goods and estates. 'To express their Creator of the World, the Egyptians described an old man in a blue mantle with an egg in his mouth, which was the emblem of the world, and expressed their notion of divinity by an eye on a sceptre, by an eagle's head, etc. . . . For eternity the Egyptians painted the sun and the moon, as things which they believed to have had no beginning, nor were likely to have any ending.'

was as thick as a man's arm. Through these grates, Sethos saw a long walk, to which he could perceive no end: on the east side of it was a long row of arches or vaults, from which came a great light of lamps and torches; and from the bottom of these vaults he heard the voices of men and women, which made a very harmonious noise. Amedes informed him that the walk he saw through the grates ran below the other pyramids, which were real tombs; and that the arches led to a subterranean temple where the priests and priestesses, whose voices he heard, performed every night different sorts of sacrifices and ceremonies, which could not be revealed to him because he was not yet initiated.

All this speculation suddenly found itself with a solid basis of fact for the most unexpected of reasons: Napoleon invaded Egypt. Although he quickly secured the country, after landing near Alexandria on July 1, 1798, the expedition became a strategic and political fiasco: Nelson destroyed the French fleet at Abukir Bay on August 1; Napoleon fled back to France in August, 1799; the army floundered about until it negotiated its own evacuation in 1801. But Napoleon had originally taken with him a Commision of Arts and Science, a party of scholars, scientists and artists charged with the task of investigating every aspect of contemporary Egypt and its antiquities. During their three years in Egypt the Commission carried through an incredible amount of work, sketching, measuring, collecting. They eventually published the results of their researches, beginning in 1809,

As likely as not, these earlier exegeses depended on pseudo-hieroglyphic texts that were themselves the invention of some artist or the error-ridden product of an unenlightened copyist. During the second half of the eighteenth century, the German traveller Karsten Niebuhr did begin collecting accurate hieroglyphic inscriptions, and the Commission, too, took copying seriously. Egyptologists could at last assume that the texts they pored over would prove intelligible if they ever could decipher them. Then, completely by accident, some of Napoleon's soldiers stumbled across the clue that would make all the difference.

A detachment of soldiers working on some fortifications near Rosetta in the western Delta happened to turn up a slab of basalt, a fine-grained black stone, rather over 1 metre (3 ft.) high, somewhat less broad and about 30 centimetres (1 ft.) deep. The soldiers noticed that the face carried inscriptions and sent the stone, the Rosetta Stone, to the members of the Commission in Cairo. The Rosetta Stone itself ended up in the British Museum, as spoils of war, but Egyptologists all over Europe got hold of reproductions. Their excitement stemmed from the fact that the inscription came in three bands. The topmost, half broken away, consisted of fourteen lines of hieroglyphs; the middle had thirty-two lines of demotic script, a simplified form of Egyptian writing; the bottom section, fifty-four lines of it, was in Greek. They could translate the Greek; it recorded a decree of the Egyptian priesthood in 196 BC, and this gave them hope of deciphering the hieroglyphic version.

Even with this key, finding the solution took a further twenty years and involved a number of scholars sifting through many more inscriptions than just that on the Rosetta Stone. Some of them mislead themselves by clinging to the idea that hieroglyphs had to be symbolic, purely a picture language; others handicapped themselves by refusing to admit any link with Coptic, the later language of Egypt; others, still, went so far with their researches and then drifted off to take up other interests. One man in particular pulled together everything that was known about hieroglyphs, Jean François Champollion, born in Figeac in the south-east of France in 1790.

Jean François, who called himself Champollion the Younger in deference to the older brother who roused his interest in Egyptology, set himself to learn all the languages that might be useful, including Coptic, before, at the age of eighteen, he turned to the Rosetta Stone, starting with the demotic inscription. Fourteen years later, in 1822, he was able to publish a *Letter regarding the Alphabet of the Phonetic Hieroglyphs*. Champollion went on correcting and extending his ideas until his death in 1832. By then, he had made an expedition to Egypt and prepared a dictionary and grammar of Ancient Egyptian. His work has been the basis of all subsequent study of hieroglyphs.

Hieroglyphic writing mixed together different ways of representing words. Some of the signs really were pictures: the picture of a face meant a face; an eye was an eye; a circle with a dot at the centre was the sun; a rectangle, the plan of a house, was a house. Some, although still

Jean François Champollion is commemorated as the man who solved the secret of the hieroglyphs in the early years of the nineteenth century, making use of the inscriptions on the Rosetta Stone.

159

Giovanni Belzoni drew the interior of Ramesses II's temple at Abu Simbel in 1817, after clearing it of sand.

pictorial, expressed more abstract concepts so that the picture of a sceptre implied the idea of ruling. These picture signs could also stand for the letters of the word they represented, so that the sign for a house denoted the letters *pr*. By extension, this same sign could then stand for any other word, such as 'to go out', that was associated in meaning and built around the same consonants: Egyptian writing left out the vowels which made the difference between various words with the same consonants.

Many of these phonetic signs referred to groups of two or three consonants but twenty-four of them, signs like a basket with a handle which corresponded to *k*, represented single letters and made up an alphabet. These phonetic signs might be joined together to form words or they could be added on to a symbolic sign to show how to pronounce it. Further hieroglyphs, called determinatives, placed at the end of a word indicated its sense, the kind of meaning it had. The determinative might show that this was

an abstract word, or one referring to a particular activity or kind of person. In this way a single group of consonants plus various determinatives might suggest the idea of purification or cleanliness, a priest, clean clothes, or an embalming place or tomb.

In writing hieroglyphs, the Egyptians usually worked from right to left or top to bottom, although they could set them out from left to right or in other patterns if necessary: they turned the signs round so that they always faced the beginning of the message. Decipherers hit further problems because the Egyptians ran words together rather than leave unsightly gaps; they rarely included any equivalent of 'the' or 'a'; they made virtually no distinction between 'the sun rises', 'the sun rose', 'the sun will rise'; and so on and so on. When people did learn to read ancient Egyptian, and ultimately the problems are similar to translating any dead language, they found a rich vocabulary, involving over 700 signs with two or three meanings each, a clarity that came from brevity and strict word order, and a kind of formality that reflected the force of tradition. To an extent, modern Egyptologists can reconstitute

*The sarcophagus in this view of the chamber in Mycerinus'
pyramid was lost when a ship carrying it to Britain sank.*

some of the ancient pronunciations by working
back through Coptic, but when this does not
apply they insert a weak vowel such as *e* where
they have to in order to make a word sayable.

During the nineteenth century, and continuing
on to the present day, interest in Egypt grew and
grew. Some travelled to Egypt intending to rip
out as many antiquities as they profitably could;
some went to study its ancient civilization,
although one great Egyptologist, Samuel Birch
of the British Museum, never had the time
actually to visit the country; some went as tourists;
others turned to Egypt for more esoteric reasons.

Henry Salt, British consul general in Egypt for
eleven years until his death in 1827, set the
standard for appropriation in competition with
the French consul general, Bernardino Drovetti.
His consular income totalled £1500 a year after
taxes but this, he felt, could not meet the expenses
of a palatial establishment in the new French
quarter of Cairo. The rent might be only £50 a
year but to entertain visiting dignitaries and

Egyptologists he hired a staff of two janissaries,
a steward, a cook, two footmen, a gardener, a
camel and driver to fetch water from the Nile,
an ass for odd jobs, a bullock for the garden and a
washerwoman. He set out to bridge the gap by
trading in antiquities, relying on the goodwill of
the governor, Mohammed Ali, who was looking
for allies in his campaign to make Egypt his
personal domain. Henry Salt formed and sold
three collections of antiquities (one provided
the basis of the British Museum display, another
went to the king of France, the third was auctioned
off after his death) but he never really made the
fortune he wanted.

Giovanni Belzoni, a two-metre (6 ft. 7 in.) tall
strong man and engineer, acted as one of Henry
Salt's agents and as a collector on his own account.
Giovanni Belzoni, who had been born in Italy
in 1778, travelled through England and Europe,
fetching up in Egypt in 1815. In just a few years
he accomplished more than virtually any other
plunderer, specializing in moving the apparently immovable, whether obelisk or vast statue.
He opened up Chephren's pyramid at Giza,
he discovered the extensive and beautifully-
decorated tomb of Seti I in the Valley of the Kings,
he excavated at Karnak and cleared the great
temple of Abu Simbel of sand.

In one most impressive feat, Belzoni shifted a
giant, 7-tonne (ton) head of Ramesses II out of the
Ramesseum at Thebes, delivering it eventually to
the British Museum. Even after it had been
levered on to a roughly-constructed wooden
framework, hauling it down to the river required a
couple of weeks' effort. Belzoni was so pleased
when the statue, which he knew as the young
Memnon, reached the bank of the Nile that he
gave all the Arab workers an extra present of one
piastre, or sixpence, about a day's wages: 'They
well deserved their reward, after an exertion to
which no labour can be compared. The hard task
they had to drag such a weight, the heavy poles
they were obliged to carry to use as levers, and the
continual replacing the rollers, with the extreme
heat and dust, were more than any European
could have withstood: but what is still more
remarkable, during all the days of this exertion, it
being Ramadan, they never ate or drank till after
sunset. I am at a loss to conceive how they existed
in the middle of the day at a work to which they
were totally unaccustomed.'

Even as Henry Salt, Giovanni Belzoni and the
rest dragged their trophies out of Egypt, others
settled down to the longer haul of trying to

In 1816, Giovanni Belzoni recorded the efforts of the Egyptian labourers as they dragged the statue he called the young Memnon, actually Ramesses II, to the Nile.

understand the civilization that produced these giant monuments – as well as making their own collections of antiquities. Robert Hay, a Scottish landowner, extended the idea of the gentleman traveller by returning to Egypt a number of times between 1824 and 1838. He employed artists to record the antiquities as they found them and he made accurate copies of hieroglyphic inscriptions. His collection of drawings provides a remembrance of monuments that have disappeared even since his time; ancient blocks of stone were still a handy source of building materials. Robert Hay described a visit he made to the pyramids of Giza: 'The sun was just setting, all the western sky was illuminated, colours of gold and purple of the purest nature softening as it rose and tinging the edges of the smaller clouds. Three pyramids I could only see, with much shade about that part of the country. Near, the green fields became lighted up with a bright light, the people seemed all returning home and the oxen taking leave of their ploughs.'

Sir John Gardner Wilkinson established the real

foundation of British Egyptology, spending twelve years in Egypt, from 1821 to 1833, and revisiting it later. He worked among the tombs of Thebes, studied hieroglyphs, made a survey of the main archaeological sites and wrote a monumental and yet popular account of what was known of ancient Egypt in the three volumes of *The Manners and Customs of the Ancient Egyptians* first published in 1837.

Colonel Howard Vyse concentrated on pyramids, spending £10,000 on surveys and excavations during the late 1830s and publishing the results in a book *Operations carried on at the Pyramids of Gizeh in 1837*. Colonel Vyse adopted a somewhat rough and ready approach. He bored into the Sphinx to see if secret passages connected it with the Great Pyramid. Tradition held that a spiral staircase of twenty-two steps led down to the entrance of a labyrinthine network of passages that only initiates could thread: Colonel Vyse did not find it. He used gunpowder to blast his way into the higher construction spaces above the King's Chamber, discovering hieroglyphic markings left on some of the hidden blocks by the original work gangs. One contained the name of Cheops, showing that he had built the Great Pyramid. Colonel Vyse forced his way into some of the smaller pyramids at Giza but his most beneficial contribution was probably to send John Shae Perring, a civil engineer, to travel to many of the other pyramids, opening them, measuring them and copying inscriptions he found within them.

Although Colonel Vyse achieved much, in some ways he suffered great disappointment. He made clear, when he began his operations, that his real hope was to find new systems of passages within the masses of stone: 'The Pyramids, particularly those of Gizeh, attracted my attention; from the grandeur and simple majesty of their forms, from the remote antiquity and uncertainty of their origin, and also from the peculiarity of their mysterious construction; since, after the investigation of many ages, doubts were still entertained, not only as to the purpose for which the passages and chamber already discovered were originally intended, but in a much greater degree respecting any other passages or apartments, which might reasonably be supposed to exist in these enormous structures.'

Karl Richard Lepsius, one of the greatest Egyptologists of all, led the Prussian Expedition to Egypt during 1842 to 1845. This was one of the most serious expeditions mounted; Richard Lepsius himself spent years in preparation, visiting the main collections of Egyptian antiquities in Europe, learning the ancient languages and working to extend Champollion's interpretation of hieroglyphs. Over the years the expedition collected more than fifteen thousand Egyptian antiquities and plaster casts of inscriptions, publishing its discoveries in the *Denkmäler aus Aegypten und Aethiopen*, twelve huge volumes of illustrations and a further five for the text.

One man, Joseph Bonomi, an English artist, worked for several of these scholars. Robert Hay took him along on his travels and he then stayed in Egypt for over eight years; he helped Sir Gardner Wilkinson with illustrations; and he returned to Egypt with Richard Lepsius' expedition. While working near Thebes he actually lived among the tombs he was studying. Travellers reported that he had converted one into a commodious dwelling where, like Robinson Crusoe, he kept his boat, his cat, his dog, his goats and hens, and his pet ostrich: his income of £100 a year allowed him to live like a gentleman. In one of his letters, however, he did express a wish to exist again among the living. He was most impressed by Egyptian art. In one tomb he found an entire wall given over to depicting the moving of

a huge statue. Four rows of figures pulled the colossus on a sledge, others carried forward baulks of timber while some poured water in front of the runners to lessen the effect of friction. The drawing was detailed enough to show how the cords holding the statue on the sledge were tightened by twisting them with sticks. 'Egyptian,' wrote Bonomi, 'is more excellent as an intelligible descriptive representation of a subject than a beautiful picture according to the modern notions of painting. It was the aim of the Egyptian artists to render the subject intelligible to the meanest capacity, not merely to make a good picture which their ignorance of perspective would in great measure preclude.'

Joseph Bonomi also recorded the jollier side of Egyptologizing. At Christmas-time, in 1842, the Prussian Expedition was working at Giza. On December 26, they assembled in the Great Room of the Great Pyramid where they had placed a date tree in the sarcophagus and hung it with festoons of figs, dates, raisins: 'We all sang our national anthems and drank a bottle of hock to the memory of our friends.'

Even the tourists made their contribution. Henry Westcar, that young Englishman, collected an Arab tale spun around the mock doors the ancient Egyptians carved in stone. While passing round the temple of Denderah an Arab showed him a kind of false door and told him that, during the time the village was inhabited, the door had been seen open by a man in whose garden it was, that he had entered and found immense riches, that he had got a camel and loaded it with gold, but that just as he was coming out a mad buffalo entered and he was obliged to fly, leaving the camel. Upon returning he found the place stoned up and verily believed the devil must be there.

Henry Westcar also climbed the second pyramid at Giza, Chephren's, a brave act, for him and the accompanying Arabs, as it still had its topmost cap of smooth facing stone: 'At the bottom of the casing my Arabs endeavoured to persuade me not to go, and I was almost of their way of thinking when one told me none but Englishmen went up. This determined me. I took off my shoes and commenced. The third step was a very long one sideways and I stood some time to think of it. If I once passed that step I must proceed, and if I fell, what difference would a few feet make? Having gained the summit I happened to cast my eyes down the casing below, smooth as glass as far as it extended, but nothing was to be seen till the eye met the earth below, strewn over with immense blocks of stone, which appeared about the size of bricks and the asses and men like mice and babes.'

Photographers made their way to Egypt almost as soon as the new process came into being. Frédéric Goupil-Fesquet, a French view-taker, captured the pyramids at Giza for what was almost certainly the first time on daguerrotypes, silver plates, on November 22, 1839, the second day of trying: 'It seemed very humiliating to me to come back to Cairo without bringing any souvenir of the most famous monuments in the world; in spite of the disparagements of my companions, who threatened to throw the daguerrotypes in the Nile like so much excess baggage, I had the patience to prepare a further ten or so plates which I polished as well as I could and with all speed possible. I presumed to do the opposite of the instructions of M. Daguerre, and thanks to this expedient I obtained successively four and five proofs, both of the Sphinx and the pyramids, leaving the pictures exposed to the sun for 15 minutes.' A few years later, C. G. Wheelhouse, a medical man with Lord Lincoln's Mediterranean yachting party, produced a panoramic view of the plain of Karnak, with the ruins dotted around, that still shows just how wild and bleak the place could be. Wheelhouse noted in his album of photographs that he had heard one of the Colossi of Memnon speak, just as it did in antiquity.

One particularly intriguing account of an ascent of the Great Pyramid, foreshadowing the twentieth-century interest in pyramid power, came from Werner von Siemens, founder of the electrical firm Siemens and Halske. Werner von Siemens, while on his way to the Red Sea to lay a telegraphic cable, broke his journey at Cairo long enough to visit Giza on April 14, 1859, taking with him ten of his engineers. While they were climbing the Great Pyramid, hauled up by about 30 Arabs, a cold wind raised the desert dust into a white mist. On the summit, copying one of the Arabs, Werner von Siemens pointed an outstretched finger in the air; this produced a sharp singing sound and a prickling sensation in the finger. He was just the man to recognize an electrical phenomenon and he and his companions experimented away: 'By wrapping a piece of damp paper around a full wine bottle, which had a metallically-coated neck, I transformed it into a Leyden jar (an electrical accumulator), which became strongly charged when held high above one's head. It was possible to obtain loud cracking sparks of about 1 centimetre (0.5 in.) range.'

At this point, the Arabs, who thought the playful engineers must be magicians, tried to drag them from the summit. The chief of the tribe took on Werner von Siemens himself: 'I held the well-coated bottle in my right hand high above my head. I waited my moment and lowered the neck of the bottle slowly towards his nose. When I touched it I myself felt a strong concussion, to judge from which the sheik must have received a violent shock. He fell speechless to the ground, and several seconds elapsed, making me somewhat anxious, before he raised himself and sprang howling down the steps of the pyramid with gigantic leaps.'

All this activity affected Europe and America. Europe made the Egyptian style part of both Empire and Regency design; it lingered on into Art Nouveau. In France, the ex-Empress Josephine, with the help of firms such as George Jacob and his sons, filled her chateau at Malmaison with furniture sporting winged lions and sphinxes. In Britain, Thomas Hope published drawings of the Egyptian Room he laid out in his own home; another furniture designer, George Smith, borrowed both elegantly simple basic shapes and the sphinxes, lions, palm trees and crocodiles with which to embellish them. He modelled one set of chairs, in the Royal Pavilion, Brighton, on an Egyptian throne. In 1821 Giovanni Belzoni staged a successful exhibition in London's Egyptian Hall, displaying full-size impressions of some of the rooms from Seti I's tomb together with many other curiosities.

Sometimes the interest in Egypt showed up in odd places. Joseph Bonomi wrote to Robert Hay about a manufacturer with grandiose ideas: 'My dear Sir, There is a man at Leeds (in England) who proposes to build a portico to a large cotton mill after the fashion of the Temple of Philae and has written to me to make him out working drawings.' Bonomi went on to help plan the Egyptian Court for the Crystal Palace which opened in South London in 1854. Among the attractions, besides tombs and temples (reduced in scale), the decorated walls, and the pair of figures 22 metres (72 ft.) high, were the names of Queen Victoria and Prince Albert rendered into hieroglyphs.

America, too, joined in enthusiastically: Memphis, Tennessee, and Karnak, Illinois, (north-east of Cairo and south-west of Lake Egypt) really are

Pyramid theorists such as Piazzi Smyth, who published these maps in 1864, have suggested that the Great Pyramid lies at the centre both of Egypt and of all dry land.

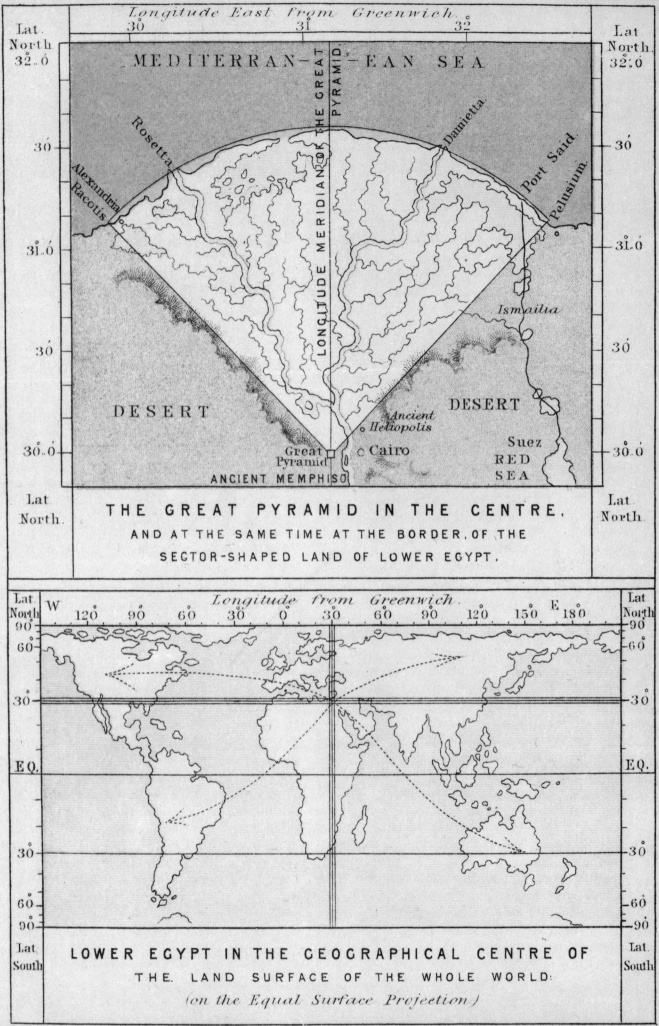

PLATE II.

Longitude East from Greenwich.

Lat.
North.
32°.0

MEDITERRAN— —EAN SEA

Rosetta.

Damietta.

Port Said.

Alexandria
Racotis

Pelusium.

Ismailia

DESERT

DESERT

Ancient
Heliopolis

Suez
RED
SEA

Great
Pyramid

Cairo

ANCIENT MEMPHIS○

LONGITUDE MERIDIAN OF THE GREAT PYRAMID.

Lat.
North.
32°.0

Lat.
North.

THE GREAT PYRAMID IN THE CENTRE,
AND AT THE SAME TIME AT THE BORDER, OF THE
SECTOR-SHAPED LAND OF LOWER EGYPT.

Longitude from Greenwich.

W
120° 90° 60° 30° 0° 30° 60° 90° 120° 150° E 180°

Lat.
North.
90°

Lat.
North.
90°

EQ.

EQ.

LOWER EGYPT IN THE GEOGRAPHICAL CENTRE OF
THE LAND SURFACE OF THE WHOLE WORLD:
(on the Equal Surface Projection)

PIAZZI SMYTH, DEL.T

A. RITCHIE & SON, EDIN.R

called after their Egyptian namesakes; New York City seized on the style to build their massively monumental House of Correction, nicknamed 'The Tombs'; and the Philadelphia Centennial exhibition in 1876 featured a life-like wax model of Cleopatra, tastefully adorned in as little as possible.

Every country that could grabbed an obelisk. Italy already had several, shipped there by the Roman emperors: Augustus used one as a giant sun dial and calendar. Another had found its way to Istanbul. One, lifted by Giovanni Belzoni from the Temple of Philae, graced the grounds of a private house in Dorset, England. In the 1830s, the French took one of Ramesses II's obelisks from the Temple of Luxor and set it in the Place de la Concorde, Paris. The Romans had shifted a pair of Tuthmosis III's obelisks from Heliopolis or On to Alexandria: in 1878 the British took one to London, placing it beside the River Thames and christening it 'Cleopatra's Needle'; the Americans made away with the other in 1880, moving it to New York City's Central Park. Even nineteenth-century technology was hard-pressed to manipulate these 200 tonne (ton) masses in safety, underlining the achievements of the ancient Egyptians themselves.

As a final tribute to the seductive power of the myths of ancient Egypt, Scotland's premier duke, Alexander, tenth Duke of Hamilton, had himself mummified. Alexander, reputed to be the proudest man in Britain, felt that what suited the pharaohs might do for a man who could trace his pedigree back to the thirteenth century. He spent some hundreds of thousands of pounds on Hamilton Palace and Mausoleum near Glasgow; he purchased a costly and unique sarcophagus, made from basalt, covered with exquisitely carved hieroglyphs and said to have contained the body of an Egyptian princess; and he persuaded the surgeon Thomas Pettigrew, who had unrolled a number of mummies, to undertake the wrapping-up. After the duke died, in 1852, Thomas Pettigrew embalmed the body, chopping off the feet to reduce its height, and swathed it in bandages. The London *Times* concluded its account of the funeral with the mourners departing 'leaving the body resting on a dais in front of the sarcophagus. The workmen, headed by Mr Pettigrew, the embalmer, and Mr Bryce, the architect, then took possession of the chapel, when the coffin was opened and the body placed in the sarcophagus. The lid, which weighs 15 hundredweight [$\frac{3}{4}$ tonne], was then lowered, and the world and all its concerns closed for ever on Alexander, the tenth Duke

of Hamilton.' As it happened, the mummy-bearing sarcophagus was later buried in the local cemetery: there it remains, although it has been relocated by soil resistivity tests, because if dug up it would, apparently, attract various forms of capital taxation.

All this stirred up the theorists, people who felt the ancient Egyptians had been trying to tell us something when they built the pyramids. Some claimed them as repositories of ancient wisdom; some as part of God's revelation; some as aids to magic.

A number of theorists started with measurements, although they tended to juggle other people's figures rather than collect their own. One of the first was John Wilson, a British writer on astronomy, who brought out *The Lost Solar System of the Ancients Discovered* in 1856. He began with a belief that pyramids, obelisks and temples of any description symbolized in geometrical form 'the laws, formed by the Creator for the government of the celestial bodies'. He described Giza: 'The plain on which the pyramids at Gizeh stand is a dry, barren, irregular surface. On this platform of rock stand the massive pyramids – monuments of the skill of man and the antiquity of science – temples of a remote epoch, where man adored the visible symbols of nature's universal law, and through that the invisible God of creation. Here the pyramid of Cheops indicates the half circumference of the earth and the half diameter of the earth's orbit. Its towering summit may be supposed to reach the heavens, and the pyramid itself to represent the law of the time of a body gravitating from the earth to the sun. . . .'

From here, John Wilson leapt into double-jointed gobbledegook; picking numbers out of thin air; throwing in the supposed measurements of the Great Pyramid, other pyramids, obelisks, the temple at Karnak and even the length of railway line open in Great Britain in 1850; multiplying everything by virtually everything else; and finally coming up with the size of the earth, the distance to the moon and sun, the orbits of Jupiter and Saturn and all the other things the ancients had known.

Next came John Taylor, a literary critic and editor, who decided to concentrate on the Great Pyramid because 'it was not only the largest of the three most important structures but was, probably, the most correct and exact of them all in its proportions.' In *The Great Pyramid: Why Was It Built? and Who Built It?*, published in 1860, he suggested that the ancient Egyptians constructed such a pile because 'in the form of a Pyramid, all those truths might be declared which they had taken so much pains to learn; and in that form the structure would be less liable to injury from time, neglect, or wantonness than in any other.' A typical truth apparently incorporated in the Great Pyramid by its founders, and revealed by John Taylor, represented the diameter of the earth as equal to the lovely round number 500 million English inches (about 12700 kilometres) which is about the actual size of the earth.

Charles Piazzi Smyth, Astronomer Royal for Scotland, picked up these ideas in *Our Inheritance in the Great Pyramid* which appeared in 1864. Piazzi Smyth hoped to keep Britain from going metric, that 'great attempt of the French people to abolish alike the Christian religion and the hereditary weights and measures of all nations'. In this he was backed by Sir John Herschel, himself a respected English astronomer and Master of the Mint, who however, saw no reason to drag in pyramids.

Piazzi Smyth held that the Great Pyramid enshrined God's fundamental standards of measurement; all other pyramids were but pagan imitations. He believed that the sarcophagus in the King's Chamber was never a coffin but a measure for corn; the weight of water that would just fill it he called a Pyramid ton, a quantity rather greater than an ordinary ton. He went on to show that the fundamental unit used by the builders of the Great Pyramid derived from their knowledge of the length of the earth's polar axis: the despicable metre related itself to the earth's circumference. He called this unit the Pyramid inch and claimed it as a highly democratic measure beyond the influence of kings and despots: 'The inch is roughly a thumb-breadth to any man who has ever lived on earth for the last four thousand years.' This Pyramid inch, he calculated, equalled 1.00099 English inches (2.543 centimetres). In other words, the English inch was just a little on the short side but Piazzi Smyth explained that 'our hereditary unit of measure' had been worn away by 'the friction of ages'.

On he went, concerned to show just how accurately the pyramid builders had worked and how extensive was their knowledge. John Shae Perring had estimated the base of the Great Pyramid as 764 ft. (232.9 metres) and its height as 480 ft. 9 in. (146.5 metres). Oddly enough these figures do not quite agree with the angle of 51° 50' of slope he gave and perhaps he should have noted the height as 486 ft. (148 metres): this would match the scale diagram he drew. In any case, Piazzi Smyth, who had not yet visited the Great Pyramid, decided he needed greater accuracy. He recast Perring's measurements, added the results of a French survey, averaged and re-averaged, and finally came up with new values for the base at 763.81 ft. (232.8 metres) and the height at 468.2567 ft. (148.2 metres). This is roughly the equivalent of estimating the height of Mount Everest to the nearest snowflake.

From these new, super-accurate figures, Piazzi Smyth computed the ratio of the height of the Great Pyramid to twice its base as one to 3.14159 which, he triumphantly pointed out, was an astonishingly accurate value for *pi*, the ratio of the diameter of a circle to its circumference. Sir John Herschel was less than impressed: 'It by no means follows from anything which the dimensions of the Pyramid indicate that the ancient Egyptians did possess a knowledge of the ratio of the circumference of a circle to its diameter, even approximately. By a very remarkable coincidence, the same slope, or one practically indistinguishable from it (51° 49' 46" as opposed to Piazzi Smyth's calculated 51° 51' 14.3") belongs to a pyramid characterized by the property of having each of its faces equal to the square described upon its height. This is the characteristic relation which Herodotus distinctly tells us it was the intention of its builders that it should embody.'

Undaunted, Piazzi Smyth set off to survey the Great Pyramid for himself, adopting a theory, first suggested by one Robert Menzies of Leith, Scotland, that the internal passages, when measured in Pyramid inches, revealed God's plan for the entire past and future of the world. By the time the fourth edition of *Our Inheritance* came out, in 1880, he could write: 'Exactly when that Second Coming which will put an end for ever to all wars is to take place is a question towards which the Great Pyramid suggests, in the Grand Gallery's Southern low passage, that a beginning of the Divine preparations for it may be, in 1879, within only three or four years; though the full and grand event may not take place until after a further interval of time.'

Others took up and extended the idea of the Great Pyramid as 'the Bible in Stone'. Two English brothers, John and Morton Edgar, rushed off to Egypt and reported in *The Great Pyramid Passages and Chambers*, published in 1910, that 'the Grand Gallery symbolizes the Gospel Age: its length coincides with the duration of the Gospel Age, from the death of Christ in 33 AD till

Autumn of the year 1914 AD, when the lease of power to the Gentile nations will terminate and Christ will take to himself his mighty power.' In choosing 1914 as the year of decision, the Edgar brothers followed the lead of the American preacher Charles Taze Russell, of Pennsylvania, who founded the Jehovah's Witnesses. He believed that the Bible and the Great Pyramid showed that the Second Coming of Christ had happened in 1874 and that 1914 completed the forty years of preparation for the Millenium.

In *The Great Pyramid: Its Divine Message*,

which appeared in 1924, David Davidson, an English engineer, provided 568 pages of closely packed analysis. According to him the Great Pyramid embodied such scientific truths as the law of gravitation but he was more concerned to point out that the Pyramid's external features were designed to attract and direct attention to a further message of greater importance. . . .

Adam Rutherford, author of the four monumental volumes of *Pyramidology* and founding President of the British Institute of Pyramidology until his death in 1974, held that 'when the Great

Pyramid is properly understood and universally studied, false religions and erroneous scientific theories will alike vanish, and true religion and true science will be demonstrated to be harmonious.'

Some typical points made by Great Pyramid theorists are: that it lies virtually on latitude 30 degrees north, exactly one third of the distance from the equator to the pole; it also lies close to longitude 30 degrees east; these two lines, of latitude and longitude, cross more dry land than do any others, so the Great Pyramid defines the

Occult practitioners, and others interested in esoteric knowledge, have often adopted Egyptian symbols such as the sun disc containing the eye of Re, the Sun-god.

centre of the habitable world; the Great Pyramid is oriented only a fraction of a degree away from true north; reflections of sunlight from its smoothly-polished faces once provided a giant sundial and calendar; the Descending Corridor was aligned with the lowest position in the sky of the star that was the pole star at the time the Great Pyramid was built; the number five runs through all aspects of the construction in a way that could not have been accidental; a raised boss on one of the stones in the antechamber to the King's Chamber measures exactly 5 Pyramid inches (about 12.7 centimetres) across, or one-fifth of a Pyramid Sacred Cubit; the length of each side, in Pyramid Sacred Cubits, equals the number of days in a year; a change in the floor surface at the entrance to the Queen's Chamber shows that 1979 may mark the end of one age and the beginning of the next. Perhaps, they add, it really was divine inspiration that put the Great Pyramid on the reverse of the Great Seal of the United States and on the back of the one dollar bill.

From such observations, people have gone on to develop symbolic interpretations of the structure of the Great Pyramid within the framework of an integrated spiritual system. One group which has made the message of the Great Pyramid part of its teachings is the Church Universal and Triumphant, which has centres in a number of communities in the United States. For the Church Universal and Triumphant, which distils a unity of religious belief from East and West, the Great Pyramid is an outer manifestation of the inner pyramid within each person. Christ came to show the path of perfection and, having done so, made his ascension. Many others, too, before and after, have found how to fulfil the divine plan, how to reach a state of balanced karma, how to win permanency for the soul. These ascended masters show that ascension is possible for everyone; and now is the time when all is being made clear through the understanding of secret mysteries. The Great Pyramid is one among many sources of revelation.

For the Church Universal and Triumphant, the Great Pyramid represents the mystery of being, of the four lower bodies, the physical, emotional, mental and etheric. The centre of the pyramid is equivalent to the heart, the top equals the third eye, and the cap-stone, which has yet to be placed on the Great Pyramid's apex, is the all-seeing eye. The passages leading into the King's Chamber become a series of halls and temples of revelation; in the King's Chamber itself all should be humble before the open tomb which symbolizes resurrection and death overcome. But the Great Pyramid is also a reminder that each person is a living pyramid. Ultimately, members of the Church Universal and Triumphant work towards the point at which the inner person becomes a perfected pyramid.

While the Great Pyramid theorists and other groups see the influence of God in this vast mass, others have gone further into mysticism. The Reverend Robert Taylor, writing in Oakham Gaol, England, in 1829, said: 'Bind it about thy neck, write it upon the tablet of thy heart, "Everything of Christianity is of Egyptian origin." ' Gerald Massey, in *Ancient Egypt: The Light of the World* which was published in London in 1907, asked who is the bread of life, the light of the world, the door of the sheep, the good shepherd, the resurrection and the life, the way, the truth and the life, and the true vine? He answered that the prototype was Horus, or Jesus in the cult of Atum-Re.

Sarah, wife of Giovanni Belzoni, refers to links with Freemasonry. 'Let the Masonic Brethren search,' she wrote, 'and they will find that the Egyptian Masonic Key will unlock the hitherto unrevealed mysteries of Egyptian Wisdom.' She analysed the paintings discovered by her husband on the walls of the tomb of Seti I, explaining that they showed the initiation of the young king into the sublime mysteries of Masonry and describing how he was presented to the High Grand Master by one whose head was covered with a mask representing the head of a hawk.

Masonry crept into another book, *The Great Pyramid and the Time of God*, written in 1891 by someone identified only as W.E.S.T. The pseudonymous author reinterpreted biblical prophecies in the *Book of Zechariah* to show that one day the order of Freemasonry would recase Cheops' Great Pyramid, completing it for the first time with a pristine cap-stone set at its apex. The ancient Egyptians had apparently left off this finishing touch. On a practical note, when the Americans raised their obelisk in Central Park, in 1880, the Grand Master of the New York Freemasons laid the foundation stone.

Rosicrucians hailed the pyramids as altars raised to the divinity Fire. The stone tower was, as it were, a stationary flame. In *The Rosicrucians: Their Rites and Mysteries*, published in London in 1887, Hargrave Jennings asked 'Is it at all reasonable to conclude that all these indomitable, scarcely believable, physical efforts were devoted to a mistake?' He answered 'No! Place a light upon the summit, star-like upon the sky, and a prodigious altar the mighty Pyramid then becomes.

Madame Helena P. Blavatsky, the Russian-born seer who founded the Theosophical Society in New York in 1875, claimed that the passageways of the Great Pyramid represented 'the strait gate which leadeth unto life' and added that externally it symbolized the creative principle of nature and illustrated also the principles of geometry, mathematics, astrology and astronomy. Internally, she revealed, it had been a majestic temple, in whose sombre recesses were performed the sacred mysteries, and whose walls had often witnessed the initiation scenes of members of the royal family. The sarcophagus was the baptismal font, upon emerging from which the neophyte was 'born again' and became an adept.

Others found mystery still alive within the Great Pyramid. In the 1930s, Paul Brunton, who believed that every opening of an ancient Egyptian tomb could release invisible forces of a dangerous character as punishment for disturbing the grave of an advanced soul, arranged to spend one night in the Great Pyramid. He fasted for three days to prepare himself, entered, was locked in, climbed the steep galleries to the King's Chamber, sat beside the sarcophagus and put out the light. In the silence and the darkness he felt that he was no longer alone, 'something animate and living was throbbing into existence.' Ghastly elementals circled about him but then came two benevolent beings wearing the regalia of High Priests of an ancient Egyptian cult. They led him on a journey through secret passages of the pyramid that correspond to the secret passages of the mind: he learned, through revelation and vision, that the soul can exist apart from the body. When he finally re-opened his eyes, in inky blackness, he found that it was just midnight.

Aleister Crowley, the English adventurer and mage, had been another who stirred up secret forces within the Great Pyramid. He took his first wife, Rose Edith Kelly, to spend a night in the King's Chamber while on their honeymoon. By the light of a single candle Aleister Crowley began reading a 'preliminary invocation'; soon the whole chamber was aglow with astral light and he was able to snuff out the candle. Later, however, he found that the polished floor made a hard bed.

Modern practitioners of the occult often hark back to the great magician and alchemist Hermes Trismegistus, identified with Thoth, the Egyptian god of wisdom. The ancient Egyptians themselves had already formulated such basic concepts of magic as the hidden power of the word. In particular, they believed that Thoth had set down in books 'written with his own hand' the most potent secrets of all. They related the story of Setne Khamuas, the son of a pharaoh, who had ventured into a tomb near Memphis in search of one of these primers. The book lay between the bodies of Neneferkaptah and Ahure, his wife and sister. They, the children of another pharaoh, had defied their father to marry each other for love. Ahure told Setne how they had acquired the spell-book, which had been sealed in a box set in the midst of the sea and protected by every kind of serpent. When Setne persisted in taking it, Neneferkaptah deployed his own magical powers to confuse and bamboozle the thief.

Inspired by such tales, a number of present-day occult groups and individual magicians have drawn on ancient Egyptian myths for emblems such as the Eye of Horus set in a blazing Pyramid of Fire. Aleister Crowley found his own symbol in the Cairo Egyptian Museum. Crowley regarded himself as the Beast of Revelation; the number of the Beast is 666; exhibit 666 in the museum was a painted tablet commemorating a Twenty-sixth Dynasty priest, Ankh-f-n-Khonsu: Crowley confided that he had been Ankh-f-n-Khonsu in a previous incarnation.

Reincarnation has apparently produced one astounding phenomenon: a modern speaker of ancient Egyptian. In the 1930s, Rosemary, a young girl living in the north of England, spoke in strange tongues during a series of trances supervised by Frederic H. Wood, a teacher of music. Phonetic transcriptions of these declamations reached A. J. Howard Hulme, compiler of a dictionary translating ancient Egyptian into Esperanto. He recognized that Rosemary was actually speaking ancient Egyptian.

As Howard Hulme and Frederic Wood explained in *Ancient Egypt Speaks*, published in 1937, they gradually realized that Rosemary was the reincarnation of a temple dancer, named Vola, of the time of the Eighteenth Dynasty king, Amenophis III. The voice with which she usually spoke, identified at first as the Lady Nona, belonged to a Babylonian princess called Telika who took the Egyptian name Ventiu when she was married off to Amenophis III. The princess remembered well the ghastly struggles between the domineering Queen Tiye, chief wife of Amenophis III, and her 'wise, clever, mild and gentle' son Amenophis IV, who changed his name to Akhenaten when he changed his god from Amun to Aten. Ventiu's end was sadly brutal: priests who hated her cast her into the Nile.

Rosemary produced about five hundred phrases in all, over a period of five years. On May 4, 1936, she made a gramophone record, while in a trance, at the International Institute for Psychical

Research, London, that preserved 'the true pronunciation of ancient Egyptian'. Howard Hulme emphasized the value of being able to identify the vowel sounds that gave groups of words with similar consonants their various different meanings.

Over the years Egypt and its pyramids have turned up spasmodically in films and books. A series of horror pictures started in 1932 with *The Mummy*: Boris Karloff played Imhotep, a high priest buried alive after stealing a magic scroll that would revive a dead princess. He returns in modern times, disguised as an archaeologist, to stalk his reincarnated love. Boris Karloff went on to do *The Ghoul*, then Lon Chaney and others came up with *The Mummy's Hand*, *The Mummy's Tomb*, *The Mummy's Curse*, *The Mummy's Ghost* and a remake of *The Mummy*. Elizabeth Taylor's *Cleopatra*, in 1962, provided glamour. Laura Mulvey and Peter Wollen's *Riddles of the Sphinx*, in 1977, and Agatha Christie's *Death on the Nile*, in 1978, both used the ancient ruins of Egypt as a background, the one looking at a woman's struggle for autonomy, the other performing the brittle minuet of a whodunnit. Probably the most astounding of the pyramid films was *Land of the Pharaohs* directed by Howard Hawks in 1955. The story, partly written by William Faulkner, set a cast of thousands building a pyramid for a dying pharaoh played by Jack Hawkins. With the pyramid completed, those who constructed it found themselves forcibly entombed along with their pharaoh. Some of them, however, led by Joan Collins as Princess Nellifer, rebelled against this unforeseen requirement to share his death and worked their way out.

H. Rider Haggard drew on an Egyptian apparatus of hieroglyphs and burial places, of embalmments and resurrections, in writing *She*, in 1887. This story of a paradoxically four-sided romantic triangle spanned two millenia and promised only tragedy to Ayesha, she-who-must-be-obeyed, her love, the priest Kallicrates reincarnated in his own descendant Leo Vincey, and the Egyptian princess Amenartas. In another book, *Cleopatra*, H. Rider Haggard had his hero Harmachis take Cleopatra by secret passage-ways into the pyramid of Mycerinus at Giza so that she might strip the still-existent mummy of its valuable jewels, using them to pay for the defence of Egypt against Rome.

By the end of the nineteenth century, Egyptologists had begun to develop methodical approaches to archaeology instead of the earlier hunt for trophies: this scene shows the French archaeologist Albert Jean Gayet at work.

Harmachis described their entry to the pyramid: 'Stones having been piled up on a certain spot at the base of the pyramid, to somewhat more than the height of a man, I climbed on them and searched for the secret mark, no larger than a leaf. I found it with some trouble, for the weather and rubbing of the wind-stirred sand had worn away even the Ethiopian stone. Having found it, I pressed on it with all my strength in a certain fashion. Even after the lapse of many years the stone swung round, showing a little opening, through which a man might scarcely creep. Then, having taken counsel of the plan of the passage that I had brought with me, which, in signs that none but the initiated can read, was copied from those ancient writings that had come down to me through one-and-forty generations of my predecessors, I led the way through that darksome place towards the utter silence of the tomb.'

Rider Haggard, in writing stories like this, was responding to the ever-rising interest in ancient Egypt, and drew on an increasing amount of real knowledge. More and more people were actually going to Egypt and adventurous travel was settling down into tourism. By now the traveller found a well-beaten route to the pyramids: across the Nile from Cairo; up to the plateau of Giza; and then a swift ascent of the Great Pyramid, dragged up by the waiting Arabs. 'You recollect perfectly how you commenced the ascent,' said one satirical guide-book. 'You have a dim remembrance of having got halfway up. But how you reached the top, you have not the slightest conception. At length you recover your self-possession and take a look around at the world. After which you descend.' Photographs show people taking afternoon tea atop the Great Pyramid, the summit is about 10 metres (33 ft.) square. There they sit, in basket chairs, gazing casually over towards Chephren's pyramid, while servants hand round cakes.

People who could not visit Egypt for themselves clamoured for travel books. One of the best and most popular was *A Thousand Miles up the Nile* by the English novelist Amelia Edwards, published in 1877. She reached Egypt almost accidentally, taking refuge, she said, 'to get out of the rain'; but she became an enthusiast, travelled extensively, researched thoroughly and had the text of *A Thousand Miles* checked by the British Museum. She felt that, at first glimpse, the pyramids looked small and shadowy, too familiar to be startling. But when she took a carriage out to the edge of the desert the prospect changed: 'The Great Pyramid in all its unexpected bulk and

This circlet from Tutankhamun's tomb bears the cobra of the goddess Wadjet and the vulture of the goddess Nekhbet, symbols that have haunted later tales about ancient Egypt.

majesty towers close above one's head, the effect is as sudden as it is overwhelming. It shuts out the sky and the horizon. It shuts out all the other pyramids. It shuts out everything but the sense of awe and wonder. . . . The colour again is a surprise. Few persons can be aware beforehand of the rich tawny hue that Egyptian Limestone assumes after ages of exposure to the blaze of an Egyptian sky. Seen in certain lights, the pyramids look like piles of massy gold.'

Back in Britain, Amelia Edwards toured and lectured, devoting herself to the cause of Egyptology. She made herself an energetic focus for the growing concern over the destruction and looting of Egypt's spectacular antiquities. In 1882, she became the catalyst for the setting up of the Egypt Exploration Fund. Its first president was Sir Erasmus Wilson, a surgeon who had paid to bring Cleopatra's Needle to London; Amelia Edwards was one of its secretaries. The Fund, nowadays called the Egypt Exploration Society, aimed at excavation without exploitation, research into the history of ancient Egypt in preference to digging for gold and saleable antiquities.

With reports of excavations circulated widely by the newly-founded Egypt Exploration Society; with stories freely available from a growing number of lending libraries; with accounts of travels in Egypt by Amelia Edwards and others crowding each other off the presses; the public was ready for sensation. The sensation it got was the Curse of Tutankhamun, or King Tut as the newspapers headlined him.

People had known of curses inscribed on Egyptian tombs and temple gateways, and even admired their all-embracing ferocity. One typical warning against violating a tomb ended with the malediction 'As for anyone who shall disregard it, Amun, king of gods, shall pursue him; Mut shall pursue his wife; Khonsu shall pursue his children; he shall hunger, he shall thirst, he shall faint and sicken.' Egyptologists pointed out, if they commented at all, that the curses mainly threatened those who misappropriated the endowments that provided for offerings and prayers for the dead rather than just anyone who entered the tomb. And, after all, any curse was thousands of years old and called on the vengeance of gods who had long since lost their dominion.

One death revitalized thoughts of curses, but it

was a particular death, that of a rich, high-ranking British aristocrat, and it happened in the full blaze of world-wide publicity. The man who died was George Edward Stanhope Molyneux, fifth Earl of Carnarvon. He had been paying for the explorations carried out by the archaeologist Howard Carter which led to the discovery of Tutankhamun's tomb in the Valley of the Kings late in 1922. In the weeks that followed, they and the world realized how rich the find would prove to be. On February 17, 1923, Lord Carnarvon watched while Howard Carter broke open the inner chamber, revealing the outermost golden shrine. Shortly after, while he was still in Luxor, a mosquito bite on the right cheek, aggravated by a cut while shaving, became infected and produced blood poisoning. Lord Carnarvon, already weakened by severe injuries suffered in a motoring accident in Europe, succumbed to pneumonia and died in Cairo on April 5. It was enough for the newspapers who claimed that above the door of King Tutankhamun's tomb could be read the inscription: 'Death shall come to him who touches the tomb of a Pharaoh.'

Somehow the romance of the Curse took over. Lord Carnarvon's son revealed that as his father died the lights went out all over Cairo. It is said that, at the moment of his death, his dog, left at home at Highclere Castle near London, gave a terrifying howl and died. Lord Carnarvon was buried on a hill overlooking the Castle so that the setting sun sinks behind his grave. From time to time people tick off those who appear to have died young after some involvement with Tut and his tomb; from time to time others scornfully dismiss the idea. In 1970, Richard Adamson, an Englishman who had been a security guard during the original excavation, appeared in a television interview, denying that there was a curse. The taxi taking him home from the studio crashed. 'In the past,' he said, after his mishap, 'when I have disclaimed the curse, disastrous things have happened in my family. You can say this has given me food for thought.'

As it happens, brave Egyptologists have disregarded the threat of curses to concentrate on research. Sir Flinders Petrie, who looked into as many pyramids, tombs and graves as anyone, set another kind of example in living to the age of eighty-nine years old. His own reports show the effort the search for knowledge has called for. In *The Royal Tombs of the First Dynasty*, published in 1900, he casually mentioned collecting between ten and twenty thousand pieces of vases made from the more valuable stones, eventually putting together parts of about 200 vases. So much pottery lay about the area that the Arabs called Abydos Um el-Qa'ab, 'the mother of pots'.

One equivalent modern project concentrated on a temple built at Karnak by the Eighteenth Dynasty king Amenophis IV or Akhenaten. Later kings had thoroughly destroyed the temple, recycling its blocks of stone to provide the foundations and core fillings of their own constructions. As archaeologists restored these other monuments, Akhenaten's blocks came to light. Starting in the late 1960s the Akhenaten temple project, funded by the University Museum of the University of Pennsylvania, photographed the carvings on 36000 of these blocks and used a computer to piece the pictures together. Over a period of eleven years they have recovered thousands of scenes and have been able to make new discoveries about Akhenaten's move towards worshipping the Aten, the glorious disc of the sun.

As for the pyramids themselves, Sir Flinders Petrie, when in his late twenties, spent around ten months in all taking the measurements that enable him to make accurate estimates of the size of the three Giza pyramids that he published in *The Pyramids and Temples of Gizeh* in 1883. Curiously, he had been inspired by reading Piazzi Smyth's theories although he had rejected them by the time he actually went to Egypt.

Sir Flinders Petrie's figures for the Great Pyramid were slightly modified by measurements taken in 1925 by James Humphrey Cole of the Survey of Egypt and published as the nine-page Paper No. 39: *The Determination of the Exact Size and Orientation of the Great Pyramid of Giza*. James Humphrey Cole extended the line of the edge of the casing blocks that was still traceable on the pavement on each side of the Great Pyramid. In this way he was able to fix the position of the corners and measure the length of the sides with an error of less than 4 centimetres (1.6 in.). His figures, as he published them, gave the following lengths for the sides:– North 230.253 metres (9065.1 in.); South 230.454 metres (9073.0 in.); East 230.391 metres (9070.5 in.); West 230.357 metres (9069.2 in.). This made the difference between the longest and shortest sides 20.1 centimetres (7.9 in.) and the mean length 230.364 metres (9069.4 in.). He gave the orientations of the sides as:– North 2' 28" south of west; South 1' 57" south of west; East 5' 30" west of north; West 2' 30" west of north. In other words, he found the 'worst' oriented side was less than a

tenth of a degree off true north. James Humphrey Cole made no attempt to estimate the original height of the Great Pyramid but he accepted that the faces sloped at approximately 51° 51′ and this gives a figure of 146.65 metres (5774 in. or 481.1 ft.)

Other scientists have involved themselves with the search for hidden chambers in the pyramids, applying high-technology where previous investigators used gunpowder. One group suffered a mild fiasco in 1974 when they tried to probe both Cheops' and Chephren's pyramids with radio waves. Nothing got through although the apparatus worked well enough in the laboratory. Unexpectedly, the limestone of the two pyramids turned out to be saturated with water soaked up from the ground and the humid north wind: water blocks radio waves. Later techniques using sound waves or measuring electrical resistivity may prove more successful.

One venture did produce useful results, although at a cost of more than a million dollars. This was the Joint Pyramid Project established by the United Arab Republic of Egypt and the United States of America. Led by Nobel Prize winner Luis Alvarez, it lasted from 1966 to 1970 and showed, almost certainly, that no hidden chamber exists near the centre of Chephren's pyramid. The group placed a cosmic ray detector, a spark chamber, in the vault beneath the pyramid and then, for twenty-four hours a day for more than a year, recorded all the cosmic rays passing through the pyramid. Any empty space in the pyramid should let through more cosmic rays than expected and would show up in comparison to the solid areas.

When the scientists came to analyze their recordings everything fell apart: the computer plotting the data threw up results that vacillated wildly from day to day. One member of the group, Dr Amr Goneid of Ein Shams University, Cairo, actually said: 'It defies all the known laws of science and electronics. This is scientifically impossible. Either the geometry of the pyramid is in substantial error, which would affect our readings, or there is a mystery which is beyond explanation. Call it what you will, occultism, the curse of the pharaohs, sorcery, or magic, there is some force that defies the laws of science at work in the pyramid.' However, they decided the real problem lay in the spark chamber itself. Amongst

The Earl of Carnarvon, who paid for the investigations that uncovered Tutankhamun's tomb, took this photograph of the excavators at work in the Valley of the Kings.

other things, it depended on neon gas to operate and any contamination of the gas made it unreliable. Eventually they discarded the records of about a third of their one million 'cosmic ray events' and announced that no large chamber exists in the central part of the pyramid.

In a practical experiment, Thor Heyerdahl, who led the *Kon-Tiki* expedition that drifted by raft across the South Pacific Ocean, showed that the ancient Egyptians could have sailed to America. The idea of cultural diffusion, that the ancient Egyptians spread their civilization across the world, had always been attractive. One eighteenth-century English scientist, John Turberville Needham, argued that they had exported their hieroglyphs to China and so Chinese picture writing should provide the key to Egyptian inscriptions: Jesuit missionaries in Peking rejected the possibility. Others thought that the civilization of classical Greece began with Egypt. One man, Robert Deverell, a member of the British parliament in the early nineteenth century, took cultural diffusion to extremes with the insubstantial suggestion that the name Saccara (Saqqara) showed that the ancient Egyptians were closely in touch with America and the West Indies because these countries produced sugar or saccharum.

Modern-day diffusionists have looked for connections between ancient Egypt and South America, arguing that both societies erected pyramids and other monumental buildings, that they had similar religious customs and that some outside influence must have triggered off the sudden cultural advance that seemed to happen around the Gulf of Mexico and in Peru around 1300 BC and after. In 1969, Thor Heyerdahl, working close by the Great Pyramid itself, built *Ra I*, a boat constructed from papyrus reeds along the lines of ancient Egyptian designs. Setting off from Morocco, he sailed more than 4300 kilometres (2700 miles) in eight weeks before abandoning the boat because the lashings were wearing through. In 1970, with *Ra II*, he sailed over 5000 kilometres (3000 miles) in fifty-seven days and reached Barbados, showing that the ancient Egyptians could have done the same.

Engineers with an interest in Egyptology sometimes speculate about how the ancient Egyptians raised blocks weighing 5, 10, or 15 tonnes (tons) and more into position. One suggestion actually had these blocks hauled aloft by legs set at different levels on the pyramid, the lifting rope running down through a series of pulleys to a giant capstan at ground level. Egyptologists say that the Egyptians never had pulleys: the most that has been found is a sort of stone rope guide.

A French architect, Auguste Choisy, suggested that the Egyptians used twin levers to lift the blocks straight up before sliding them sideways on to a higher level. The diagrams explaining this have a horribly unstable look. A recurrent theme has been the balance arm: a stout beam supported on a pivot about 2 metres (6 ft.) high. The block is slung from the shorter arm of the beam, which is about 1 metre (3 ft.) long, and the workers then hang counterweight rocks from the longer arm of the beam, which is about 5 metres (16 ft.) long. This swings the block into the air and allows them to position it on a sledge or other support. One of the latest engineers to argue for this device, Norwegian-born naval architect Olaf Tellefsen, has said that gangs of 25 or 30 men then pulled the laden sledges up greased slipways set directly against the sloping face of the pyramid. He also felt that the Egyptians could have made a simple pulley by running the rope round a cut-down tree trunk wrapped in a loose leather sleeve.

A number of Egyptologists have suggested that the Egyptians hauled the stones up mud-brick ramps. They point to a tomb painting of the Eighteenth Dynasty showing a ramp in use for erecting temple columns; to the remains of ramps found at Giza, Meidum and Lisht; and to a papyrus calculating the number of bricks in a ramp 366 metres (1200 ft.) long, 27 metres (90 ft.) wide and 30 metres (100 ft.) high. The jump between a 30 metre (100 ft.) high ramp and the 147 metres (481 ft.) of the Great Pyramid is, however, still daunting. Some people think the Egyptians relied on subsidiary ramps winding round the pyramid: an objection is that these would provide too insecure a base for levering large blocks into position. In 1978 a Japanese television company demonstrated ramps in use by building a replica pyramid maybe 50 metres (165 ft.) high on the banks of the Nile in order to make a film: behind the scenes the builders relied on cranes and lorries. One condition set by the Egyptian government was that the company should remove its false pyramid leaving no trace.

Some Egyptologists have drawn inspiration from Herodotus, who mentioned machines that raised the blocks step by step. Sir Flinders Petrie thought that blocks placed on sledge-like rockers could be lifted by slipping planks beneath the runners as block and rocker swung backwards and forwards. John Fitchen, Emeritus Professor of the Fine Arts at Colgate University, New York, extended this idea with the proposition that the builders purposely made part of the face of the unfinished pyramid into a giant stone staircase: gangs of workers jacked the blocks up step by step from the main ramp to the construction level.

Unfortunately, no ancient Egyptian drawing or description of how the pyramids were built has ever come to light and this may be one secret they are fated to retain. The only certainty is that captured by an American civil engineer, August Mencken, in a book published privately in Baltimore, Maryland, in 1963: 'The one indisputable fact about the building of the Great Pyramid is that it was built.'

And, being built, it has power. The first person to make the claim was the Frenchman Antoine Bovis, an ironmonger and practitioner of radiaesthesia or divination by pendulum. On a visit to Egypt he climbed into the King's Chamber and found there the mummified corpses of animals. Back home in France, he constructed scale models of the Great Pyramid and confirmed to his own satisfaction that they would mummify animals. A Czechoslovakian radio engineer, Karl Drbal, took the next step. He made a cardboard model about 15 centimetres (6 in.) high and placed within it an ordinary razor blade. The blade was supported at one-third the height of the pyramid above its base, the same level as the King's Chamber, and both blade and pyramid were oriented north-south. Karl Drbal achieved upwards of a hundred shaves with that single blade. In 1959, after ten years of effort, he acquired a Czechoslovakian patent for his razor-sharpening device.

Musicians form one particular group that has experienced the energy fields of the pyramids. The percussionist Sun Ra visited the Great Pyramid to play tapes of his music within the King's Chamber. The Grateful Dead played at the foot of the Great Pyramid in 1978 and reported that the experience was surreal. Nik Turner, with Sphynx, has laid down tracks with titles such as *Horus*, *Osiris* and *The Pyramid Spell*. He found himself playing his flute on top of the Great Pyramid at midnight on Christmas Eve, 1976: 'I'm sure I felt it move.' The classic album, however, has come from the American Paul Horn with *Inside the Great Pyramid*. There it is: solo flute with all the echoes off the polished walls of the King's Chamber.

Others have tested out pyramid power and found a number of effects. Some of the claims for what can happen with a model pyramid, whether closed in or just a frame work, are: dry-cell batteries regenerate; water seems tastier; food keeps longer; seeds germinate faster; pets and house plants are happier; crystals grow in unusual forms; children appear calmer; sleep is better; menstrual cramps diminish; meditation is more concentrated; mental acuity improves; sex drives increase; dowsers using a pendulum, dowsing rods or a forked switch can sense the force field of the pyramid; natural healing processes may be aided; prayer becomes more effective; and all psychic phenomena are stronger.

Alan Geffin, who runs Pyramid Energy Products, London, distributes all sorts of pyramids, from a 15 centimetre (6 in.) base length cardboard version, in the experimental kit produced by Pyramid Power V of Santa Monica, California, to his own 1.8 metre (6 ft.) base length open steel meditation frame. He talks of the universe as made of energy and composed of geometric patterns. The pyramid becomes a life-force symbol. He feels that to become a successful dowser, a water-diviner, or its equivalent, you have to believe in whatever you are doing: pyramid energy works regardless. He himself has shaved for over six months with one razor blade; has seen a glass of wine turn bubbly; and once ate a soft, white French cheese after it had been on display beneath a pyramid for ten days in a warm exhibition hall. He believes that scientists who reject such findings have very closed minds.

Pyramid energy possibilities have stimulated people into constructing pyramidal buildings. One particular example is the Unity Church of Christianity in Houston, Texas, opened in 1974, which is a model version of the Great Pyramid, oriented due north and rising to about 25 metres (75 ft.) high. The structure is the result of a vision which came to the Church's minister, John D. Rankin. In choosing a pyramid, the congregation combined practicality with symbolism. As a building in use, the shape provides an unobstructed interior of awesome height. As a temple of revelation, the four walls of the pyramid refer to the inner circle of Jesus' disciples – Peter, James, John and Andrew – who symbolize Faith, Wisdom, Love and Strength. Each of the four walls is, in

Over 4500 years of history link this view of modern Cairo with the distant pyramids of Giza: throughout that time the pyramids have fascinated all who have experienced their influence, from the ancient Egyptians themselves to the present-day investigators who probe their secrets.

179

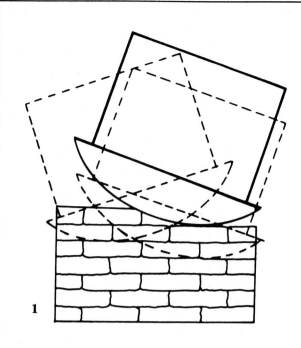

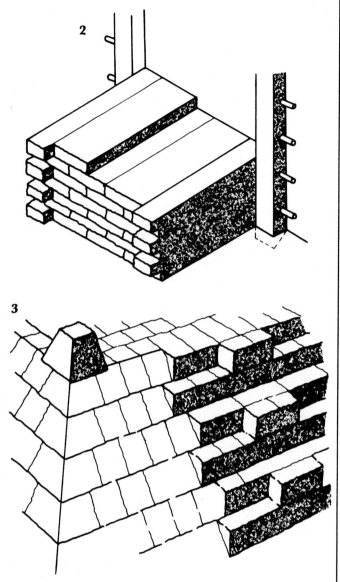

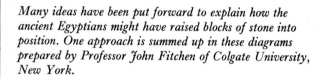

Many ideas have been put forward to explain how the ancient Egyptians might have raised blocks of stone into position. One approach is summed up in these diagrams prepared by Professor John Fitchen of Colgate University, New York.

1) Each block is mounted on a wooden rocker. Workers lever this to and fro, slipping planks of wood beneath the runners to raise it.

2) A wooden framework set against blocks already in position holds the planks firm.

3) To provide a 'staircase' up the pyramid some of the casing blocks are left rectangular and chipped to shape during the final smoothing of the pyramid surfaces.

turn, a triangle, the classic expression of the Trinity. Although the pyramid form works well for a church, John D. Rankin warns against constructing a pyramid home as the additional energy input over long periods would be too great: over-exposure to any form of radiation is as likely to produce undesirable effects as desirable.

In the early 1970s, the world missed its chance to find out what actually does happen when people work within a large and truly pyramidal building. Britain's Northampton County Council announced a competition for its new municipal offices: the prize went to architects Jeremy and Fenella Dixon for a design taken straight from Cheops' Great Pyramid. 'It's one of the lesser-used shapes,' said the Dixons. 'It's a strong and banal shape that survives being pulled apart. It's a sensible shape for keeping water out. It's an economical shape. It's also a hierarchical shape, with large open-plan areas at the base rising to the council chamber and chief executive's offices at the top.' They set it high on its ridge-top site, orienting it, in the English landscape tradition, to ancient landmarks such as an Iron Age hill fort. They used glass and plants to make it the hanging gardens of Babylon by day and a city of light floating in the sky by night. They even had jokes: on the day that marked the beginning of the financial year the sun would shine down through a shaft into the accounts department. The Council voted for it – and then the money ran out.

Perhaps that is the one true mystery of the pyramids of ancient Egypt: what effect did they have on the society that built them?

Summary chronology of ancient Egypt

Egyptologists render ancient Egyptian names into English in a variety of ways. This book follows a convention that draws mainly on the traditional Greek forms of the names of Egyptian kings and gods as these are often more generally familiar than a direct transliteration of the Egyptian original. As an example, the god who is scribe of the gods is called *Thoth* and the kings named after him *Tuthmosis*, rather than *Dhwty* and *Dhtwy-ms*. In this list alternative names are sometimes given in brackets as for King Cheops. Khufu is the Egyptian form of Cheops. In addition the Sun-god appears simply as Re although this name is sometimes written as Ra or R'.

Dates	Period/Dynasties	Major Kings	Events
Before 3100 BC	Predynastic		Occupation of the Nile valley; development of agriculture, village settlements and common culture; formation of the kingdoms of Upper and Lower Egypt
3100 to 2686 BC	Early Dynastic Period First and Second Dynasties	Narmer (who may have been the legendary Menes)	Unification of Upper and Lower Egypt; extension of influence through trade and conquest; building of royal tombs at Saqqara and Abydos
2686 to 2181 BC	Old Kingdom Third to Sixth Dynasties	Zoser, Sneferu, Cheops (Khufu), Chephren (Khafre), Mycerinus (Menkaure), Unas, Pepi II	Building of first pyramids and of major pyramids at Giza; consolidation of centralized government and tax system; development of hieroglyphic writing; rise of Sun-god Re (Ra) as royal god
2181 to 2050 BC	First Intermediate Period		Political disunity with power in the hands of local governors
2050 to 1786 BC	Middle Kingdom Eleventh and Twelfth Dynasties	Mentuhotep II, Ammenemes (Amunemhet) I, Sesostris I and II, Ammenemes III	Reunification of Egypt and regrowth of Egyptian influence; resumption of pyramid building; irrigation systems extended and land reclaimed; rise of Amun of Thebes as major god
1786 to 1552 BC	Second Intermediate Period		Political disunity with foreign rulers, the Hyksos, in Lower Egypt: last known royal pyramid built
1552 to 1080 BC	New Kingdom Eighteenth to Twentieth Dynasties	Ahmose, Amenophis (Amunhotpe) I, Tuthmosis I & II, Queen Hatshepsut, Tuthmosis III, Amenophis IV who became Akhenaten, Tutankhamun, Ramesses I, Seti (Sethos) I, Ramesses II	Highest point of Egyptian power and prosperity; extensive building in temples at Karnak and Luxor; royal burials in Valley of the Kings, during Akenaten's reign, emphasis on worship of the Aten, the disc of the sun
1080 to 30 BC	Late Period		Political disunity with numerous rulers; conquest by Persians in 525 BC and by Alexander the Great in 332 BC; death of Cleopatra in 30 BC; occupation by Rome

Books for Further Reading

Readers who want to go more deeply into Egyptian archaeology and
pyramid lore will find literally hundreds of books to study.
Those listed here provide a wide-ranging introduction and are
generally available from libraries or bookshops,
often as paperbacks.

GENERAL HISTORY

Cyril Aldred, *Egypt to the End of the Old Kingdom*, Thames
and Hudson, London 1965

Margaret Murray, *The Splendour that was Egypt*, Sidgwick and
Jackson, London, revised edition 1964

John Ruffle, *Heritage of the Pharaohs*, Phaidon, Oxford, 1977

PYRAMIDS

I. E. S. Edwards, *The Pyramids of Egypt*, Penguin Books,
Harmondsworth, revised edition 1961

Ahmed Fakhry, *The Pyramids*, University of Chicago Press,
Chicago, 1961

MUMMIES

E. A. Wallis Budge, *The Mummy*, Cambridge University
Press, Cambridge, 1925

EGYPT THROUGH THE AGES

Brian M. Fagan, *The Rape of the Nile*, Charles Scribner's
Sons, New York, 1975

PYRAMID LORE

E. Raymond Capt, *The Great Pyramid Decoded*, Artisan Sales,
Thousand Oaks, Calif, revised edition 1978

Peter Tompkins, *Secrets of the Great Pyramid*, Harper and
Rowe, New York, 1971

Max Toth and Greg Nielsen, *Pyramid Power*, Warner Destiny,
New York, revised edition 1976.

Readers able to visit a specialist library might start by looking
out for these books:

Somers Clarke and R. Engelbach, *Ancient Egyptian Masonry*,
London, 1930

Amelia Edwards, *A Thousand Miles up the Nile*, London, 1877

Adolf Erman, *Life in Ancient Egypt*, (translated) London, 1894

W. M. Flinders Petrie, *The Pyramids and Temples of Gizeh*,
London, 1883

C. Piazzi Smyth, *Our Inheritance in the Great Pyramid*,
London, 1864

Howard Vyse, *Operations carried on at the Pyramids of Gizeh
in 1837*, (3 vols.), London, 1840-2

Index

Acknowledgements

I wish to thank every one who has helped in the preparation of this book, and in particular:

Jeremy Dixon for information about the Northampton County Council project;

Robert Douwma (Prints & Maps) Ltd, 93 Great Russell Street, London WC1, for making available David Roberts' lithographs of Egypt taken from *Egypt and Nubia*, (3 vols.), 1846-9;

Richard Elen of *Sounds International* for information about musicians;

John Fitchen, A.I.A., Emeritus Professor of the Fine Arts, Colgate University, New York, for making available the diagrams on page 180 which first appeared as figures 1 and 2 illustrating his article *Building Cheops' Pyramid*, pp 3-12, Journal of the Society of Architectural Historians, Vol. XXXVII, No. 1, March 1978;

Alan Geffin, Pyramid Energy Products, 20 Bride Lane, London EC4, for information about pyramid energy;

The German Archaeological Institute, Cairo, for making available the manuscript of Henry Westcar's Diary;

The Griffith Institute, Oxford, for making available a copy of Joseph Bonomi's Diary and Mrs Anthony de Cosson for giving permission to quote from it;

James Rutherford, editor of *Pyramidology Magazine*, The Institute of Pyramidology, Harpenden, Hertfordshire, and Bill Cox, editor of *The Pyramid Guide*, P.O. Box 30305, Santa Barbara California, for copies of their magazines;

University College, London, for permission to draw on Sir Flinders Petrie's writings.

Humphrey Evans

Picture Acknowledgements

George W. Allen: 14/15
Ardea/Sue Gooders: Endpapers
Brian Brake/John Hillelson Agency: 149
British Museum: 63
Denise Bourbonnais: 36, 109
Peter Clayton: 57T, 78, 79, 108, 118, 159, 160, 162, 174
Cooper-Bridgeman Library: 10/11
C. M. Dixon: 110, 134T(British Museum), 139L&R
Courtesy Robert Douwma Maps and Prints Ltd: Contents, 12/13, 86/7, 123
Humphrey Evans: 89, 105
Mary Evans Library: 93, 146/7, 150, 153, 172
Professor John Fitchen 'Building Cheops Pyramid', Society of Architectural Historians Journal XXXVII, March 1978: 180
John Freeman/British Museum: 158
George Gerster/Magnum: 21
Giraudon (Louvre): 23
Robert Harding Associates: 81, 82/3, 116, 124

Michael Holford Library: Title, Title verso, 26(British Museum), 28/9(British Museum), 32(British Museum), 40/1, 47, 56/7(British Museum), 64, 67, 72/3(British Museum), 88, 90/1, 100/1, 111(British Museum), 114(British Museum), 121, 128/9, 134B, 137, 138, 157, 168/9
Hirmer Verlag Fotoarchiv: 59L&R, 112
Lehnert and Landrock, Cairo: 16, 89
Erich Lessing/Magnum: 39
William McQuitty: 57B, 76, 97, 122, 126, 136
Popperfoto: 120
Mauro Pucciarelli: 25
George Rainbird Ltd/F. Kennett: 34, 125
Rijksmuseum van Oudheden, Leiden: 53
Royal Photographic Society: 176
Adam Woolfit/Susan Griggs: 179
Roger Wood Studio: 49, 50, 140, 144
Spectrum Colour Library: 99
Zefa: 154